The Americas Overland

Toby D. Smith

Blue Mountain Press

Library of Congress Control Number: 2020921980

ISBN 978-0-9996892-2-6 (paperback)
ISBN 978-0-9996892-3-3 (e-book)

Edited by Tatiana Wilde
Cover photograph by Timon Studler

Blue Mountain Press
Philadelphia, Pennsylvania
www.bluemountainpress.net

Manufactured in the United States of America

AUTHOR'S NOTE

What follows is based on actual occurrences. Although some elements have been changed for dramatic effect, it should be regarded in its essence as fact.

Security is mostly a superstition. It does not exist in nature, nor do the children of men as a whole experience it. Avoiding danger is no safer in the long run than outright exposure. Life is either a daring adventure or nothing.

- Helen Keller, *The Open Door*

The Americas
Overland

PART I

A trip, a safari, an exploration, is an entity, different from all other journeys. It has personality, temperament, individuality, uniqueness. A journey is a person in itself; no two are alike.

- John Steinbeck, *Travels with Charley: In Search of America*

1

INTO THE MIDNIGHT SUN

The train snaked through a dense forest of birch, alder, and spruce, which encroached on the railway like a velvety sea. Overnight, snow had fallen at the higher elevations and I glimpsed white-dusted mountains of the Chugach Range through wisps of morning cloud. Where the occasional road crossed the tracks, it was dirt or gravel, washboarded and rutted. For a moment the train broke free of forest. Broad ecru-colored mudflats, like unbleached linen, stretched toward a ribbon of water. Beyond the mudflats a line of peaks, all covered in a layer of fresh spring snow, jumbled the horizon.

I had come to Alaska believing the landscape would resemble northwestern Montana, where I last lived, except with many more glaciers and snow-covered mountains and far fewer people. The wide skies, open vistas, and rugged beauty of Montana's Rockies had enchanted me. I was mesmerized by gorges, waterfalls, and alpine meadows where grizzlies grazed and bighorn sheep clung to cliff edges. Montana's jagged peaks and glacier-carved valleys, so different from the gentle ridges and forested lowlands of the Appalachian foothills where I grew up, spoke to me about the possibility of even grander landscapes, and that is when I heard the proverbial call of the wild from Alaska.

I now found myself aboard the Alaska Railroad, which was carrying me north past the mudflats of Knik Arm, through marshes and bogs, beyond the boreal forest, into the taiga–Russian for land of little sticks–and toward Alaska's interior. When we passed snow-capped mountains reflected in an unstirred lake, the passengers 'oohed'. Like me, they were spellbound. I find art to be so subjective; some understand a work, others don't. But with mountains, sunsets, landscapes, nearly everyone speaks the same language. Even the teenagers aboard stopped pretending they were not excited.

The locomotive climbed out of the birch and cottonwood forests, past scattered stands of ever-smaller spruce, and across a vast treeless landscape surrounded by towering mountains. After eight hours the train called at the remote Denali depot in the heart of the Alaska Range. I stepped off and stood on the open platform with my bags in hand. As I watched the railcars plod forward and rattle around the bend, I felt like I was in a scene in an old-time black and white movie when a stranger arrives in a dusty frontier town.

I found my way to a former roadhouse along the Nenana River. The original owner, Jim Crabb, and his daughters had made something of the place in the 1950s. They offered a sparse room and basic meal to the few travelers who drove past on the Denali Highway, a gravel road that until the 1970s was the only one spanning Alaska's interior. I later learned from a local that, "old Crabbie died from the cancer" and that his daughters were bought out and moved south. Business at The Village, as their roadhouse came to be known, continued to grow.

A graveled remnant of the Denali Highway still climbed upward from The Village to Karma Ridge, along which cabins hidden in the woods housed a few locals who hunkered down there through the long winters. Twenty miles south was Cantwell, a flag stop where the train stopped on request.

Twenty miles north lay Healy, a coal-mining town with less than a thousand residents. Nearby loomed the snow-shrouded flanks of Denali, North America's highest summit, named long ago by indigenous Athapaskans. All else in the surrounding region was a rugged landscape of taiga, tundra, and mountain. Alaska, I quickly realized, was vaster than I ever imagined.

I had been hired to tend bar in The Village lounge. Though my thirst for adventure ran deeper than serving cocktails, I thought it a convenient means to explore the surrounding environs. Since the lodge had not yet opened for the season, I found myself alone on that first night. Even at midnight, traces of light lingered in the night sky. I sat on the river's edge, contemplated mountains brooding in the distance, and considered the events that brought me to such a wild place.

I learned that over the years everyone from trappers, miners, and hunters to dreadlocked park employees, rafting guides, bush pilots, Athapaskans, and locals from Karma Ridge, Cantwell, and Healy had come to consider The Village lounge a worthy watering hole on their way to somewhere. The lounge's décor, which encompassed pool tables, dartboards, a stone fireplace, makeshift corner stage, smoke-yellowed walls, and beer-stained carpet had changed little since Crabbie's day. Most nights I served drinks from behind the long wooden bar to a motley collection of locals smoking cigarettes and drinking Budweiser or tequila or Yukon Jack. I had dreamed of coming to Alaska for years. Now, night after night, the characters that populated my dreams came slowly to life.

A few people, like my coworker Nellie, asked what I was running from.

"Most people up here have left something or someone behind," she said. "What about you?"

"I'm not running from anything," I replied, "but I might be looking for something."

"Like what?"

"I'm not sure. Freedom, maybe. Not the kind of freedom where I can do whatever I want. Something else. Maybe I'm looking for inspiration."

For me, the lands most conducive to reflection are those yet unmarred by humanity. My version of utopia is a place where nature rules, humanity's influence is insignificant, and you can be whomever you wish to be. Alaska seemed a promising place to start that search. Indeed, what struck me about most people I met in Alaska was that they seemed unafraid to be themselves, however strange or quirky that might be. I had tasted this kind of freedom in Montana and even Colorado, but Alaskans took self-expression even further.

A month after I arrived I had a taste of such freedoms when a handful of coworkers managed to get two days off on both sides of summer solstice–the longest day of the year–to road-trip up the Haul Road. Their goal was distant Prudhoe Bay, which sits isolated and alone along the Beaufort Sea on the northern edge of Alaska. Two of the road-trippers, Luke and Dave, convinced me to join them. The idea of driving over six hundred miles across the northern half of Alaska to the Arctic Ocean sounded like a crazy scheme, but a tantalizing one. Luke, always prone to wild ideas, cornered me at the start of one evening lounge shift.

"Are you in?" he asked.

"If I get all four days off," I said, "I'm there."

In the kitchen, Dave was plating a Ketchikan sauté and an order of Crabbie's Crossing Crabcakes. He had worked his way across the country, followed the Grateful Dead for years, and elevated vagabonding to a permanent lifestyle. From those experiences flowed a seemingly endless repertoire of stories.

"Dude," he said when I stepped into the kitchen to pick up the order, "we're leaving Wednesday night after work. We've got me, Dan, Jen, Michelle, uh, Anne Marie, and Luke. If you come that's, like, seven people."

"That's a lot. Maybe I'll back out."

"Oh no, you're in. You're going."

I agreed to meet him Wednesday night at eleven near the Outbacks, a cluster of employee cabins nestled in the spruce forest. Later that night I stopped by the Shoebox, the cramped employee dining room. I explained our plans to my friend

Tony, who was a longtime Alaskan and currently the lodge's maintenance supervisor.

"That should be a great trip," Tony said. "Bring lots of tires. Spend the money and buy another spare. Don't try to do it with just one."

"Why not?" I asked.

"That road is all dirt and rock. You'll have some blowouts."

Next I mentioned the trip to my roommate, Jeremiah Johnson. When we first met and he told me his name, I thought he was joking. He didn't laugh. He had never heard of Vardis Fisher's novel *Mountain Man,* which inspired a 1972 movie about a 1880s wilderness pioneer named Jeremiah Johnson. Yet there before me stood a modern-day mountain man. He had been born a few miles up the road, hunted moose, and climbed mountains. The year before I met him, he had barely survived a snow-machine collision with a moose and had to crawl half-paralyzed for a mile through snow and subfreezing temperatures to the nearest cabin for rescue. His left arm still hung useless at his side, but that didn't slow him down. He had already regained mobility in his left leg. The moose, on the other hand, died on impact.

"You're going to Prudhoe?" he said. "Bring lots of tires. I've known people who blew all four tires on that road."

On Wednesday night Luke and I sat in the Shoebox getting a last bite to eat.

"We'd better leave by eleven," he said.

Lynx Creek Grocery, the only place to refuel, was eight miles up the road and closed at midnight. If we didn't get there by then we would have to wait until the next morning to leave.

"If anyone holds us up I'll harass them so hard the whole trip," he vowed. "They'll hear it from me!"

At eleven I met Michelle and Anne Marie at Dave's battered van near the Outback cabins. Twenty minutes later Luke came around the corner.

"You guys ready?" he shouted.

"We're ready," I answered, "but I talked to a few people, and I think we should get more tires."

7

"We'll be fine," Luke assured me as we tossed our gear into the van and climbed aboard. I let it go.

We found Jen and Dan up the road glugging a pitcher of beer, and stopped at Lynx Creek to fuel up. There, Luke plotted another of his schemes.

"I'll pay for the first tank of gas," he said before putting thirty dollars' worth into the van. When the tank was full he went inside to pay.

"How much did you give them?" Michelle asked after we had returned to the main road.

"Fifteen." He smiled. "There's no meter in the store."

Luke's methods irked me at times, but I kept silent. The trip had hardly begun, and I was, after all, the newcomer.

Darkness never falls in the middle of the night on the longest day of the year in the mountains of interior Alaska. We had plenty of daylight remaining when the seven of us headed into the midnight sun with a full fuel tank, one bald spare, two cans of Fix-a-Flat, and no extra tires.

Fairbanks, a few hours to the north, was our last chance for supplies. When we arrived the stores had already closed, so at three in the morning we pitched our tents in the woods near the university to wait. At daybreak a patrol jeep stopped. I heard a radio dispatcher squawk Dave's vital stats over an officer's radio but he was clean, it seemed, and they told us to get moving.

When the liquor store opened we bought cases of beer, bottles of whiskey, and jugs of wine. I mentioned again the possibility of purchasing more tires, but everyone ignored me. We soon left the last vestiges of civilization behind. Two rode in front, I sat in one of the middle Captain's Chairs, and three were crammed in back amidst piles of gear. Thirty miles north the asphalt disappeared, and from there we bumped along a narrow dusty road.

Past Livengood, where the Elliott Highway ends, we turned onto the Haul Road. Officially known as the Dalton Highway, the dirt and gravel track stretches more than four hundred miles across the North Slope of Alaska and ends near the

Arctic Ocean at a place called Deadhorse. The road was cut through the tundra during the 1970s to reach the oil fields that brought Alaska prosperity and formed the basis of the state's boom and bust economy. Since then, only permit holders and semi-trucks hauling supplies were allowed on the road. The year before our journey, access was granted to the public for the first time. Only a few intrepid travelers attempted the drive that first year. If we made it to Deadhorse on this road, one of the most isolated and rugged in the United States, we would be among the first travelers to do so.

The Dalton carried us to Yukon Junction and across the Yukon River. Dave was determined to make good time. He blew past a gas station-cum-restaurant but later swerved onto the shoulder near a sign proclaiming we had reached the Arctic Circle, still a long way from the ocean. After a few snapshots of the sign and taiga forest we continued. Dave pushed the beat-up overloaded van with its four worn tires around blind corners, nearly colliding with oncoming truckers, and overtook every vehicle going in our direction. By the time we reached Finger Rock everyone, including Dave, was half-pickled from the alcohol.

Luke and I climbed to the top of the slanted granite formation that jutted forty feet above a high hill and overlooked the sweeping tundra. Nothing around us grew more than a foot tall. The weathered rock seemed to be pointing, like a decrepit crone jabbing a finger in the air to show the way—or warn against it. As I sat atop the rock and took in the expansive view, which stretched to distant horizons in every direction, I thought about the girl I had left behind.

"I don't understand," she'd said before I headed north. "Why would you want to leave me, to go to Alaska, of all places? I thought you loved me. I thought we had something."

The truth was I had never felt about anyone the way I felt about her. "I don't want to leave you," I had said. "I don't entirely know why I'm going. I guess I feel I have to."

"But why?"

"I don't know," I said. "I can't really explain it."

I had met Tamara after my first summer working in Montana at a lodge on the shores of Sacred Dancing Lake. After I returned home I found a job tending bar at a neighborhood pub. I soon had my eye on the petite brunette who waited tables upstairs. Tamara sometimes forgot my name, but I knew she had grown up nearby, moved to the city, and recently returned home.

One wintry night after her shift ended she stopped by the pub for a glass of wine and, to my surprise, became smitten with me. Not long after we started dating she revealed that she had never been west of West Virginia, and I promised her a real road trip. That summer we drove to Colorado, visited friends in Boulder, and continued on to Sacred Dancing Lake.

A few months after we returned home I mentioned my longtime desire to see Alaska. "After living in Colorado and Montana," I explained, "a summer in the wilds of Alaska feels like the next destination." But Alaska did not entice Tamara as it did me, so I flew to the Great Land alone.

When I called her from a pay phone on a deserted dust-blown street in downtown Anchorage the evening before I caught the train to The Village, I had never felt so far from home. That feeling had waned prior to this drive across the Arctic, but during our road trip my thoughts often strayed to Tamara and what I may have lost by leaving her behind.

"Why" was a question I still struggled to answer, as was "what", not only in regard to leaving Tamara but also in other unresolved aspects of my life, such as what my future should hold. However, in the wilds of northern Alaska, where nature ruled and the struggle for simple existence dominated everything, the answers to my persistent questions seemed slightly more within my grasp.

My thoughts were interrupted when Dave called out that he was ready to get moving. An hour later he stopped the van again on the narrow dirt road so everyone could relieve themselves. As we filed into the brush, a hissing sound filled the air. As long as we moved the tires held but whenever we stopped, they seemed to spring another leak. Dan pumped in our last can of Fix-a-Flat. I hoped it would hold, for we had long ago used our only spare.

At the single service station in Coldfoot, usually frequented only by long-haul truckers, we spoke to the man in charge. He had an extra tire, two sizes too large, that he sold us for ten bucks. He removed our shredded spare tire from the rim and replaced it with the oversized secondhand one. Meanwhile, Luke and I shot half a dozen games of pool in the most northerly bar in North America. Summer solstice came and went, though we barely noticed.

In aptly named Coldfoot, we got cold feet. The signs read: *Private Vehicles May Not Drive to the Arctic Ocean*, and *No More Services*. Deadhorse still lay hundreds of miles away, with no fuel, services, tire repair, or any other amenities in between. We had no tools or maps and our new oversized spare tire would damage the van's differential if we drove too far on it.

Some of us in the group wanted to turn back; others insisted we continue to the Arctic. In the end, we all crawled inside the van and headed north, into the yawning emptiness. With tires a dominant source of concern, everyone hit the beer bottles and wine jugs even harder.

Many hours later the Brooks Range rose from the tundra like a monstrous insurmountable wall. We climbed slowly upward amongst the snowy peaks to Atigun Pass. From the pass we descended to the treeless plain of the North Slope. Halfway between Coldfoot and the Arctic Ocean, when we paused for another bathroom break, air began hissing from the right rear tire. As we stumbled out of the van a light rain began falling. Except for the patter of drops on the dirt, stillness surrounded us.

We filled the tire with a can of Fix-a-Flat we had bought in Coldfoot, but after a few miles it went flat. We had no choice but to replace it with our oversized, secondhand spare. The only tool we had was a pair of vise grips. Soon the lug nuts were almost stripped, but remained tight as ever. The tension in our group exploded. Stranded in the middle of nowhere, everyone argued over what to do.

"Okay, take a deep breath everybody," I heard Dave say, "and just relax."

Following his advice, I soaked up the scenery while contemplating our situation. The light rain kept falling as broken clouds drifted overhead. To the south, the Brooks Range loomed. The seemingly never-setting sun hovered over vast plains of treeless tundra and I could see caribou grazing in the distance. I gazed at the landscape surrounding me and was overwhelmed by the grandeur. A wave of emotion and gratitude welled up inside me. I closed my eyes and inhaled the subtle tundra aroma–an earthy mixture of lichen and berries and moss and Labrador tea intermingling in the crisp clear air–and realized life had never felt more full. John Muir must have felt the same when he counseled, "You should never go to Alaska as a young man because you'll never be satisfied with any other place as long as you live." I wondered if this would be my fate.

After a while, something alien intruded upon the landscape. I watched the thing move slowly towards us–a hulking beast of metal and chrome rumbling down the gravel track. When the semi-truck reached us, the rushing sound of its air brakes seemed almost deafening after the empty silence. We hadn't seen any other vehicle for hours and never expected an eighteen-wheeler to show up right when we needed it. Dave explained our situation to the truck driver as Luke and I pushed against the front of the unstable van to prevent it from toppling off the jack stand. Within minutes the driver had our flat tire off and the oversized spare on the hub.

Gravel crunched reassuringly beneath the van as we returned to the dirt track. Dave had become less manic since leaving Coldfoot, mainly because Dan had taken over the copilot seat from Luke, who fueled Dave's impatience. As we rolled along the gravel, Dan looked out his window, checked the tires on his side, and said, "Yikes, the front tire is *really* low." He tried to show just how low with his hands.

Dave looked out his window while Dan held the steering wheel. "Wow, my front tire is really low too," said Dave.

This went on for miles, at times with both sticking their heads out their windows at the same time.

"Well, if yours is lower than mine, we're in trouble," Dave said. Dan crawled behind Dave to check the driver's side front tire on the driver's side.

"Mine's *way* worse than yours!" he insisted.

Slow but sure, we continued rolling over the North Slope with no more spares or Fix-a-Flat. A snaking cloud of dust kicked up by the dirt-caked van lingered behind us on the endless tundra. Emptiness stretched away in all directions. At three in the morning the midnight sun still hung high in the sky; it would not set for another month. We had reached the roof of the world, it seemed, where the land was flat on all sides and clouds slanted into the horizon at peculiar angles. It was difficult at times to see where the sky began and the land ended. Everyone fell silent as untrammeled tundra unfolded before us on the longest day of the year.

At four in the morning we entered a desolate maze of machinery and metal sheds. A speeding pickup truck tore around the corner toward us. We flagged the driver down and learned from him that Prudhoe Bay and Deadhorse were essentially one and the same. This was Deadhorse, a small settlement where oil field workers lived, and many worked. Most oil rigs were located a few minutes up the road in Prudhoe Bay. The Arctic Ocean still lay eight miles away, but for security reasons the U.S. Army guarded the two access roads that led to the sea and denied entry to all private vehicles.

The driver of the pickup truck, Sam, told us to pitch our tents in the gravel along Lake Colleen. At five, a different truck stopped beside us. We figured they were running us out of the area, but earlier Sam had used his CB radio to contact the dispatch office, telling them we needed tire work. The driver of this truck told us to follow him. I rode in the van with Dave to the tire shop, where a mechanic named Milton patched the tires and gave us air and advice. We gave him beers, more valuable than cash when the closest bar was in Coldfoot, and slipped him a twenty.

"I come on at six tomorrow night," Milton said. "If you're still around I can get you about twenty pounds of sandwiches."

That sounded too good to pass up. Dave and I were tired and started back to camp for some shuteye, but with the sun already high in the sky, we drove instead to the very end of the road to make sure the checkpoints really were as far as we could go. They were. We inspected a tiny supply store, then tossed a Frisbee we had brought along.

But the Arctic Ocean beckoned.

"We have to find a way there," I heard Luke say.

Sure enough, he located a guy who would fly five of us to the ocean's edge for eighty dollars each. That evening Dave, Luke, Dan, Michelle, and I buckled into the six-seat twin-prop. We lifted off, soared over tundra flatlands, lakes, caribou, and herds of grazing musk oxen, and angled towards the very edge of Alaska. Chunks of ice floated in dark blue waters. I could see the Arctic icepack, which in winter froze solid to the shoreline but in summer receded a few hundred yards offshore. This seemingly endless ice stretched a thousand miles to the North Pole.

Thoughts of friends and family came to mind. Memories of places and moments in time flashed past. Every prior experience seemed so distant. How remote we are, I thought. I remembered the string of planes, trains, and automobiles I had ridden to be in this place. I wondered whether it was good or bad that I pushed forward on such adventures without always knowing why.

The pilot banked the plane, circled, and landed on a short gravel runway a few dozen feet from the Arctic Ocean. He said we could stay for fifteen minutes. Despite the stiff breeze, Luke and I tore off our clothes and dove into the near-freezing water. We swam to an iceberg twenty feet out and climbed on top. As I ogled the Arctic icepack, my mind filled with an overwhelming sense of wellbeing. We had done it! The euphoria didn't last long in such frigid conditions. We hustled back to shore and, although my feet hurt for the next hour, the pain meant they were not frozen and served as a reminder that

I had done something I would not soon forget.

A massive storm front followed the plane back to Deadhorse. While surveying the landscape below, an epiphany struck me. I wondered what the world looked like on the other end of the Americas, at the tip of Argentina. And I realized, with a sudden jolt, that I would very much like to find out.

We landed just before the sky burst open. While we were gone Jen and Anne Marie had taken down the tents and washed the mud-covered van. We fueled up, replenished the Fix-a-Flat supply, and made one last stop at the tire shop. Milton the mechanic ran over to us through the rain and said to meet him at our campsite. There we waited for twenty minutes with only an Arctic fox trotting past to keep us company. At last Milton appeared and handed a bag through the window, then two more, and finally a fourth. They were filled with sandwiches, chips, grapes, fruit, and hot dogs. He beamed as we laughed in delight.

As Deadhorse receded in the van's rearview mirror, I read a blurb aloud from a small map, printed the year before, that I had picked up at the supply store.

As 1995 is the first year the 413-mile Dalton Highway has been opened for public access–you folks are the "trail blazers" so to speak. We hope you enjoy your adventure and the time you spend here at "The End of the Road," and that this map has made it easier. Thank you and have a good trip home, wherever that may be.

With six hundred miles to go the journey was far from over, but everything I saw felt different–clearer, or perhaps sharper in some way. The storm ended, the sun appeared through the dark clouds, and a full rainbow arced overhead. A few minutes later a half dozen snowy owls flew in front of the van, then circled around us before flying away. Farther on a huge white wolf appeared. He stopped, watched us, moved off, stopped again, and then continued, slowly, before disappearing over a shallow rise. These sightings seemed to me like good omens. I knew we would be okay.

The great white wolf exuded a grace and elegance akin to human nobility, I thought. As I watched him disappear into the solitude of his domain, I realized I did not want to be a lone wolf. I had found a form of freedom in this Alaskan wilderness, but I missed Tamara terribly. There is great value in sharing poignant moments with those we love. I wanted to try again. I needed to find a way to make it all up to her, and suddenly I knew how. I would take her with me to the other end of the Americas.

2

THE LATIN LEGACY

Alaskan summers tend to be dishearteningly short. Only a few months after my drive to the Arctic Ocean, the call of migrating cranes sounded overhead, golden cottonwood leaves fluttered to earth, and the snow line crept down the mountainsides. With startling speed, summer ended. *Closed,* read the signs tacked to the locked doors of the lodge where I worked. *Reason: it's freezin'.*

A friend had left her car at the lodge and flown home early. As a favor, I drove it down the length of the Alaska Highway and delivered it to her in Oregon. Then, with her and another friend, I wound my way up the coast to Seattle, and there boarded a train bound for the East Coast.

Despite my intention to reconcile with Tamara, our relationship remained rocky. I told myself that Alaska had driven a wedge between us, but in truth my decision to leave her behind had ushered in our undoing. Her intellect, progressive ideas, striking looks, and refined yet practical sensibilities had drawn me to her. Plus, we always had fun whenever we were together. But we could not quite resolve our differences, and two years after I first took the train to Denali, I returned with a heavy heart to the land of midnight sun.

During my absence The Village owners had added more rooms and remodeled the rustic bar. A few old timers still came by, such as Crazy Carl, a longhaired unkempt freelance whitewater rafting guide who lived twenty miles south in a cabin on a bend of the Nenana River. Crazy Carl had taken up with Kim, a hard-drinking forty-something south Floridian. Kim's Outback cabin sat a few steps from mine and most nights the two partied into wee hours.

One afternoon, Kim and Carl were in the lounge drinking bottles of Bud and throwing back shots of Jägermeister, laughing raucously as I served them from behind the bar. I overheard Carl say he was selling an old Datsun he had—the same boxy gray vehicle I noticed parked outside.

I looked up. "How much?"

"I don't know," Carl answered. "Three hundred, maybe."

The next day we rode in Carl's van to his cabin.

"It's a Datsun 510," he said as we climbed out of the van. "I bought it last week from a local guy."

"What year is it?"

"1973, I think."

The Datsun had no paint, just gray primer on bare metal. The passenger door didn't open, and the interior was a shambles. It was cute, though, and petite, and I decided that it was a she. Like my relationship with Tamara, she needed some attention. When I turned the key she started, so I stomped on the gas and raced her the two miles to the end of the mud road. I noticed the odometer was stuck at 99,949, and neither the speedometer nor any of the gauges functioned, but she had plenty of heart and spirit. I let her idle and then cut the engine.

As I looked over the worn interior, a not so deeply buried memory dislodged itself. A dozen years earlier at the age of fifteen I had emerged with a group of friends from thick-forested wilderness after spending a week in the West Virginian backcountry. At the trailhead were a few ramshackle cars—one a boxy, gray early model Datsun. She was rugged, mud-smeared, and wonderfully battered. Inspired, I saved enough the next summer to buy a silver 1976 Toyota Corona. I drove the car until my junior year of college, thinking then that I needed to upgrade. Since then I had owned several cars, but none had yet moved me like that Toyota.

I remembered that Carl was waiting, but when I turned the Datsun's key the engine wouldn't turn over. After five minutes I managed to get her started, and by the time I returned to Carl, my decision was made.

"Sold," I said, and handed him three crisp hundred-dollar bills. I had found my dream car, and a suitable successor to my beloved Toyota.

The next day at the lodge I told my old-timer coworker, Baldy, that I bought Crazy Carl's 1973 Datsun 510. He stroked his white beard and his eyes twinkled.

"You're crazy yourself for buying such a clunker!" he laughed.

She ran, though admittedly like every trip might be her last. To be ready for anything, I picked up a tattered Chilton repair manual at a used bookstore. She never again failed to start, but was not without her quirks. She had no working headlights, which on summer solstice was okay but by August would be a problem. Carl tested a few wires, but was stumped on how to fix them. One night, a few weeks after I bought her, I realized the high beams worked. I decided the issue was resolved.

Though little else functioned, I drove the old Datsun from Fairbanks to Anchorage a few times and made lots of local runs to Black Bear coffee shop and Cruisers bar for live music. Mostly I bounced over gravel roads, mud up to the windows, as fresh snow blanketed the peaks and clouds skirted round them.

When the summer tourists left and solitude prevailed, the lodge closed for the season and I once again headed south. On my way out of Alaska I stopped in the village of Talkeetna to visit my coworker, Nellie. She was looking for land to buy in the area and was staying in a trailer belonging to Todd and Kristy—mutual friends of ours—but had no vehicle to get around in. I had not yet titled or registered the Datsun so was driving with expired tags and no insurance.

"Feel free to use the car if you like," I said as I handed her the key. "Plug that leak in the left front tire if you can. Pull the cable off the battery if you head out for the winter. And enjoy the ride!"

I hitchhiked into Anchorage to catch a flight to Bangkok. Over the winter I visited Bangladesh, trekked through the Himalaya, barely survived a pilgrimage to Tibet, encircled the Indian subcontinent, and traversed Eastern Europe as the region emerged from the grip of the Cold War.

I liked going where tourists rarely ventured, and getting lost in whatever country I was in—not the kind of lost where I couldn't find my way back to my bare-bones hotel—but a kind of wandering lost where I could soak in my surroundings and be utterly absorbed by my environment. I enjoyed living out of my rucksack with only a few essentials. There were so many other things about my style of travel that I loved: sleeping in places most people had never heard of, living simply and on my own terms, meeting people so different from myself, learning about their cultures, histories, and ways of life. I got a thrill when I was submerged in different languages, seeing things I could never have imagined, and trying things I had only ever dreamed about.

While I had discovered a quirky kind of survivalist escape in Alaska, it was in Eurasia that I found another kind of freedom. The ability to explore exotic lands and live amongst strikingly different cultures was, for me, exhilarating.

Along the way, I wondered why Asia and Europe were regarded as separate continents when they are clearly one geological entity. Africa's size and uniqueness justify its stand-alone status, I thought, but the Americas are divided into a north and south despite the Isthmus of Panama, which connects the two. Australia—considered a continent because it sits upon its own tectonic plate—is three times smaller than Greenland, considered the world's largest island. None of this made sense to me. The earth's surface is actually a trio of cultural landmasses—Eurasia, Africa, and the Americas—all surrounded by one ocean and dotted with thousands of islands, including Antarctica. It was a simplistic, but for me logical and manageable way of viewing the world's geography.

Ideas for my second 'landmass excursion'—the first being across Eurasia—simmered in my subconscious while I traveled through India. The optimal route across the Americas remained unclear until I walked the cobblestone streets of Prague a few months later. There, I happened upon a shop with a map of the Americas posted in the window. Captivated, I stared at the map through the glass over the next half hour while finalizing my route.

Six months after flying into Bangkok, I returned to Alaska. This time, Tamara came too. As I had earlier realized on the drive from Deadhorse to Denali, I held no desire to be a lone wolf. I was ready to understand my shortcomings and learn how to be a better partner. We had corresponded during my Eurasian journey and reconciled to the point that she was ready to join me in Alaska. We shared a snug Outback cabin, and during long walks in the woods and talks late into the night in our tiny one-room space, we gradually resolved most of our differences. One night, I told Tamara about my dream.

"I've already ridden from here to the Arctic Ocean and back," I began. "So, next I want to travel the length of North America, cross the border into Mexico, wind through Central America to Panama, continue into South America, and follow the spine of the Andes to the Strait of Magellan at the southern tip of Argentina."

She didn't say anything.

"Where the land ends I'll turn north and continue up the east side across Uruguay and Paraguay and through the jungles of Brazil. Hopefully, I'll end up in Venezuela. The only roadless stretch is the Darien Gap, which separates Central and South America. It's all wilderness there. Apart from that section, I want to travel overland by car, bus, train, ship—whatever the locals use."

Tamara still said nothing. She took a sip of wine and sat

quietly. When I thought about it, the idea *was* rather daunting. Canada and America are both immense. Mainland Latin America stretches from Mexico to Argentina and includes sixteen Spanish-speaking nations, a Portuguese-speaking one, and one-fifth of the world's exposed land mass. The idea suddenly sounded a bit nuts.

"Well," I struggled on. "What do you think? Will you come along?"

At this, she perked up.

"I thought you'd never ask," she replied, her face glowing with excitement. "Absolutely!"

At last, our paths were merging.

To prepare for our adventure, we scoured the used bookshops in Fairbanks and came away with a few works on Latin American culture and history. This seemed a good place to start. The more I learned, the more I understood the importance of Tamara's role on our journey. When we first met, I knew nothing about politics, but Tamara's deep passion for the subject and many related conversations had taught me much. We didn't always agree, but in such moments we agreed to disagree. I realized that Latin America's political complexity would be easier to untangle together.

In order to ground myself in the larger picture, I started at the beginning. I knew from my grade school days that tens of thousands of years ago huge sheets of moving ice covered most of the earth's northern reaches, and so much fresh water was frozen into the mile-thick glaciers that ocean levels were hundreds of feet lower than they are today. The Bering Strait, now an icy waterway separating present-day Siberia from Alaska, was then completely exposed, and as animals wandered across the land bridge, hunter-gatherer humans followed.

Over the course of thousands of years, bands of early humans populated the Americas from present-day Alaska all the way to Argentina. Most indigenous cultures—the Yu'pik Eskimo and Athapaskan peoples of the Arctic, the Cherokee and Blackfoot tribes of North America, the Aztecs and Mayans of Mesoamerica, and the Inca and Nazca of South America, among hundreds of others—evolved from these ancestral migrations. We would follow in their footsteps.

Norsemen are the first known Europeans to have reached the Americas. Centuries after their first arrival, the competition for spices and colonies motivated seafaring nations to seek new trade routes to resource-rich Asia. When Christopher Columbus dropped anchor off the beach that he famously believed to be the edge of Asia, just a few million individuals living in far-flung nomadic tribal groups inhabited most of North America.

Latin America, by contrast, was composed at the time of some thirty million people organized into complex societies. Regional powers traded over great distances; empires rose and fell. Many of the most powerful were based in Mesoamerica—an area stretching from present-day central Mexico to Costa Rica. A second power base emanated from present-day Peru.

"Columbus was ruthless," Tamara announced one evening as she perused one of the books we had purchased.

"Probably so," I replied, "but the conquistadors were even worse. Columbus might not have understood what he found, as suggested by his persistent belief that he'd found a new route to Asia, but he sparked a whole new era of European expansion. And violence."

When Muslims from North Africa, known as Moors, invaded Spain and Portugal in the eighth century, Christian armies retaliated. For seven centuries Spanish and Portuguese soldiers fought against the Moors, and in 1492, the same year that Columbus convinced Ferdinand II, the King of Spain, to finance his initial expedition, the last of the Moors were driven out. Seeking new glory, these hardened Spanish and Portuguese soldiers—known as conquistadors or conquerors—advanced on Latin America like a well-oiled military juggernaut.

"It says here that Spain experimented with colonial rule, first in Hispaniola, by implementing a slave-plantation economy, two-class caste society, and absolutist Catholic-influenced political regime," Tamara recited. "Though little gold and silver was found, they left the local population decimated. Spain then turned towards present-day Cuba and Puerto Rico. When precious metals and limited labor supply were again exhausted, Spain looked to the mainland."

Once the Aztec Empire collapsed, present-day Mexico and Central America fell under Spanish control. After the Inca Empire was toppled, Ecuador, Peru, Bolivia, and Chile came under Spanish rule. The Spanish fanned out across Paraguay and Argentina, while the Portuguese gained a foothold in Brazil. In less than a century all of Latin America was conquered. And during the course of that hundred years, over fifty million indigenous people were killed.

"It didn't get much better after that," Tamara continued. "Once any resources were extracted, the conquistadors instituted an authoritarian system based on the elitist, hierarchical, Christianized power structure of their homelands. Local Spanish rulers claimed to receive their mandates from God. Landowners and the military elite obeyed any edicts. On the bottom rung, peasants and workers had few if any rights. The Roman Catholic Church decided after lengthy debate that indigenous peoples did have souls, and in the course of being Christianized, would work as serfs. Africans were brought in for slave labor, but they were considered lacking any souls or rights." She stopped reading. "I don't know how they could do that and not see the hypocrisy," she said.

"I guess God approved," I quipped. "Does it say why they are known as 'Latin' people?"

Tamara skimmed the page.

"According to this, 'in the nineteenth century countries within the Spanish and Portuguese colonial empires were linked to Roman culture and Romance languages, and considered people of the 'Latin race'. English and Dutch-speaking nations such as Belize and Suriname were not considered part of Latin America, nor were French-speaking ones such as Haiti and French Guiana.'"

Over the next three centuries the church, armed forces, landowning elite, and business interests all fell under state control. Interwoven into this structure was the notion of patronage. If a gift was given, one was expected in return. At low levels it kept the wheels of government turning; at high levels and in its worst form, patronage degenerated into corruption.

Tamara and I learned that the medieval values and feudal-era systems that Spanish and Portuguese conquerors imported to Latin America enabled them to maintain a continuous, stable, and bitterly cruel rule for three hundred years. The age of the conquistadors etched an indelible imprint upon the fabric of Latin American heritage and history. In fact, though times have changed, this five-hundred-year-old legacy still influences much Latin American culture.

As Tamara observed, "In democracy it's your vote that counts. Under feudalism, it's your count that votes." For centuries ordinary Latin Americans, like their medieval counterparts, had little say in their destinies.

Needing a break from our lessons, we decided to hitchhike a hundred miles south to Talkeetna, where we pitched our tent on sandy banks of the Big Su River, and found my old Datsun 510. Nellie had left it parked near a friend's cabin. After I installed a fresh battery, the car roared to life. The clutch didn't engage, but a local kid filled the dry cylinder, and with a can of Fix-a-Flat in the left front tire, we were underway.

Before Crazy Carl owned her she had belonged to Pete, a long-time local. Pete had practically lived in the car for many years, having driven her the length of the Alaska Highway eight times. He had covered her headlights with wire screens to protect them from gravel kicked up on the long drives, equipped her with air shocks, rebuilt the original engine with a cobbled-together assortment of second-hand parts, installed a 280Z five-speed transmission, and with all that, raced her on the southern California 510 circuits.

By the time Carl sold me the car all hints of her former glory had faded. Yet whenever I ran into Pete I learned something new. He loved talking about her, and always reminded me of a boy reminiscing about the girl that got away.

Tamara named her Anastasia, after the Russian Romanov princess who, according to legend, escaped the assassin's bullets that killed the rest of her family. Time and again Anastasia, the car, lived up to her namesake. During one of our late night conversations, I raised a new topic with Tamara.

"I've been thinking about Anastasia's role on our journey," I began.

"I have too," she replied.

"Do you think we should drive her to Maryland?"

"Yes!" she responded. "Absolutely."

"It'd be a long drive for the old girl. Well over five thousand miles. She might not be up for it."

"We can't leave her behind," Tamara decided. "She's a part of this now. She's coming along."

3

ANASTASIA

Summer wound down quickly. Scurrying squirrels chattered nervously from the spruce tips, the Northern Lights shimmered overhead on moonless nights, and quaking aspen leaves fluttered on autumn breezes. The next phase of the journey was nearly upon us. We had decided that once the season ended we would drive Anastasia across North America to Maryland, on the East Coast, and from there sort out the next phase of our adventure. The idea seemed a bit madcap, considering Anastasia's rough state, but we felt certain she could make it.

"In that car?" the naysayers usually scoffed.

"We'll drive her as far as we can, then pull the tags and leave her behind if we have to," I usually responded, though I didn't believe that would ever happen.

One morning as we were driving along, a loud *ka-thunk* rattled Anastasia. She stuttered to a stop as I steered her onto the shoulder. We had no choice but to leave her for a few days, unsure of what had happened or how to get her back to our cabin. My friend Paul, a local bus driver I knew, later noticed

Anastasia sitting on the roadside. The next time he saw me he shook his head.

"Are you still driving that thing?" he asked. "Give it up already."

"No way," I insisted. "She's coming with us."

The truth is I was having doubts, but wasn't going to give up on Anastasia yet. The lodge closed in three weeks, so our time was running short. I determined that one of the drive shafts had snapped, but getting parts in the Alaskan interior was a challenge. Scott, one of the lodge waiters, helpfully towed Anastasia to our cabin with a length of rope attached to his Toyota. The next day Tamara and I borrowed a battered pick-up from Baldy, my old-timer coworker, to visit the Cantwell auto body yard. We found Crazy Carl there, who on occasion helped the semi-retired proprietor. Unfortunately the shop had no Datsun parts. Luckily, on the way home we noticed another junkyard, where the owner said he could get the part we needed. A week later, with a little help, we installed the replacement drive shaft.

In the meantime, one of the brake calipers had frozen. The only way to free the caliper was to jack up the car, remove the tire, and use a bent screwdriver to pry the brake shoe from the wheel cylinder. Otherwise, smoke poured from the overheated assembly. I wondered what else was wrong with our tired old girl, so we made a service appointment in Fairbanks. I managed to drive the hundred and twenty miles to Fairbanks without once using the brakes.

The shop quoted us three hundred dollars to fix Anastasia, before labor, but he didn't have the necessary parts in stock. Fortunately the kindly mechanic provided numbers for various junkyards, parts stores, and even someone who had a few early model Datsun carcasses rusting in his front yard. We had no luck until we arrived at one particular salvage yard.

"Sure, we got an old 510 out back," the man said. "Still has the calipers, too. Go ahead and pull one and you can have it for thirty bucks. By the way, need a drive shaft? I pulled it for a customer who no longer wants it. You can have it for forty."

Tamara and I stared at the same part we had just paid $150 for. We shook our heads regretfully and headed into the auto yard armed with the wrenches and sockets the man had loaned us to extract the parts we needed. We had never scavenged parts in a junkyard, unaccompanied, before. I found the Datsun, upside-down and covered in rust, and climbed on top. I tried prying the brake caliper from the wheel, but it wouldn't budge. Tamara wandered away to sit in the morning sunshine as I struggled and sweated.

"You have that piece yet?" the junkyard owner asked when I returned empty-handed. I shook my head. He gave me a different wrench and an oily can of Liquid Wrench.

"Try this."

Within minutes I had the part in hand and, beaming, held it overhead like a trophy. It seemed I was on my way to becoming a true grease monkey. We stopped by another shop on the way home and explained our situation to Chris, the mechanic on duty.

"This is worthless!" he declared when I pulled the caliper from the trunk. He called around to find a decent part.

"There aren't any in Alaska," he finally admitted, "but they can ship one from Seattle. It'll take about a week."

"I have to go to work in the morning..." Tamara hinted.

He looked at the part again.

"Maybe we can make this thing work. Are you two sure you want to do this? There aren't any more of these things on the road. This ain't even probably worth it."

"Just fix her!" Tamara exclaimed.

"Okay, Leon," he said, turning to another mechanic standing nearby. "These kids need some brakes."

Hours later, we drove back to our cabin with brakes intact.

A week later we headed north to the Fairbanks repair shop one last time. Chris replaced the u-joints, various hoses, and the muffler. Driving Anastasia across the continent now seemed ludicrous. While Chris worked, I paced the waiting room. An Alaskan housewife, sitting amongst the clutter of greasy automotive magazines, watched me.

"He needs to relax," she said to Tamara. "This drive'll be difficult, but enjoy it. Few could do what you're doing, but you're both young and life is short. So enjoy the moment."

"Thank you," Tamara replied, smiling. "He's worried that we're going to get stranded somewhere."

"Of course," the woman said. "But remember, cars have personalities. Know your car. Trust your car. You'll be okay."

On our return to Denali we stopped for fuel in the town of Nenana and I noticed puddles of green fluid under the car. Probably the water pump, I thought, but maybe Chris overfilled the radiator. An hour later, Anastasia overheated. As we puttered to a stop, a bus rumbled past. My friend Paul looked down from the driver's seat and shook his head.

"I don't know about this trip," I sighed to Tamara as I propped open the hood. While I poked at various hoses, she reminded me what the Alaskan housewife had said.

"I think she's right," Tamara said. "We'll be okay."

I wasn't so sure. That night at the lodge's closing party the Denali Cooks, a popular local band, played late and drinks flowed heavily.

"Give it up," Paul said when he saw me. "Let it go. At some point you have to move on."

I laughed. "We're not leaving Anastasia behind."

"Okay," he said. "Then I've got something for you." Twenty minutes later he returned with an empty five-gallon fuel can. "At least take this with you."

"Thanks, Paul."

"Take care," he said, clapping me on the back. "You've got a long way to go."

The next day, after I replaced the three inches of faulty, worn out radiator hose, we packed the last of our belongings and left the lodge behind. The first stop on our journey was Talkeetna, where we visited our friends Todd and Kristy.

I mentioned our need of a roof rack. "I have something that might work," Todd said, and pulled a warped piece of plywood from his garage. I bolted it to the roof and strapped a spare tire and Paul's fuel can on top. Now Anastasia looked ready for a road rally. Later, as we cast for salmon on the Big Su, we chatted about our plan to drive across North America. Kristy threw her head back and roared with laughter. When she realized we weren't kidding, she turned serious.

"Canada is huge. Took us a week to drive south in our truck. If the snow had been any deeper and the temperatures any colder, I don't know what would have happened."

I looked at Tamara. The thought of being stranded in Canada in a blizzard a thousand miles from anywhere in a car that didn't run and had no heat was the last straw.

"We shouldn't do this," I said. "It seems crazy."

"You want to do this," she said softly. "And so do I. What's the worst that can happen?"

"How about the ferry?" Kristy suggested. "That's a blast!"

Besides the Alaska Highway, the other overland option was to take a ferry through the Inside Passage, a waterway that follows Canada's western coastline and connects Alaska to Washington State. We could still travel overland, but with a reduced risk of breaking down hundreds of miles from the nearest town. I looked at Tamara and she nodded. Later that day I used Todd and Kristy's old rotary phone to make a ferry reservation for Anastasia, Tamara, and myself.

The next day we said goodbye and headed south. The only way to reach the ferry terminal, a thousand miles away, was by driving through a corner of Canada to the town of Haines on the Alaskan coast. We drove past snow-capped mountains, lit gold and crimson by morning sun. Fog filled the hollows and sunshine peeked forth from a deep blue sky. I promised myself I would return. We passed through Anchorage, where I forgot to fill Paul's fuel can. The next outpost of any significance was Glenallen, nearly two hundred miles farther on. I hoped we'd be able to stop for fuel before then, but the only station along the desolate Glenn Highway turned out to be closed. We continued onward. Twilight fell and with it the temperature. On the rises Anastasia faltered. The broken fuel gauge always registered empty, but I figured the fuel tank, relocated by a past owner to the trunk, likely held ten gallons.

31

"We should make Glenallen easily," I told Tamara. "I think we have a couple gallons left. It's probably just the altitude."

Minutes after I said this, Anastasia sputtered to a stop. As an eighteen-wheeler roared by in the damp darkness, I pushed her off the road.

We walked in the dark with Paul's empty fuel can. Though I felt like a fool, neither of us said a word, for Tamara seemed to accept that such moments were part of the adventure of traveling with me. After a mile of empty road we came upon a cabin, the first structure we'd seen on our walk. We knocked and a little old lady pulled away from her black and white television long enough to lead us to a barn where gallon milk jugs filled with gasoline lay piled together.

"Take whatever you need," she said to me, and then turned towards Tamara. "If you run out again, come back here and I'll give him a scolding."

I wondered how many other wise women would save me from myself on this trip. There were no open hotels in Glenallen, so that night we slept in Anastasia. In the morning we slipped and slid on slick tires through a snowstorm on our way to the remote outpost of Tok, and then continued over the border. Blowing snow raged mercilessly around us in the mountains of Canada. Every twenty minutes Anastasia rolled to a stop, forcing me to pull over into the drifts. Each time I removed the air filter, thawed a layer of ice, and dried the element. After another dozen miles we stopped and repeated the process. The drive seemed endless.

At last we cleared the highest passes, crossed the border back into Alaska, and arrived in Haines. We boarded our waiting ferry, unrolled our sleeping bags, and through sheer exhaustion fell asleep in the open air of the solarium deck amongst our fellow passengers. For four days the ship hugged the coastline of the Inside Passage as porpoises and orca whales skimmed alongside. Todd and Kristy were right. We had a blast.

We disembarked near Seattle, and from there drove around Mt. Rainier, past Mt. St. Helens, through Portland, and down the Oregon coast. We walked among Redwoods, toured wineries in Napa, and drove into Yosemite Valley at sunset. Anastasia seemed to be running hot, but we made it through Death Valley and only lost fourteen dollars in the Vegas slot machines. We were feeling lucky. Now that we were in the Lower 48 I was feeling more confident. And I was getting to know our car, as the Alaskan housewife had advised.

Soon after leaving Vegas, the clutch started feeling soft. I knew that getting parts in the barren Nevada desert would be nearly impossible, so I asked a mechanic in the town of Mesquite to take a look.

"You can't adjust these," the old-timer said, wiping grease from his hands.

"Sure you can," I countered, and grabbed my tattered Chilton manual from the trunk. He rubbed the stubble on his chin, studied the pages I showed him, and got to work. The old-timer managed to repair the clutch and we continued on to Boulder, where some recently-married friends recommended a mechanic for a tune-up and clutch adjustment.

"The clutch is fine," their mechanic said, "but the transmission rings are worn and failing."

"Will we make it home?" I asked.

"Easily," he said.

A few days later, we departed Boulder for the idyllic pastoral farmlands of the Midwest. Thirty miles west of Illinois, as we rolled into Memphis on a Saturday afternoon, a loud THUNK took us by surprise. I could no longer put Anastasia into any gear.

"Your clutch is finished," said Dynamite, a local mechanic who towed Anastasia to his junkyard shop. "Cost you about six hundred fifty bucks. But I got a '79 Olds out back for sale for five hundred."

That night at a motel Tamara and I talked about what to do. The Oldsmobile Dynamite wanted to sell didn't run and had weeds growing around the engine block, so that was a poor option. Yet I had to face the fact that it wasn't worth fixing Anastasia, which might take a week. Paul was right. It was time to let go. But we needed a way out of Memphis. The next morning we came across a '87 Toyota Celica for sale at a used car lot for nine hundred dollars. I asked Dan, the dealer, about the leak I had noticed.

"Just power steering fluid," he reassured me. "Nothing to worry about."

"Are you sure that's not oil?" I asked.

"Guarantee it!"

We traded Anastasia to Dynamite for the towing fees and labor costs we owed him, and mournfully cleaned her out. We had been through a lot with the little car. I felt like I was giving up a member of our family, but I couldn't invest any more in the old girl. I thought of the Alaskan housewife. She was right. Cars do have personalities, and on road trips they're a central part of the journey. My eyes felt a bit blurry.

"You never cried like that for me," Tamara murmured.

At the dealership we paid for the Celica, signed the papers, and turned the key. The car had started when we test-drove it, but this time nothing happened.

As Dan's mechanic pulled the starter, he broke the already weak neck of the radiator. Late the next day he got the "new" used parts in. Puddles of oil appeared under the car when we stopped for fuel and when I turned the key the starter still did not work. Dan's mechanic slopped black goo on the underside of the engine, to plug the oil leaks, but we had to wait another night for the concoction to dry.

"This stuff will seal anything," he said. "Works even better than a real gasket."

I doubted it.

Next morning, the car leaked oil as bad as ever.

"Oh, Dan?" said a lawyer on the corner who we visited to see what recourse we had. "He's notorious. Not much you can do though. His cars are all as-is."

A week after Anastasia broke down, we got into the Celica we had named Memphis and drove away. Every fifty miles we had to stop to add two quarts of oil. Whenever I started the motor nothing caught, so Tamara had to climb out and rock

Memphis back and forth until the solenoid brushes found the right spot.

When we reached the Maryland border a few days later we felt hopeful; when we crossed the county line we cheered. We had made it home. We rented a third-floor turn of the century apartment near the restaurant where we had met. I sold Memphis to a quirky Armenian and over the winter we worked, saved cash, and planned the next phase of our adventure. From Maryland, we planned to head south by bus to the Mexican border, and from there make our way across Central America. My excitement grew by the day.

Tamara read Tim Cahill's *Road Fever*, a fast-paced account of an overland adventure stretching from the southern tip of Argentina to the northern edge of Alaska–the reverse of our route. The story opened Tamara's eyes to the danger and high levels of crime we might encounter in Latin America. Her enthusiasm began to wane.

"How are you feeling about this trip?" I asked her a few days before we readied to depart.

"Not great," she said. "These places sound *dangerous*."

I couldn't deny her concerns. Civil wars, violent crime, and social unrest pervaded most of the places we were going. I had no desire to put Tamara in harm's way, and began to reconsider the whole idea. I could not help but wonder: were the risks worth it?

4

AN AMERICAN DICHOTOMY

The day arrived for us to continue our journey. On a sunny April morning, the only dark clouds hanging over our heads were Tamara's doubts about the trip. We picked at rubbery pancakes and runny eggs at Elmo's, a roadside diner that used disposable everything–plastic forks, Styrofoam plates, and paper coffee cups–whether customers sat at one of the half-dozen Masonite-topped tables or took breakfast to go.

"Bacon," I joked. "You either love it, or you're wrong."

Tamara seemed not to notice.

"This place is an environmentalist's nightmare," she murmured, reaching for her paper coffee cup.

Her father chuckled. Honest, laid-back, and generous, I wondered what Dave thought of me dragging his only daughter across the Americas. Despite Tamara's somber mood, he seemed excited for us.

"What's your first stop?" he asked.

"The plan is to take a bus from Baltimore to Texas, where we'll try to make it over the border, into Mexico," I said. "From there, we'll see. Maybe Monterrey."

Tamara set her Styrofoam plate aside. Her eyes, like the eggs, were watery. Dave picked up the tab and then drove us to the local station, where trains ran on the half hour to downtown Baltimore. When Tamara struggled to lift her overflowing rucksack, Dave and I tried to help but she refused all offers. She walked into the station with her back bent beneath the burden.

"I can do this," she said, when I again offered to help. Then her rucksack wedged in the turnstile. She couldn't move backward or forward. She closed her eyes, lowered her head, muttered something, and dragged the load through.

None of us spoke on the train. From the station we walked to the downtown Baltimore bus depot, and amongst the graffiti and boarded-up storefronts, said our goodbyes. I reached for Dave's hand and wondered when I would see him again, knowing it would likely not be for half a year.

As he readied to leave, I glanced at Tamara's overstuffed rucksack. I had suggested she take a walk around the block with it the night before we left, to test the weight, but she hadn't time. Now I asked her what she could live without. After rummaging through the rucksack she handed a jacket and an extra sweater to her father. He hugged her and headed towards the exit with the bundle. In the doorway, he stopped and turned.

"I remember reading somewhere that to live is to risk dying. And to hope is to risk despair. To try anything at all is to risk failure. But risk we must, because when we risk nothing we do nothing, we have nothing, we are nothing."

At this, Tamara brightened a bit.

"Thanks, Dad," she said.

"Be careful you two, but have fun. That's what life's about."

With that, he was gone. Tamara sat in a blue plastic seat and stared at the blank television screen attached to the armrest until the tardy Greyhound bus arrived. We found seats and settled in for the long ride—halfway across the country—to the Texan border. She pulled out a book, gazed out the window, and wiped away a tear.

"I'm glad we're doing this," she said after a time. "Thank you for bringing me."

"You're welcome," I said. "I'm glad you're coming along."

She sighed deeply, smiled, and opened her book. We were underway, but had a long road ahead of us. Our next challenge was the crossing into Mexico. Borders were going to be among our potential obstacles and one of my largest concerns. If one closed, a grumpy guard denied us entry, or we had a visa in our passports from the wrong country, we might have to detour around or find another way in.

"What's the real purpose of borders?" I wondered aloud.

Tamara looked up from the book she was reading.

"Control?" she suggested.

That much was true. While some were invisible lines in the sand, I knew others were tools that states and sovereigns used to exercise authority over citizens and outsiders.

"Borders have probably been around since before the first civilizations," she said, marking the page with her bookmark. "People probably wanted protection from disease, war, famine. They were afraid."

"That's probably *why* civilization began," I reflected. "The temple promised salvation and immortality, for a donation. The marketplace offered goods that allowed more leisure time, for a price. And the palace provided stability, for subservience. All three offered a better standard of living, but with tradeoffs."

"They still do," Tamara mused. "History over the past couple thousand years is the story of the church, corporations, and the state competing with each other, and factions within each fighting for dominance. They're the infrastructure of society. Think about it. Christians and Muslims have been at war for centuries. Products that beat the competition permeate our lives. Presidents and dictators fight for land and oil."

"And too often the needs of the individual get lost in the clutter. Where's the balance between control and individual freedom?" I wondered.

"Have you read *The Social Contract*, by Rousseau?"

"I haven't, but his idea that people are born free, yet everywhere are in chains, is to me one of his most compelling."

"He believed that people aren't good or bad," Tamara continued, "but as society degenerates, we must compete with others, while growing increasingly dependent on them. This double pressure threatens our freedom." Gazing out the window, she thought about this further. "In Rousseau's view, it's *society* that corrupts pure people. So he proposed that people join together–without complex social structures–to preserve themselves and remain free."

The world began to change after the conquistadors invaded Latin America. Feudalism collapsed in England and Holland. The idea of limited government over absolute rule had gained favor and in Europe the Protestant Reformation destroyed much of the prevailing religious orthodoxy. In eighteenth-century Europe the Industrial Revolution sparked the fires of entrepreneurship and dampened those of mercantilism. Science changed how Europeans saw the world around them and a new multi-class society emerged. It was against this backdrop of sweeping change that North America's colonization unfolded.

"Rousseau's ideas even inspired the signers of America's Declaration of Independence," Tamara added. "They believed the legitimacy of government derives from the consent of its citizens, rather than inherited power or military strength. In a world dominated for millennia by authoritarians, oligarchies, and monarchies, and shaped by wars and regimes, America's founding fathers advocated a truly revolutionary idea. The United States was, in a sense, born free."

"Unlike Latin America."

"Yes, but though noble in intent, America was not really born pure," Tamara added. "Rousseau argued that any political entity should be a direct democracy, because citizens should never, he believed, elect others to represent themselves. And, he believed a nation should not be too large. The bigger the territory, the more strength the government must exert to maintain control."

As the United States grew under Manifest Destiny—the belief that settlers were destined to expand across the continent as part of a mission to remake the world in America's image—the United States diverged further from a size Rousseau believed could best serve the public's interest.

"And one thing I've learned traveling with you," she added, smiling, "is that this country is *huge!*"

Our philosophical ponderings took a pause in Virginia when our bus driver turned onto Route 29. The road paralleled the interstate but wound among multi-generational farms of the Old Dominion State and held more appeal for overland travelers like us than tedious interstate freeways. As twilight descended, the Carolinas and signs of the Deep South emerged. Long spells of wakefulness, interrupted by short bouts of restless sleep, comprised our night.

In Atlanta, the driver roused us at four in the morning for a rest stop. Outside Columbus, Georgia, he gave us enough time to grab two tall coffees. We ran late, and our short breaks shrank such that there was no time to find food before the bus roared off again.

The driver negotiated narrow rural roads and slumbering towns drawn from musty, sepia-colored library books. For miles, squat porch-front flats with peeling paint, rusting early-model automobiles and machinery, and faded clapboard storefronts with empty shop windows drifted past. Between the towns lay mile after mile of unbroken pine forest thriving in shallow sandy soil.

When we reached Mobile, on the Alabama coast, we were far behind schedule but our connecting bus had thankfully waited. With no time for food, we crammed our rucksacks aboard and continued on, ravenous. In Mississippi we stopped long enough to grab a few morsels before pushing on, into Louisiana. On the lengthy ride through Texas, beneath brooding black skies, long flickers of lightning reached down from the heavens and highlighted the sleeping passengers with flashes of white light. Someone at the previous stop had said the bus went all the way to Laredo on the Texas border so we relaxed, but at Houston everyone piled off the bus. We blinked sleepily and confusedly.

"Your bus is waiting at gate five!" the driver hollered.

We dashed across the terminal and found our bus just in time. Sleep was impossible, so I stared into the darkness and found myself thinking about America's role, and the impact of capitalism in particular, upon the countries we were about to visit.

"Have you read *Wealth of Nations*, by Adam Smith?" I asked a bleary-eyed Tamara.

"I have," she replied. "It's interesting that he published a treatise on capitalism in the same year the Declaration of Independence was signed."

"A harbinger of things to come, I suppose."

"As I recall, Smith claimed that the goal of capitalism is freedom from government interference. Every individual should be able to participate equally in the economy, kind of like how voting gives everyone a voice in the political process."

"Yes. In Medieval Europe a person was born into a certain class, worked within a specific guild, and lived a life based on rules set by the church. But as money and capital became more of a driving force, the medieval system unraveled. The race to accumulate wealth was on, and Europeans exported this mindset to the American colonies. Smith's ideas, plus the influence of religious freedom and democratic rule, set the stage in America for the rise of the modern corporation."

"The world would never be the same."

"True. It seems the corporation has overtaken the church and the state as the dominant social and political force. But here's my issue with capitalism. Nothing grows indefinitely, yet corporations are expected to turn a profit year after year. The only way to do *that* is to sell more stuff. So, advertisers work harder to convince us we'll be happier, wealthier, or better looking if we buy their products."

"If people want what's being sold," Tamara countered, "then what's the problem? I imagine millions of people would love to have the choices we have."

I thought about this. She made a good point.

"You're right," I continued, "but it seems to me that marketing takes advantage of peoples' insecurities, and they then subscribe to the false dreams that advertisers so often sell. If someone doesn't know what they want in life, they might be convinced to *buy* something to find happiness, rather than *do* something more fulfilling, like read a book, travel, or spend time with family. People too often consume rather than have experiences and build positive memories."

"That's their choice, isn't it?"

"Yes," I opined, "but I still feel the big con of Western society is the promotion of products—regardless of whether or not people want, need, or can *afford* what's being sold—with the promise that those products will make them happier."

"Choice is a form of freedom. And you're a big advocate for personal freedom. People have the right to choose how to make themselves happy."

"The whole system feels disingenuous to me."

"Where are you going with this?"

"I'm thinking about America's role in the countries we're going to, and I guess I'm a little bothered by it."

After the end of colonialism Latin Americans were free, but three hundred years of Spanish and Portuguese rule had left them unsure how to govern themselves. In the absence of political parties or solid institutions, many nations slipped into anarchy or dictatorship. Cut off from the modernizing world, the mid-1800s were a time of turbulence for Latin America.

"As Latin America struggled to find its identity, the United States needed resources—lots of them—to support corporatism, capitalism, and consumerism, and sustain the illusion that things bring happiness," I said to Tamara. "Businesses needed raw materials to manufacture the goods that people wanted. And Latin America was one of the easiest places for the United States to get those resources."

"Makes sense," she replied. "What's the problem? This is why America became an economic powerhouse, and is what provides the lifestyles we both enjoy."

"It's the hypocrisy that bothers me. As the power of the United States grew, its influence over Latin America also grew. The United States nominated itself as the benevolent protector of democracy and freedom. But, in practice, successive administrations have supported any Latin American government that best enabled the flow of resources to the United States corporations that needed them. The problem with this policy is that it usually led to the support of autocratic dictators and military regimes."

"*Now* I see where you're going with this."

"Funding coups and backing overseas armies greatly contributed to the rise of the guerilla organizations, military dictatorships, and civil wars that tore much of Latin America apart throughout the twentieth century. The way I see it, the conflict between an increasingly wealthy and militaristic America and a subjugated and powerless Latin America created an American dichotomy which, to varying degrees, shaped the history of every nation in Central and South America."

"I guess we'll find out soon enough," said Tamara.

"I'm not sure if it was ever really about democracy."

I have never felt overly patriotic or espoused an especially strong sense of national pride, yet I have been grateful to live in a land where so many freedoms prevail. I wanted to believe that America's positive influences have outweighed the negatives. On this journey I hoped to witness, firsthand, how United States policies and corporations had affected the people and cultures of Latin America, for better or worse.

Another part of me wanted to believe that underdogs could always overcome powerful oppressors, that David could always defeat Goliath, that anyone, no matter how disadvantaged, could rise to the occasion and tackle whatever obstacle arose. The struggle might not be easy and there could be much to lose and sacrifice, but triumph would be possible. I wanted to believe this, but wasn't certain of its veracity. The best way to find out, I had decided, was to travel overland across the Americas, for I knew that immersing myself in a place was the best and sometimes only way to truly know that place.

5

MEXICO'S MARXIST ROOTS

The bus deposited us in Laredo, on the Mexican border, at four in the morning. Tamara dozed on a wooden bench inside the bus depot, while I pulled a stack of briefs published by the U.S. Department of State from my rucksack, and perused the warnings for each of the countries lying ahead. The destinations on our Mexican route–Mexico City, Oaxaca, and Chiapas–all posed a fair amount of danger.

Crime across Mexico had turned increasingly violent in the months before our arrival. So-called "express" kidnappings–attempts to get quick cash in exchange for the victim's release–on well-traveled highways outside Mexico City did not exclusively target the wealthy, so any traveler was at risk. Two resistance groups operating in the states of Guerrero and Oaxaca, the Popular Revolutionary Army and the Insurgent People's Revolutionary Army, had recently attacked police and military targets, and kidnapped civilians. Tourists were advised to avoid demonstrations and other activities that might be deemed political by Mexican authorities, in light of tensions in the state of Chiapas.

I roused Tamara before dawn. She was growing a little more used to her rucksack, though the narrow straps still cut into her tender shoulders. Around the corner from the bus depot, near a plaza of eucalyptus trees that was filled with a cacophony of birdcalls, we ordered coffee and *chilaquiles rojos*—fried tortillas smothered in red salsa—before cleaning ourselves up in the restaurant sinks.

With no banks or money changing kiosks, called *casas de cambios*, yet open we walked through Laredo, over the bridge spanning the Río Grande, and into the Mexican border town of Nuevo Laredo. The authorities ignored us, though as I had learned, searches and delays more often arose on the way home than when entering Mexico. A smattering of shops had begun to open, and a few vendors called out to passersby from damp sidewalks and grimy stalls.

We hopped aboard one of the battered local buses headed to the main bus station that was revving in a cloud of exhaust fumes on the east side of the main plaza, and cruised along twisting streets, punctuated with unfinished and partly demolished concrete buildings with rebar poking skyward. Trash littered every gutter and open space. At the Central Camionera we caught a long distance bus, and at midday reached the city of Monterrey.

There, Tamara and I meandered along a seedy strip of *cantinas*—sometimes-raucous Mexican watering holes—where Monterrey's budget hotels were also congregated. Tamara bore the weight of her rucksack during the long walk without saying a word. The first hotel was more expensive than I had expected. Though the peso's value had dropped since I'd last visited Mexico, inflation had evidently driven prices skyward. All the other hotels we checked were of a similar price, so we had little choice but to choose one and settle in.

While we unpacked, a woman's cries of pleasure wafted through our window. After seeing Tamara's expression, I explained to her that, in this conservative Catholic country where entire extended families lived beneath one roof, cheaper places such as ours often doubled as brothels, or pay-by-the hour hotels for young lovers needing a hideaway. Either way, we both felt like we were invading the woman's privacy, and so we escaped into the streets.

We celebrated our arrival in Mexico, the first country on our Latin American odyssey, with free pours at a local brewery. Two young well-heeled European men joined us, and we all laughed at our contrasts. Their hotel cost seven hundred pesos, ours one hundred sixty. They had flown up from Mexico City; we had arrived by bus, from Baltimore.

"We're visiting two *chicas* we met in Paris on holiday," one of the jetsetters explained. "Berta and Ana."

"We'll probably dance with them until dawn at one of the discos in the Barrio Antiguo district," added the other. "Come join us!"

We laughed. "We'll likely read in our room," Tamara said.

After the young men left to meet Berta and Ana, Tamara and I wandered the Zona Rosa district amongst thousands of locals. Music blared from speakers atop the Governor's Palace along the Plaza de Armas as the sun dipped behind towering mountains of the Sierra Madre Oriental. A wedding procession filed out of the old stone cathedral. Groups of young locals strolled past fountains shooting into the sky.

To me, the Spanish language is a romantic one, flowing from the tongue without a single harsh syllable; passionate, forgiving, and gentle. I enjoyed the simple formalities of the language, greeting passersby with a polite "buenas noches" and equally solicitous "buenos días" in the morning. Before getting down to business, acquaintances would always enquire about the other's wellbeing. "¿Cómo estás?" one might ask. *How are you?* "Bien, gracias." *Good, thank you.*

Elderly men and women sitting on stoops and benches greeted passersby with wide smiles. In the parks and plazas teenage lovers kissed and embraced. And wherever we went, youngsters' wide brown eyes, a mixture of Spanish and indigenous heritage, brimmed with questions.

As evening fell, we circled back to our hotel, where a child's wailing had replaced the woman's moans. The setting wasn't peaceful, but I was comforted by the fact that we were surrounded by regular people living their everyday lives—in some ways identical to, and in others entirely different from, the life I knew. Such moments were why I loved to travel.

Lying on the bed beneath the whirring fan, other thoughts infiltrated my mind. Already I was worrying about our funds. Now that we had reached Mexico, it was apparent that prices were higher than I expected, and we heard rumors that costs had exploded across the whole of South America. I worried whether we would have enough cash to reach the southern edge of Argentina and make it home again. Even if we had enough money in our bank accounts, I feared running low thousands of miles from home with no way to get additional funds. We had barely begun and already I sensed the dream starting to slip away.

In the morning, I dispelled my worries and we pushed forward by bus towards San Luis Potosí. South of Monterrey, the land turned dry and desolate and the parched terrain was dotted with cacti and yucca. We occasionally came across men wearing ten-gallon cowboy hats repairing sections of tarmac. Occasional cafés or truck stops stood by the roadside, though most were abandoned or half-built. No dwellings dotted the shimmering desert that stretched to the horizons. Sometimes, our bus would stop at a desolate place and passengers would disembark in the searing heat and walk into the emptiness. I wondered what lurked out there and what kinds of lives they lived in such an inhospitable landscape.

We reached the city of San Luis Potosí in late afternoon. At the first hotel we encountered, Tamara wrinkled her nose. I admittedly had hoped to cut a few corners, but Tamara simply wanted some basic comfort and cleanliness. She made no secret of the fact that she detested bugs, vermin, and filth anywhere in her life but particularly in her living quarters.

"Let's try somewhere else," I suggested.

We found another hovel across the street, somewhat decent compared to many of the hotels in India where I had stayed.

"This place smells funny," Tamara said.

"Okay, let's move on."

The next hotel seemed no better than the first, but the manager showed us a room anyway.

"Let's take it," Tamara said.

"Are you sure?" I asked. "This looks like a roach motel."

"It'll be okay." She took a deep breath and nodded at the manager. The room was ours.

The streets of San Luis Potosí bustled with activity. In the main square, dancers in traditional loincloths and cloaks twirled for onlookers. At every plaza we entered, musicians played, and seemingly at every cathedral a grand Catholic wedding was unfolding. Lavish bouquets of flowers decorated the grooms' automobiles. Every corner of the city seemed to teem with life.

As darkness descended we returned to our hotel. The manager could not find our room key, and while he searched, I wondered what awaited us on the other side of the door. After he eventually found a key that fit the worn lock, Tamara stepped through the doorway. When she flicked on the light, dozens of two-inch cockroaches scurried across the filthy walls and bare floors. Baby ones poured from a hole in the wall by the broken sink.

"Ack!" she shrieked. "They're everywhere!"

Tamara stomped some of the bugs, but we were greatly outnumbered, so she gave up and plunked herself in the middle of the bed, fully clothed, with her boots still on. I knew it would be a long night.

"Leave that on!" she nearly shouted when I reached for the light switch.

"I'm sorry," was all I could think to say.

"I can't do this," she mumbled. "Maybe I could still spend the summer in Europe. France, maybe. Italy would be nice."

Then she said nothing more, and after a while switched off the light. Within minutes, loud voices began echoing off the concrete walls in the open courtyard. A woman's moans floated upward, louder and louder. Sleep was impossible. As dawn approached, the place at last quieted and we slept, intermittently.

Visiting the second floor bathroom in the morning, Tamara had to step around a large hole in the floor to avoid falling through. The water was turned off, so she couldn't wash her face or hands, the inoperable shower was like an unlit dungeon, and the toilet was filled with excrement.

"Are you okay?" I asked after she returned.

"That...was...disgusting..."

The hotel was too sleazy, even for me, and though Tamara proved she could bear it, neither of us wanted to endure six more months in such conditions. It seemed we would have to either find a way to muddle along with not enough money to afford basic comforts, or turn back. Neither option sounded appealing.

As we approached Mexico City in mid-morning, I worried about borders and budgets. Tamara was preoccupied with bugs and bandits. We were an anxious pair. Of all our destinations, Mexico City was her greatest concern. The most common crimes in Mexico City involved pickpockets, purse snatchers, and armed robbers confronting tourists. Recent media reports of Volkswagen Beetle taxi driver robberies, abductions, and even murders had unnerved Tamara and her family. She made clear that her priority was to quickly get in and out of Mexico's capital. Considering my financial concerns, I happily obliged.

Originally built in the thirteenth century on the clay bed of long ago drained Lake Texcoco, Mexico City was now home to over twenty million people–among the highest concentrations of humanity on Earth. An eclectic mixture of classical and colonial-era architecture, as well as ancient Aztec ruins surrounded the Plaza del Zócalo at the heart of the mile-high city. From the Metropolitan Cathedral's bell towers, which we climbed, the expansive view on a rare smog-free day took in a ring of 15,000 feet-high mountains and the frequently active volcano of Popocatépetl.

In the Coyoacán neighborhood we visited the former home of Leon Trotsky. A major contributor to the Bolshevik victory in the Russian Civil War, he later opposed the policies of dictator Joseph Stalin and this conflict forced his exile to

Mexico City. In Coyoacán, on 21 August 1940, acting on instructions from Stalin, an assassin smashed Trotsky's head with an ice axe. He died the next day.

We wandered through his house, a small fortress with guard towers at each corner and twenty-foot stone walls surrounding gardens and banana trees. I pondered the bullet holes that attackers pumped into his bedroom three months before his assassination, and tried to imagine living in such conditions. Though I knew that Karl Marx and Trotsky founded Marxism, I had long wondered what exactly their beliefs entailed. Though not a topic I typically brought up at dinner parties, I had begun to suspect that many critics of Marxism did not entirely understand what Marx, or his ideology, stood for. Afterward, sipping coffee at a nearby outdoor café, I picked Tamara's brain.

"What do you know about Marxism?" I asked her.

"Well, I know it started as a reaction to capitalism," she began. "Marx was a utopian who believed the capitalist model too often did not create products that are truly useful. I think one of Marx's complaints was that capitalists are motivated more by money making than by helping others." She took a sip of her coffee. "If there's no market for a new product, advertisers create one. And since production is often oriented towards meeting artificial demand, rather than real human needs, Marx believed people end up feeling alienated. They're not able to create things that have meaning to them, and they're pressured into buying things they don't really want."

A young man we had noticed visiting Trotsky's house walked past, and we invited him to join us.

"I'm a student," Rodrigo explained, "studying English and political science."

"This is why you were visiting Trotsky's house?" I asked.

"Sí. I have been before, but felt a desire to return."

"How did Trotsky end up in Mexico City?" Tamara asked.

"The Russian Revolution and the ideas of Marx, Lenin, and Trotsky influenced many Mexican people," Rodrigo said, "especially artists, intellectuals, and students. After our own revolution, painters like Diego Rivera and Frida Kahlo, and poets like Octavio Paz, all became Marxists. At Rivera's request, the president of Mexico gave asylum to Trotsky."

"And the Mexican people were okay with this?" asked Tamara.

"Oh yes. They saw Marxism as a good alternative to capitalism, and a buffer against United States imperialism."

"How do you feel about Marxism?" she asked.

"I see Americans as unsatisfied and unhappy. So many of you eat too much and buy too much and work too much. Why? You are looking for something. But you are not finding it. I think you need a different system."

"Marxism?" Tamara smiled.

"I am not a Marxist. But I do believe that too many in the West are slaves to consumerism. You work more hours to make more money but you have less time for what really matters. Like family. I don't want to live in poverty and I don't want my family to be poor. But having money does not make us happy."

"What does?" I asked.

"I think finding work that fulfills us. Or at least finding a way to enjoy the work we are doing. My uncle sells balloons every night from his cart around the plazas near his home. Seeing children having fun provides his meaning. He is happy."

"What kind of system do you think we need?"

"I am not against capitalism. You are the richest country in the world. But you are not the happiest. Even within Mexico, those in the north believe those in the south are lazy. Those in the south think those in the north have no souls. The closer you get to America, the more this is true. We all want to provide for our families. But there must be balance. Choose meaningful work. I think this is what Marx wanted for the workers and proletarians. Prosperity and fulfillment."

Rodrigo looked at his watch. "My next class starts soon," he said. "I must go."

"Thank you for chatting with us," I said.

"¡Sí!" he said. "I hope you find what you are looking for."

What Tamara and I were looking for we were unlikely to find in Mexico City. At her request we didn't linger long. In the bus station that afternoon, while I purchased tickets for our overnight run to Oaxaca de Juárez, Tamara found her way to an upstairs rest room. She always washed her hands or used sanitizer when touching anything questionable, but had nevertheless been struck low with a case of Montezuma's Revenge. Flushed and feverish, for the rest of the evening, while we waited for our bus to leave she dashed every few minutes to *el sanitario* at a cost of two pesos per poop. Worried, I wondered what to do.

"Let's get a room," I offered. "I can find one nearby while you rest here."

"No…" She said, slumping back into her seat.

"Why don't you lie down?"

She shook her head, but later gave in and collapsed on the dirty tile floor in an unmoving heap. I brought her beans and rice and soda, but nothing stayed in her drained, dehydrated body. Passing Mexicans wondered why she was lying on the floor.

"Enferma," I told anyone in the bus station that asked. *Sick.* They gazed at her with pity in their eyes.

As evening fell, I noticed a torpid haze hanging over the city like a stained muslin cloth. Our throats ached, our eyes couldn't focus properly, and our noses bled intermittently. I recalled a recent article about the 100,000 children in the Mexico City area who died every year as a result of pollution, the quarter million people who suffered from eye diseases, and fact that life expectancy in the city had been reduced by up to ten years. I almost feared we might add to those figures.

As departure time neared I roused Tamara. She hopped up from the floor in her eagerness to leave the city, and grabbed her ticket from my hand, but a wave of nausea soon overtook her. She faltered, rallied, and finally, outside the terminal, collapsed. She scuttled along on her hands and knees like a crab, rose partway, and then slumped forward. Even though she was about to puke, have an attack of diarrhea, and pass out all at once, she did not want to appear sick and be denied entry to the bus, so, I distracted the conductor while she crawled aboard. I asked him whether the bus bathroom was unlocked. "Ah," he said. "No hay un baño." *There is no bathroom.* "¡Ay, caramba!" I muttered.

When I gave Tamara the bad news, she just closed her eyes and shrank into her seat. As the bus moved forward, I watched life teem on every block. Thousands milling about bought and sold in an orchestra of cooperation. A vendor or two manned each corner, and locals gathered round feasting on tacos and tortillas. Radios blared, cars beeped, dogs barked, kids yelled, and men whistled to friends, to get one's attention, and to hail buses or VW Beetle taxis rolling along the back streets. Gradually the Valley of Mexico fell behind us. As we climbed into the Sierra Madre Oriental, a landscape of rolling hillsides covered in a million points of light filled the horizon.

We reached Oaxaca at half past three in the morning. In the cramped waiting room, Tamara pulled a two-day old Texan newspaper from her rucksack. She kneeled and spread the opened pages onto the floor. I thought she might want to scour them for something special. A flight home, perhaps? Instead, she lay down upon her paper mattress. The hours dragged as we waited for morning. At dawn I woke her. She struggled up, but said nothing as we walked into the heart of Oaxaca.

Yellow morning light played through broad trees that shaded the central Zócalo as soldiers raised an oversized Mexican flag and old men watered flowers. The Governor's Palace guarded the southern edge of the plaza across from the grand cathedral. Wrought-iron verandas and European-style wooden doors accented the surrounding houses. Countless cousins of our old car, Anastasia, rumbled past in various states of disrepair. When a battered, silver two-door passed us I stood in respectful silence, to Tamara's amusement. We left our belongings behind the desk of a hotel and found coffee and *huevos revueltos*–scrambled eggs–at an outdoor cafe. As we ate, Tamara came slowly back to life.

Afterward, we joined thousands of comely, bronzed Oaxaca townsfolk strolling through Alameda de León plaza. The indigenous influence was stronger here than in the north. The shapely young women dressed far more fashionably than us. Older Oaxaca women wore more traditional attire and, to my eyes, exuded a beauty all their own. Most were short, not over four feet tall, with stocky legs and all with deep brown skin, dark hair, and strong hands.

Part of Oaxaca's charm for me was the language, but food and music also reflected the vibrant culture. Many people we met were talented artists, and the markets bustled with handicrafts and wares. Everyone had something to sell, usually handmade. Women wearing dresses and small aprons sold roses stacked in baskets. I noticed one young girl sitting atop a wide wall, from where she sold cold drinks. Between customers she blew bubbles in the sunshine and giggled at the world. I thought of Rodrigo. This was not a capitalist culture in the sense that corporations held sway. Mexico was a nation of entrepreneurs. Here people seemed happy, and proud of their crafts and handiworks. It appeared to me that the system Rodrigo had described was alive and well in Oaxaca.

At a local bar near the main plaza we celebrated another day by sipping one-dollar Sol beers. Thunder and lightning rattled the rooftops. When the rain poured down, locals hurried past beneath umbrellas and newspapers. Later, as the sun broke free and lent a golden glow to the eastern hills, we giddily bought a tin of sardines, can of beans, and spicy tortilla chips for a picnic in our room.

Earlier in the day we had learned how to send a package to the United States. Tamara wanted to return items home that she could live without. We found an empty box to ship the items home in, bought paper at a *papelaría* shop and brown string at the open-air market, and wrapped the package before handing it to the post office clerk. As Tamara grew more comfortable, so too her enjoyment of our journey increased. I was also relieved that she recovered so quickly from her sudden illness. Maybe my dream would come true after all.

Famished, we were about to devour our picnic dinner when Tamara stopped short, having glanced at her lower legs. Above each of her Achilles tendons, and only there, were clusters of bright red rashes. We forgot about dinner, and instead scoured books seeking a bug or affliction she may have picked up. She had no pain or other symptoms. I suggested some reaction to the bus station floor. She suspected a disease. But nothing fit. Stumped, we ate in thoughtful silence.

6

THE FORGOTTEN REVOLUTION

From Oaxaca, we continued southward. Tamara's mysterious ankle rashes were still a shade of fiery crimson, but as they caused her no discomfort, we opted for a wait-and-see approach. Beyond the Isthmus of Tehuantepec lay Chiapas, a state riddled with civil unrest and revolution. We spent all night on the bus, again, traveling past subsistence plots tended by indigenous folk with work shovel in hand or bundle of firewood carried by a tumpline about the forehead, until first light, when we climbed into the clouds on the approach to San Cristóbal de las Casas.

Founded in 1528 as a military fort by the Spanish conquistador who vanquished the area, San Cristóbal served as administrative capital of Chiapas until the late 1800s and remained the region's cultural heart. In the local Tzotzil language, the town–which is nestled within a verdant valley of the central highlands–is called Jovel, "the place in the clouds."

Here we had our first taste of what I called the American Dichotomy–the historical disparity between an increasingly powerful United States and a Latin America struggling to find its identify following independence from Spain and Portugal. Three hundred years of colonial rule had left authoritarian, patrimonial, elitist values embedded in the culture. Though the church, wealthy landowners, and military wanted those values to remain entrenched, a new political culture appeared in the wake of independence, this one supported by urban intellectuals, students, and an emerging middle class. The clash between these two polarities—traditional holders of power versus reform-minded upstarts—triggered violence, instability, and civil war across Latin America during the 1800s.

In Mexico, most of the land was controlled by large estates called *haciendas*, and the villagers were forced into *peonaje*, a form of debt slavery. The son of peasants, young Emiliano Zapata grew frustrated by the ongoing theft of village land. So, he began taking disputed land by force. In 1910, the Mexican Revolution erupted, and Zapata jumped all in. His followers, known as Zapatistas, played a major role in the revolution, which eventually resulted in a new constitution.

Across the rest of Latin America, as governments gained more control over their states, they generally ruled in the same autocratic manner as their Spanish and Portuguese colonizers before them. This resulted in animosity and in part led, in the 1930s, to the shift towards socialist, Marxist, and anti-American politics among students, intellectuals, and trade unionists. Latin America's oligarchic, medieval, feudal-like hierarchies neared collapse. Politics remained divided for decades. Unrest instigated during the 1960s by peasants, workers, and left-wing guerillas throughout Latin America forced a return to military authoritarianism and led to a new wave of civil wars.

The end of the Mexican Revolution led to the creation of the Institutional Revolutionary Party, which ruled Mexico for the remainder of the twentieth century. Various counter movements formed, but few had lasting impact until the 1980s when remnant members of former factions founded the Zapatista Army of National Liberation, or EZLN, which took its name from Zapata and saw itself as his ideological heir.

After the bishop of San Cristóbal adopted an ideology called liberation theology–which critiqued society and the Church and interpreted Christ's teachings with the goal of reversing repression–San Cristóbal became a base for political activism. Six years before our arrival, on 1 January 1994, the North American Free Trade Agreement, or NAFTA, went into effect between Mexico, Canada, and the United States. At the same time, a clash between the bishop's ideology and the government's move towards free trade erupted.

On that day, a new revolution began. Impoverished indigenous EZLN fighters, some toting fake wooden rifles and all wearing black ski masks and red bandanas, stormed San Cristóbal and other villages in Chiapas. Under the leadership of Subcomandante Marcos, the ragtag group's commander, the plight of the indigenous people of Mexico was elevated to the world stage. A new generation of Zapatistas declared war against the Mexican government.

The term *guerilla* derives from the Spanish *guerra*, and combined with the diminutive *-illa*, means *little war*. Popularized in the early 1800s, when the Spanish resistance rose against Napoleon using tactics of ambush, sabotage, and hit-and-run raids, the term later described irregular bands of mobile rebels who used inhospitable terrain to their advantage, while fighting larger professional armies.

The first time I heard the word I was ten years old. I was sitting in the backseat of my father's Chevy station wagon while my uncle and father rode in front. They were discussing my father's upcoming business trip to Colombia, the war which was then happening in the jungles there, and the risks he was taking by going. I wondered why *gorillas* would want to start a war, and gradually realized they were not talking about furry apes but men with guns who might want to harm my father. This idea confused and concerned me, and I believed then that all guerillas were, by definition, bad.

Guerilla warfare is asymmetrical, in that it pits two armies of different sizes and types against each other. It is also irregular, in that the guerilla's goal is to not only defeat the enemy but also to gain popular support and generate political influence. Often guerilla groups rely on support from the populace and embed themselves within local communities. Guerillas generally only fight against small groups of established military forces, and though they might destroy infrastructure, using improvised explosives for example, they usually abide by the laws of war. Mobility, surprise, and secrecy are their main assets. Terrorists, on the other hand, do not usually confront soldiers or military units, focusing instead on civilians. The aim of a terrorist is to lodge fear in people's hearts. Terrorists use terror as their primary strategic tool for achieving their goals. Knowing this, governments often label opponents as 'terrorists' in order to turn popular opinion against them.

I could never support any terrorist group that intended to hurt innocent civilians. While traveling in Mexico, however, I wondered if my young belief that all guerillas were bad was entirely accurate. NAFTA was going to spell the end of Mexican crop subsidies without an end to United States ones. It would also potentially reduce the living standards of farmers in southern Mexico who could not compete with artificially-fertilized, mechanically-harvested, genetically-engineered United States imports. NAFTA also removed land reparations promised to indigenous groups from the Mexican Constitution. Leaders of the Zapatista movement did not demand independence but autonomy, and that a greater share of resources extracted from Chiapas more directly benefit the people. Within the movement, men and women were considered equal, just as Zapata himself had invited women to fight and serve as officers in his army. What the Zapatistas were fighting for sounded reasonable to me. But, I was not certain whether I agreed with their methods.

During the Zapatista Uprising, 3,000 armed insurgents seized villages, freed prisoners in San Cristóbal's jail, and set fire to police buildings and military barracks. The guerillas enjoyed a brief success until the military countered and a wave of fighting erupted. Hundreds of Zapatistas died and those left retreated into the jungle. Twelve days after it began, the uprising ended. Mexican army camps sprang up along major roads in Chiapas, and the movement's leaders had vanished. In the ensuing weeks the latter-day Zapatistas developed a media campaign using cell phones, newspaper *comunicados,* and the burgeoning Internet to generate solidarity and sympathy.

The Chiapas conflict, begun by Marcos and his followers, was still ongoing upon our arrival and I yearned to get a closer look at the communities the Zapatistas aspired to help. A few miles from San Cristóbal lies the indigenous Tzotzil Mayan village of San Juan Chamula. To get there Tamara and I flagged down one of the battered, vintage Volkswagen vans—*colectivos*— that served as shared taxis and shuttled passengers between villages. Tzotzil Mayan people in brightly colored wraps filled the streets. Outside the central church, children sold small toys and handmade animal figurines for a few pesos while women sold traditional clothes, blankets, and Subcomandante Marcos dolls. A troupe of men in dark woolen tunics and playing soft melodies on handmade instruments meandered through the plaza. We followed them into the church.

Instead of sitting in pews, the villagers were clustered around hundreds of candles stuck to the hay-covered floor. The high ceiling arched over a cavernous interior filled with the haze of copal resin incense. Two stained glass windows lent a hint of natural light; all else was bathed in the orange-yellow flicker of candlelight. A man in a woolen tunic beckoned us farther inside, where we mingled among the locals, some of whom were passing around sodas or clutching chickens.

A *curandero*, or medicine man, explained that locals came to the church to be healed. He and other *curanderos* would work in the church to diagnose medical and 'evil-eye' afflictions and prescribe remedies that included flower petals, feathers, and candles of any of five hues—white, tallow, green, yellow, or multi-color. In dire situations, a live rooster or hen would be called for. The prescribed remedies would then be brought to a healing ceremony during which families knelt, stuck candles to the floor with melted wax, drank cola or ceremonial cups of *posh*–a sugar cane-based liquor–and chanted prayers in an archaic Tzotzil dialect. If fortunate, the suffering spirit was healed.

Over time, the Tzotzil had evolved their own religious blend of pre-conquest Mayan and Spanish Catholic traditions. Despite centuries of European influence, I could see that they had maintained many ancestral traditions. The Tzotzil we met–who were among the landless people the Zapatistas intended to help–were simple, kind, generous folk with a proud heritage.

One morning in San Cristóbal, over a breakfast of fresh fruit, I read a few of Marcos' *comunicados*.

"We don't want to impose our solutions by force, we want to create a democratic space," he wrote. "We don't see armed struggle in the classic sense of previous guerilla wars, that is as the only way and the only all-powerful truth around which everything is organized. In a war, the decisive thing is not the military confrontation but the politics at stake in the confrontation. We didn't go to war to kill or be killed. We went to war in order to be heard."

This sounded rather different to me than the indiscriminate violence I had long associated with guerilla warfare.

After breakfast, Tamara and I explored San Cristóbal and visited a few of the shops lining the cobblestone streets, which sold everything imaginable. Low-lying clouds clinging to surrounding mountainsides drifted past. When we came across impoverished local children and women, who stood at most street corners selling handicrafts, necklaces, jewelry, and tapestries, I remembered that there is often no pleasure without a price. In this case, my enjoyment of this colonial-era town was tinged with the daily struggles the locals likely endured, despite efforts by both generations of Zapatistas. The murals scattered across San Cristóbal and throughout Chiapas that we often noticed–usually depicting Emiliano Zapata, Argentinean Che Guevara, and Subcomandante Marcos–told the story of Mexico's revolutionary folk heroes.

We walked to the Church of San Cristóbal, which stood atop a long flight of steps. Weathered shacks with tin roofs cluttered the hillside. As we climbed the stairs, darting chickens scratched at the dirt and snot-smeared children asked for money. "Un peso!" the tykes called. Sounds from the city's yellow and orange homes–most with red corrugated adobe roofs and wrought iron railings–drifted upward and caught my ear; a dog barked, roosters crowed, cars beeped.

One boy wrapped his dirt-stained arms around Tamara's leg, hoping to extract a few pesos. She tried, without success, to not look into his pleading, hopeful eyes. Considering the conditions around us, it seemed the Zapatistas had been right–that NAFTA did not benefit the common people. Even twenty-five years after the start of the Zapatista revolution, long after our journey, half of Mexico's population still lived in poverty. As subsidized corn and other crops poured into Mexico from the United States, consumer food prices rose but the prices Mexican farmers earned for their produce dropped. A glut of processed foods from the United States also helped make Mexico the most obese nation in Latin America. International companies took over land that farmers had supported their families on for generations, forcing many peasants from their farms.

Outside Mexico, the Zapatista Uprising had been largely forgotten, yet the issues that the Zapatistas had raised remained as pressing as ever. "The wall between rich and poor," former American president Lyndon Johnson once observed, "is a wall of glass through which all can see."

Watching poverty-stricken children race after us in the hope of garnering a few pesos bolstered my growing empathy for ordinary Mexicans trying to eke out an existence, and helped make that wall far more transparent. I am not a supporter of violence, but I know that the powerless must sometimes employ unorthodox tactics to get what they need to make their lives a bit more tolerable.

"If the people are unable to help themselves," I asked Tamara as we climbed the church steps, "then who will?"

"Sometimes," she responded after a few moments of reflection, "the answer, sadly, is no one."

7

CHICKEN BUS

Tamara and I fumbled about gathering our belongings in the pre-dawn darkness. We planned to catch a bus south to the Mexican border and, from there, make our way into Guatemala. As usual, uncertainty about the crossing weighed on my mind. If the bus were delayed, we might reach the border after it closed. If the guards turned us away, our dream of traveling onwards to South America may not happen at all.

A scream from the bathroom shattered my thoughts. Tamara stood, eyes wide, with her toothbrush in one hand.

"I accidentally rinsed my mouth from the tap instead of using bottled water," she said quietly. "Now I'll be sick again."

"Maybe not," I soothed. "If you only drank a little, you'll probably be fine. Don't worry." I held up her bottle of anti-mosquito spray. "At least I may have solved the mystery of the rash on your ankles."

To keep mosquitoes at bay, Tamara had been spraying the repellant all over her clothing. When sitting or lying down—as she did on the floor of the bus station in Mexico City—she often crossed her feet, so one heel rested atop the other foot.

"I think some rubbed onto your skin and you reacted to it."

"That makes sense," she said. "Maybe I don't need a doctor after all."

Despite this revelation, Tamara's spirits clearly sagged as she sluggishly packed her bag. I thought she had been adapting well to our simple lifestyle, but any journey took some getting used to. Like life, new ways of being take time to accept.

We walked to the bus station, where a black and white television in the corner broadcast news from the Chiapas interior near where we were passing through to reach the border. Several villagers had been killed and the Zapatistas were being blamed.

Tamara perked up a bit. "I've heard that police sometimes use such ploys to enter an area, gain control, and turn popular opinion against the uprising," she remarked. "It can be hard to know what's truth and what's propaganda."

On the bus we sat near a lone Australian woman named Lorinda who was happy for the company. Our ride turned out to be quite tense. On the roadsides were scores of Mexican soldiers in army fatigues, toting machine guns. Still more were hunkered down inside bunkers piled high with sandbags and protected by heavy, large-caliber guns. The soldiers stopped vehicles and questioned travelers before waving most onward.

The bus terminated at the Mexican border town of Ciudad Cuauhtémoc. An attendant slowly pulled bags from the hold—the last comfortable ride we'd have, as we were about to experience. I hustled off to find a ride across the border, while Tamara waited by the bags. There were no buses, but a boy pointed towards a battered 1970s-era Chevy Nova idling by the road. Tamara and I crawled into the backseat with two burly Mexicans while Lorinda, who was also headed to Guatemala, squeezed in front. The driver gunned the motor and we were soon climbing up into the mountains and across the narrow strip of territory that ran between Mexico and Guatemala.

On the other side of this no man's land we entered the Guatemalan town of La Mesilla, where a Swedish couple named Petra and Karl joined us. Moneychangers offered to sell us Guatemalan quetzals. I knew that remote crossings usually lacked banks or official exchanges, so moneychangers, despite their unsavory reputation, often offered the only option. We watched closely while Lorinda traded notes. I heard a man yell something from within a heap of misshapen buses.

"Huehuetenango?" I called back, referring to the next city on our route. He nodded.

The five of us threaded our way through a crowd of children and old women selling sodas, snacks, and fruit and hopped aboard the bus bound for Hue, as locals referred to the city. The roof overflowed with baskets and cabbages and sacks filled with grains and ducks and vegetables. Even after the aisle and narrow seats were full, the driver took on more passengers and possessions. It seemed that in Guatemala there was no such thing as a full bus. These so-called 'chicken buses'–ex-school buses that had been imported from the United States–were repainted in dozens of colors, and outfitted with a metal roof rack. All were tired, worn, and prone to frequent and fatal accidents.

We rolled upward into the jungle highlands of central Guatemala and paused often to take on peasants, bulging sacks of produce, chickens, and the occasional goat. Sheer cliffs dropped hundreds of feet into green valleys. The rutted dirt and gravel tracks–transportation arteries of the nation–wound through rugged, war-torn mountains with only a few rocks or cut saplings to prevent our bus from hurtling over the side. Passengers sitting three and four to a narrow wooden seat bounced into the air with every frequent pothole. Once, our seat itself was wrenched from its brackets but squeezed together as we were, we didn't fly far.

So much tossing about didn't dampen the locals' enthusiasm. Men and boys sang and tapped out rhythms on the metal seats, accompanied by local highland music that blared from a boom box. The lad in front of us danced in his seat, to our delight. Despite the mirth, I knew danger lurked beneath the surface. Frustration with a recent rise in crime had led to stories of violent vigilantism and lynch mobs.

We had been warned to avoid public gatherings, as anyone attempting to intervene in such scenarios were themselves sometimes attacked. Visitors to Guatemala were advised to stay in groups, or travel in caravans, and stick to main roads if possible due to the risk of banditry. Peace accords signed between the Guatemalan government and various leftist guerilla groups in 1996, four years before our arrival, had ended a thirty-six-year civil war, but crime remained a troubling problem due to an abundance of weapons, a legacy of violence, and a dysfunctional judiciary. I intended to closely watch our steps, as it wasn't only myself I was responsible for on this trip.

Our bus passed alongside rivers churning their way through the steep valleys. We frequently saw dubious-looking rope bridges dangling across gorges, held up by thin wires, upon which locals carried sacks and bundles. Mist-shrouded mountains canvassed the horizons beneath roiling clouds. Whenever we paused behind a long line of dusty vehicles at work zones and construction sites, which were marked by small stones and branches, brightly garbed Mayan children and women standing a few feet from the cliff edge clambered aboard to sell us sodas, bananas, and tamales.

The drivers raced their overloaded buses around blind corners and up steep mountain roads, passing belching trucks, and each other. Attempting to pass semi-trucks on sharp curves we often had to fall back in line at the last minute as another bus or truck hurtled towards us from the opposite direction. A lack of law enforcement meant any traffic rules that did exist were usually ignored.

On the outskirts of Hue we roared into a muddy yard where the driver revved his motor and killed the engine. Mayans with baskets of produce and merchants with bags of goods filed off the bus. Tamara and I shared a taxi into the center of town with Lorinda and the Swedes. The streets were rough and dirty, like those in Mexico, but more so. Litter filled dusty alleyways that ran between half-finished and abandoned buildings. Thick dust from bus and truck tires tearing around corners choked our eyes and noses.

Tamara and I preferred to wear muted clothing and carry inconspicuous, drab-colored gear in order to better blend in. We couldn't hide our foreign identities, but we thought it best to not make spectacles of ourselves. Lorinda and the Swedes, on the other hand, wore flashy clothing and carried massive, gaudily-colored backpacks. Shopkeepers, locals on park benches, vendors selling produce, and taxi drivers all ogled our eccentric procession.

At the hotel that we found, Karl and Petra got a room across from ours, and Lorinda one over. The Swedes craved fast food so we marched through the streets in search of the Campero fried chicken restaurant they noticed on the way in. None of the greasy meals matched our orders, but we were ravenous and devoured all the food on the table.

Outside, afternoon rains threatened, so Lorinda and the Swedes draped neon orange and bright blue ponchos over themselves. Tamara and I chuckled to ourselves, and I sensed the entire village staring again as we traipsed through town, this time looking twice as buffoonish. All Tamara and I could do was grin and bear it.

In the morning, Tamara and I bade farewell to Lorinda and the Swedes and rode on a series of chicken buses past mountains and volcanoes that jumbled the blue-gray horizon. After five hours, we spiraled down a mountainside and into Panajachel, a village nestled along the shores of Lago de Atitlán, the deepest lake in Central America. The caldera was formed eighty thousand years ago when a volcanic explosion hollowed out the basin that emerald waters now fill. Surrounded by olive-hued escarpments and Mayan villages, and flanked on its southern shores by three volcanoes, Prussian explorer Alexander von Humboldt called it "the most beautiful lake in the world." Aldous Huxley claimed, "It really is too much of a good thing." I had to agree.

Spanish-speaking *ladinos* ran Panajachel's restaurants and *hospedajes*–lodgings. Mayans sold wares, and barefoot hippies wearing traditional Mayan clothing and long dreadlocks plied the streets. Afternoon storms doused the village with thick torrents of rain that pounded the hibiscus and bougainvillea. I wondered if Petra and Karl's iridescent ponchos had kept them dry in Hue.

When rains slackened we attempted our first phone call home. There were black and beige public phones on the streets, but neither worked. At a shop selling phone cards our call didn't go through, and we seemingly lost minutes without making a connection. The storekeeper claimed Tamara's parents' number must be wrong or disconnected. We tried again, and again, until at last her mother answered.

While they talked I wandered down to the waterfront. Lights from the villages of Santiago and Antonio shimmered in the distance, the dark outline of a volcano loomed above the waters, and mist clung to mountain walls. We had only reached Guatemala, yet I felt like we had been traveling for months. I felt responsible for Tamara's safety, and knew that if anything happened to her I would never forgive myself. I wondered what her parents thought as they listened to their daughter describe our journey. Doubts about the trip crept into my mind.

I met Tamara back at our room. Streaks of lightning flashed through the sky like hot daggers. The power cut, and we sat for a moment in the darkness before fumbling for flashlights and venturing into the dim streets. The town had taken on a tranquil air. We found a corner eatery, drank dark lagers by candlelight, and listened to a guitarist strum Latin love songs. We forgot to eat, having earlier devoured a marvelous lunch of fresh fried fish and garlic sauce, and ended up talking into the night. Guatemala was growing on us.

At dawn, purple volcanoes stood partially clear of clouds. Fishing boats trolled past. A few lads dropped lines from the dock as locals climbed onto ferries bound for villages strung along the mist-shrouded lakeshores. We sat waiting in the hardwood seats of one until the captain leapt aboard and the first mate cast off. Puttering past obsidian-colored cliffs tumbling into azure waters, we gazed at weathered homes dotting the emerald hillsides.

On the dock leading to Santiago village, we toed a trembling pier. Children sold clay whistles and women grilled corncobs over orange coals. A path led uphill past shops selling paintings, brilliant tapestries, and hammocks. We passed grubby children splashing in puddles and playing in the dirt. Women hung bright red and blue wraps from sagging lines while men sat silent in cool shadows. At an indoor market, racks of fresh beef hung from hooks, livers and innards filled pans, and giant staring fish sat in stacks. Rows of Mayan women sold cabbages, tomatoes, and melons.

In early afternoon, black clouds gathered round Volcán San Pedro's crater and a brisk wind whisked through the village. The daily wind–the Xocomil–ruffled lake waters and stirred up the dust. From the Cakchiquel language, *xocom* meaning to collect and *il* meaning sin, legend held that this daily wind picked up and carried away villagers' sins. I hoped the Xocomil might carry mine away too.

The next day we visited another market, this one at Chichicastenango, with Dina, Brian, and Christina–fellow travelers we had met the previous evening–and an American expat named Steven. Vendors sold everything from handicrafts, pottery, and pigs, to grindstones, flowers, chickens, woodcarvings, and *pom*–a white resin burned as incense in Mayan rituals. Antique doors, trunks, masks, and wooden bread molds adorned the walls and floors of one shop. The six of us followed music floating through the streets into a nearby building where, upstairs, men played drums and flutes while in another incense-filled room two robed smiling men welcomed us in under the watchful gaze of a Mayan deity.

Afterwards, Steven invited us to his palatial home in Panajachel. Following a delectable dinner, Dina, Christina and Tamara chatted in the spacious living room before joining Brian and Steven and I in the well-appointed kitchen for four hours of spirited political discourse. I realized that Australians such as Brian and Christina had a neutral platform from which to observe North American and European politics, while many Americans, such as myself, often never realized the full extent of our government's role in foreign affairs. Gentle rains, the first hint of the impending rainy season, fell outside the open doorway as Steven lent clarity to Guatemala's unrest. He had lived in the country for several years, but graduated from Harvard and was well-versed in many aspects of academia, particularly world politics and economics. His former roles as investment banker, entrepreneur, consultant, and exporter had earned him numerous friends in the CIA and intelligentsia community. He was a former student of Secretary of State Henry Kissinger, a visitor to over a hundred countries and, now, owner of a gated estate in war-torn Guatemala. I wondered whether Steven was some sort of spy as he spoke, opening my eyes to the violence that had torn Guatemala apart over the past four decades.

"The war is over," said Steven, "but the seeds were sown as far back as the Second World War, when revolutionaries took control of the government. The United States got involved in the 1950s at the height of McCarthyism and the Cold War, when the CIA launched an operation to stop what the State Department and corporate interests feared was a communist takeover of American institutions and policies."

The resulting right-wing coup d'état, which banned labor unions and left-wing political parties, led to poverty, repression, discrimination, and an escalating civil war. Steven explained that the first phase began with an insurrection led by middle-class intellectuals and students.

"The US-trained Guatemalan army easily suppressed the uprising," he said, "but a group of junior military officers fled to the hills. Named after the date of the officers' revolt in 1960, the MR-13 guerillas based themselves in a mountainous corner of the country."

During the second phase, the United States sent Green Beret advisors into Guatemala to train the army in anti-guerrilla warfare tactics. Army members kidnapped and killed former labor union and peasant leaders, and successfully scattered the guerrillas. In retaliation, rebel forces attacked Guatemala City and assassinated multiple high-level leaders.

The third phase occurred throughout the 1970s, as more entities joined the rebels. The defining moment occurred when a group of K'iche' and Ixil farmers occupied the Spanish Embassy to protest the murder of fellow peasants. A police raid resulted in a fire that destroyed the embassy. The funeral for the victims attracted hundreds of thousands of Guatemalans. In time a civilian president, Jorge Serrano Elías, was elected though another ten years of conflict reigned before guerillas signed peace accords. I felt little wonder at Guatemalans' aloofness. By the end of the war more than 200,000 peasants were dead, disappeared, or displaced, making it the deadliest armed conflict in Central America.

"Kissinger once told me that if we can't manage Central America, it will be impossible to convince other threatened nations that we know how to manage the global equilibrium," Steven said. "Our credibility was on the line. And our government was going to do whatever it took to maintain it."

Unlike Guatemala's political climate, which had not changed in decades, the rains in Guatemala could shift at a moment's notice. By the time we returned to our guesthouse, raindrops were pounding the rooftops. The wet season had begun.

In the morning, Tamara and I took a bus that climbed back up into the mountains. More madmen drivers raced each other at breakneck speeds around uphill corners. After a night in the village of Antigua we reached Guatemala City. I asked an armed guard with a shotgun slung over his shoulder where the main bus station was. He pointed towards a market area, where a man motioned for us to follow. Vendors sold combs, watches, and handbags, stall after stall. We turned a corner, and found a dozen buses revving their engines. A group of men surrounded us.

"¿A dónde van?" they shouted. *Where are you going?*

More came, all yelling for us to board their buses. When I asked for a direct bus to the city of Santa Ana in El Salvador, a few men screamed "¡No hay, no hay!" *There is none, there is none!*

We chose one on the end and soon found ourselves sitting in a long line of belching buses that snaked its way through the market past tomatoes, cabbages, onions, and other produce.

"I think we'll have to change buses," I said to Tamara, "but at least this one will get us to the border."

On outskirts of Guatemala City I listened with one ear to Tamara as she spoke about the lack of a middle class.

"Here, a person is either very rich or very poor," she mused. "There's really nothing in between. And corruption is rampant..."

I listened with my other ear to strange sounds coming from the engine. We soon rolled to a stop. The driver lifted the cover, men crawled underneath, and tools tinkled on the pavement.

"Guess I was wrong," I chuckled.

A few overloaded chicken buses rumbled past, and some slowed down enough for one or two men to run after and then jump aboard. When a half-full one stopped, the remaining mass of passengers was up and running. One man saved a seat for Tamara. I gave mine to a woman with an infant in her arms. I remembered that Guatemala City was as far south as I had gone on my previous Central American journeys. Every bit of familiarity now lay behind us. Only the unknown lay ahead.

The same could be said for most Guatemalans. The civil war had done little to improve living conditions. Even twenty years after our visit, the same alliance of politicians, military officers, judges, and organized crime leaders still held the strings of power. Many of those in control seemed to care more about maintaining their privileges than they did democracy, poverty, and justice.

"Most Guatemalans see the political process as broken," Tamara continued, once we had moved into seats nearer each other. "They vote with their feet by migrating north rather than fight for change at home. The issues that really matter to most locals like education, jobs, and inequality are left out of the conversation outside of vague, quickly forgotten campaign promises."

Hundreds of thousands had fled to escape violence, poverty, and food insecurity.

"So what's the solution?" I asked.

Tamara shook her head. "I don't know, but the tide of immigrants arriving at America's doorstep isn't likely to stop anytime soon. The real issues are the politics and economics and social dynamics here and in other Latin American countries. People want a better life for themselves. But to solve any issue you must go to the root of the problem. You can't stop the tide with border walls. And tough talk by politicians is usually about getting votes, not creating change."

"Do you think it's America's job to fix those kinds of issues in other countries?"

"Not necessarily. But if our government truly wants to slow or stop Latin American immigration, perhaps in the future it should send advisors who can help make life more prosperous, rather than Green Beret military advisors. Regime change is clearly not the answer."

8

PLACE OF PRECIOUS STONES

After getting off the bus at San Cristóbal Frontera, which straddles the border with El Salvador, we walked through rising heat towards the edge of Guatemala. Inside a small customs office tucked off the muddy main drag, a middle-aged woman with ebony hair pulled tight into a bun sat at a wooden desk. She stamped our passports without once looking up.

A man standing in the street offered to change money. We needed El Salvadoran currency so I traded our remaining quetzals for colones. At the Salvadoran border post, a mob of boisterous Guatemalans filled the narrow corridor. We muscled our way past, thrust our damp passports through a round opening in the window, and escaped into the streets of El Salvador.

In moments, a waiting bus carried us into the countryside. Hazy mountains loomed in the distance, and farmers' fields occupied all arable land. Vultures circling overhead eyed mounds of trash cluttering the roadsides. Worn stone shacks with dirt floors and mud yards lined the roadways. The scenery reminded me of Guatemala—only more rugged.

The military-led government of Salvador and the FMLN, a coalition of left-wing guerilla groups, had only recently ended a bitter civil war. Although areas formerly considered conflictive zones were now open for travel, we had been warned to avoid unpaved roads and not to travel after dark due to random banditry. Many Salvadorans were armed and shootouts were not uncommon. Criminals turned violent quickly, especially when their victims failed to immediately cooperate. Those who argued with their assailants or refused to surrender their valuables were often shot.

We delved into the core of Santa Ana, Salvador's second largest city. Palm fronds fronted decaying colonial buildings and lent a tropical air to the broken sidewalks. Merchants packed their wares beneath black and purple clouds that rolled across an electric sky. A few raindrops fell but we escaped the deluge. Lights twinkled on downtown, darkness descended, and dank air settled upon the land. Even when sitting we sweated. A bent man asked for money, and another eyed us warily. Despite the destitute feel, the decrepit city held a simple beauty.

In our stuffy room the air was thick, like soup. I tried to start the rusty fan but could make no sense of it. One of the shirtless lads who ran the place came by and crossed two wires sticking out from the wall. Blue sparks flew, and the fan whirred to life. Darkness fell, but the rains did not.

"What have you read about Salvador?" Tamara asked, as we lay upon the thin mattress, waiting for the storm.

"Well, I know most early colonists were motivated by instant wealth, of course."

Many arrivals from Spain in the 1500s had no inheritance rights, so they sought riches in forms they could ship to Spain for their later return. Though the native Pipil people knew this land as "the place of precious stones" it in fact had few natural resources. Colonists exported cacao, but its decline led to an economic bust, which inspired a feudal system that bound indigenous folk to the land by tricking them into debts they couldn't repay. Indigo and then coffee replaced cacao.

"With each boom and bust cycle," I said, "land ownership concentrated into fewer hands, until only fourteen families controlled the whole colony."

"That doesn't sound good," Tamara remarked.

"No, and it got worse."

In the 1930s a military coup d'état overthrew the winner of what many considered the country's first freely-contested election. The new regime was especially brutal.

"In one instance, peasants led by revolutionary Farabundo Martí rose against the dictatorship. The military quickly crushed a planned peaceful gathering, and during what became known as "La Matanza" or "The Slaughter" some thirty thousand peasants and indigenous people were killed. Martí was executed."

"That's tragic."

In the 1970s a leftist party staged a coup d'état and nationalized Salvador's private companies, so the United States financed a counter-coup. Afterward, right-wing death squads killed dozens of people per day, while thousands of guerillas and militia members roamed the countryside. Then all the guerillas came together as the FMLN, named in honor of Martí, and the Salvadoran Civil War erupted.

The sound of what sounded like artillery fire startled us. We realized the clouds had let loose and rain was pounding the corrugated tin roof above our heads.

"How ironic," laughed Tamara. "How did the war end?"

"Even though the United States invested six billion dollars to prop up the government, the Civil War ended in a stalemate in 1992, after twelve years of fighting. Over seventy thousand people had been killed and more than a million displaced. Can you imagine that?"

"I just can't," Tamara whispered.

My mind swirled with images of war as we drifted to sleep, and after a restless night I stepped outside at dawn to drink in the fresh air and watch the city awaken. Elderly men watched passersby from park benches. Vendors unloaded cucumbers, radishes, and ears of corn. A Catholic priest hurried to the ornate neo-Gothic church which crowned the central plaza. Pedestrians bustled about their business and vendors hawked their wares, yet an air of calm underlay the endless motion.

After breakfast Tamara and I left Santa Ana to continue south, past wooded hillsides and jumbled mountains. The landscape held an unexpected allure. Clear blue skies and fluffy white clouds shimmered all the way to the horizon. We passed shacks with corrugated tin roofs above and dirt floors below that made up impoverished hillside villages. Trash heaps littered the roadsides, and big black buzzards scuttled amongst the smorgasbord of rubbish.

In the capital city of San Salvador we crept through downtown gridlock and thick humidity. Everything held a worn, war-weary tinge. Black smoke poured from grumbling buses. Palm trees swayed on occasional breezes. Sidewalk vendors spilled into the streets with carts of apples and lettuce that they parked in the middle of the main downtown crossroad. Taxis and buses worked their way around the merchants, who called to shoppers and passersby.

We were bound for the city of San Miguel, and on the southern side of San Salvador, caught a different bus. A smiling young man boarded and sat in the seat in front of us. Francisco was twenty-one, cheerful, and eager to chat. He was curious about the world beyond Salvador. I wondered about the war.

"Do you know many people who have left Salvador behind?" I asked.

Francisco's smile disappeared, and he gazed outside.

"I'm sorry," I said after a few moments, "if I upset you."

"Está bien," he said. *It's okay.* "I have known many. The war was very bad. Many left. It is not much better now. We are very poor. And it is not safe in Salvador. The *maras*–gangs of criminals–they threaten to kill us if we do not pay what they demand."

I had earlier read that seventeen of the twenty deadliest countries on Earth were in Latin America, and criminal gangs were responsible for many of those murders.

"I have known other students, many shop owners, parents with small children—all have left," Francisco continued, "but to leave is very dangerous. Last year my brother Óscar left. He took his wife and daughter with him. Valeria, my niece, was almost two when they went. They made it all the way to the Río Grande."

"Were they able to cross the river?" Tamara asked.

Francisco shook his head. "No. Óscar did not make it. He drowned while trying to swim across. And so did Valeria."

"Oh no," breathed Tamara, clasping her hand to her mouth.

"Sí. They found them face down in the water a few meters from the United States. Valeria was still holding tight to my brother. That little girl, she never let go." He looked out the window. "Ella era fuerte." *She was strong.*

"I'm so sorry, Francisco," I said, after we had absorbed his story. "And Valeria's mother?"

"She lived, but did not make it across. They brought her back. She lives in San Salvador now. The slums there are very dangerous. Every day someone is killed by the *maras*. They fight for power, territory, status. Life is very hard."

We were so engrossed in our conversation that we hardly noticed how frequently the locals disembarked at anonymous villages to climb dirt roads winding into the sky, or that every pothole bounce trounced us upon our metal seats that were so tightly spaced our knees touched the seats in front. Dark clouds rolled in and a heavy rain began to fall. When the downpours tapered off, a rainbow arced across the horizon. In the early afternoon we reached the city of San Miguel, where we said goodbye to Francisco.

"Good luck Francisco," I said, shaking his hand.

"Our thoughts will be with you," added Tamara.

"Gracias," he smiled. "I will manage."

After dinner, as Tamara and I walked to our hotel, I thought about United States immigration policy. The idea of building a longer, higher border wall between Mexico and the United States had long been debated. I knew that if a bigger wall were built, wildlife would suffer. Desert dwellers needed room to roam. If this wall were built, people would suffer as well. No wall would keep immigrants out. Great migrations—such as the movement of Siberian people into North America, and the migration of nomadic herders from the steppes of Asia into Europe–have been a defining feature of humankind for millennia. Human history is marked not by placidity and purity but by movement and cross-pollination. It is the story of immigrants intermingling with, and sometimes displacing, those who came before them. In a sense, and for many reasons, we are all immigrants. Human migration is inevitable.

Yet immigration had rarely been foremost on my mind while I was growing up, or even as a young adult. Talking to Francisco had brought the often-contentious issue into sharper focus, like a vintage camera that must be manually adjusted to see clearly through the lens.

"Why do you think immigration policy in America is so divisive?" I asked Tamara that night.

"Hard to say," she replied. "People want to feel safe. Perhaps it's partly a fear of the unknown. Someone strongly opposed to immigration maybe can't imagine what their neighborhood will be like if people different from themselves move in."

"Whether or not a wall stops immigrants," I said, "the *idea* of a wall probably feels more comforting to some people than no wall at all."

"Yes...and probably part of the divisiveness is fear of change. Like, once a couple chooses their dream home to raise their children in, and has found their community, they likely don't want that neighborhood to change."

"I was thinking, too, that perhaps people worry that history could repeat itself. There is more evidence that traumas experienced by our ancestors are inherited by us. If true, perhaps on a deep level some people carry the trauma of the past with them, and they wonder: 'Could the same thing that my great-grandfather did to *them* happen to *me*, my children, my grandchildren?'"

"There are also practical issues like jobs and higher taxes that people worry about. On the one hand immigrants often fill jobs that Americans don't want, but on the other hand those jobs don't pay much so municipalities have to bear part of the cost of supporting them. I'm sure there are so many reasons."

"Maybe immigration is really about freedom," I mused, "and the lengths people will go to attain it. I wonder what will happen to Francisco? Will he join a gang? Get mixed up in crime? Escape to the United States? Or find some other way out of his situation?"

"I don't know, but as long as poverty and war and violence dominate down here, young men like Francisco will continue being pushed towards the gang life. And others, like Óscar, will die trying to build a new life. That's the grim reality here."

9

BANANA REPUBLIC

Our plan was to steadily work our way south, through Central America, mostly following the Pan-American Highway, a network of roads stretching nearly twenty thousand miles across the Americas from Alaska to Argentina. Tucked along El Salvador's eastern border was Honduras, through which the Pan-American passed.

We trekked through morning heat past a swarm of eager moneychangers. Below the border bridge spanning the Río Goascoran, women washed clothes in muddy currents and left their garments to dry on thorny bushes lining the riverbank. Trees laden with orange blossoms grew in the lowlands and in the distance tawny-colored mountains filled the horizon. Having crossed over to the Honduran side of the border, we waited with the locals in a long line. An official charged two dollars each, and we were in. The land turned drier. Wind-blown clouds of dust coated the land in a layer of brown grit.

Most of the people we met proved kind, friendly, and curious despite Hurricane Mitch–the deadliest hurricane in Central American history–having ravaged the countryside the year before our arrival, debilitating an already desperate nation. Most crops, nearly all bridges and secondary roads, and some eighty thousand homes had been damaged or destroyed. After the storm, half of the population had no work and many were left homeless. The trend had been for Hondurans to migrate to cities in search of a better standard of living and employment. With both in short supply, incidents of violent crime, armed robbery, purse snatching, and pickpocketing had escalated. The president of Honduras claimed fifty years of progress had been undone almost overnight as a result of Hurricane Mitch.

As we traveled across the interior, it seemed the country's recovery had barely begun. Haphazard shacks of corrugated tin and warped plywood lined the roadways. We paused at Nacaome, then continued through Jicaro Gala to San Lorenzo, all villages with basic houses, dirt yards, and stick fences. Here kidnappings motivated by profit were commonplace, and although police had dismantled a criminal organization that preyed on travelers near the Salvadoran border, highway assaults on the Pan-American were still an issue.

Two decades after our visit, conditions were no better. Nearly three-quarters of the population of Honduras still lived in poverty. Flooding from natural disasters and hurricanes such as Mitch regularly wiped out crops and farmlands. High unemployment reinforced endemic poverty. The homicide rate was among the highest in the world. Drug trafficking and gang warfare violence drained state resources that could otherwise go towards education and increased food security.

After our visit, Honduras moved away from capitalism and towards an economy modeled on socialism and this rankled the United States establishment. Yet I wondered whether a redistribution of power, wealth, and control over natural resources might make sense in a country where most people struggled to survive on less than three dollars per day. Capitalism is about competition and profit, and it works as long as there is a level playing field. Otherwise the winners keep winning and the losers keep losing. Free trade, open markets, and private enterprise likely mattered little to the average Honduran because they simply couldn't compete. Most of the country's children were undereducated or not educated at all, while most adults were poorly trained in most basic skills and entirely untrained in those skills that were in high demand. Capitalism hadn't succeeded in Honduras, and probably wouldn't work until a solid enough foundation had been laid to bring the nation's people up out of poverty and illiteracy.

"How did Honduras fall so far behind?" I wondered aloud as Tamara and I made our way across the country.

"Honduras' long history of violence has surely not helped," she replied, gazing out the window of the latest bus we were bouncing in. "Something like three hundred rebellions and civil wars have erupted since independence from Spain."

"It's hard to imagine living in those kinds of conditions," I said. "As soon as you settle in after one uprising, another begins. That's no kind of life."

"Very true," Tamara agreed. "You can't get ahead when your world is so unstable."

"But why has there been so much instability?"

"I think a large part of the answer," she began, "is the banana." With every passing day, I grew more amazed by her knowledge. "The United States got involved in Honduras in the 1800s when an American businessman created a new market by buying boatloads of bananas from here and selling them for a 1,000 percent profit in Boston. Two 'bits' bought a dozen bananas, but only two apples. Bananas were cheap and tasty, and Americans loved them."

I hadn't realized bananas were such big business. In time three massive American monopolies exported bananas from Honduras to the United States. To promote development, Honduras gave five hundred hectares of land to banana companies for each kilometer of railway they laid. By the late nineteenth century, American exporters not only dominated the cultivation, harvest, and export of bananas in Honduras, but they also controlled the road, rail, port, telegraph and telephone infrastructure that they had built. By manipulating land use laws, keeping locals landless, and employing them as low-wage workers, exporters kept banana prices low. But, political instability, a struggling economy, and billions in debt hampered the Honduran government's ability to even function.

Honduras had become the quintessential 'banana republic', a term coined at the turn of the nineteenth century by American writer O. Henry in *Cabbages and Kings,* a fictional collection of short stories based on his experiences in Honduras.

To the Honduran people the United Fruit Company was El Pulpo, the Octopus, because it thrust its tentacles into everything. El Pulpo controlled transportation, infiltrated all aspects of society, was the nation's primary employer, and sometimes altered national politics.

The Cuyamel Fruit Company went a step farther. When Sam Zemurray founded the company he entered into a business and political alliance with Manual Bonilla, ex-president of Honduras, and General Lee Christmas, an American mercenary. Cuyamel's army, led by General Christmas, executed a coup d'état and installed Bonilla as president. The United States ignored this manipulation of Honduran politics by a private army, because the deposed president had allowed Honduras to become heavily indebted to Great Britain, which the United States considered a risk to its dominance of Honduras and Latin America as a whole.

A long history of military rule, corruption, poverty, and crime left Honduras among the least developed and most unstable countries in Central America. At one point, the homicide rate in Honduras was the highest in the world. In San Pedro Sula, one of the deadliest cities in the world, gang violence, shootouts, and armed raids dominated the lives of locals. Tens of thousands of young Hondurans traveled to the United States to plead for asylum from the violence of drug gangs. It was from this city that the first migrant caravan gathered. By the time the group set off from the bus terminal, more than a thousand Hondurans had joined them. Many other caravans and thousands more migrants followed. At the root of Hondurans' problems was poor governance, which had defined the country for most of its history.

In the village of San Lorenzo, while finding a bite to eat, a smiling Honduran no more than ten years old with wide and inquisitive eyes stopped us to ask a string of barely comprehensible questions. Tamara flashed me a look. As I was learning, dialects in Latin America differed from country to country and region to region. I deciphered Gaby's questions as best I could.

"¿Por qué están aquí?" she asked. *Why are you here?*

"Estamos viajeros." *We are travelers.*

"¿A dónde van?" *Where are you going?*

"A través de Centro America." *Across Central America.*

Gaby stared a moment. "¿Por qué?" *Why?*

It was a good question, and one I found challenging to translate into Spanish.

"Why are we here?" I asked Tamara.

"Tell her we're here to learn about her country."

"Ah," Gaby responded when she heard this. She slowly took in our surroundings, as if seeing them for the first time, and then looked at us, her brow furrowed.

"Loco," she said. *Crazy.*

Tamara and I laughed. Even Tamara knew what this word meant. I asked Gaby how many gringos she had met before us. The girl shook her head.

"Cero," she said. *Zero.*

It seemed not many travelers showed up in Honduras.

Webster's Dictionary defines a banana republic as any politically unstable country dependent on export of a single limited-resource product. A ruling oligarchy controls the large, impoverished working class and exploits large-scale plantation-style single crop agriculture. Favored multi-national foreign monopolies collude with the state and reap large profits from the use of public lands, while debts incurred by the corporations remain a public responsibility.

By not investing in public infrastructure, the economy remains crippled, the national currency devalues, and the country remains ineligible for foreign investment. Kleptocratic government employees use their posts for personal gain through embezzlement, fraud, and bribery. With no recourse, the working poor remain mired in a foreign-owned corporate-controlled plutocratic morass. This was the world Gaby had been born into.

Before we left her, Tamara asked me to inquire about the girl's parents.

"¿Dónde está tu madre?" I asked. *Where is your mother?*
She shook her head.

"¿Tu padre?" *Your father?*

"No sé." *I don't know.*

"¿Hermanos o hermanas?" *Brothers or sisters?*

"Nada." *None.*

"¿Dónde está tu casa?" I asked. *Where is your home?* Gaby pointed towards a cluster of wooden shacks that seemed barely habitable to Tamara and me.

"Vivo con mi tía," she said. *I live with my aunt.*

We bought Gaby a few items of food from a local stall before continuing back to our hotel. As with Francisco, I wondered about what her future would be like.

"What do you think will happen to her?" I asked Tamara. "Will she someday have children? Maybe a daughter of her own? Will she try to make her way to the United States? Or will she cling to life somewhere here in Honduras?"

"I don't know," Tamara sighed. "But people here seem resourceful. She'll figure it out. I think she'll be okay."

Such unanswered questions, of course, were part of the mystery of travel. I could only hope that the inquisitive young girl and so many others we met in Honduras and elsewhere would find peace and prosperity wherever they landed.

I thought of an O. Henry line. *If a person has lived through war, poverty, and love, he has lived a full life.* Small comfort, to be sure, but true nonetheless. From that perspective, Gaby and many others like her would at least seem to have many a story to tell.

10

RISE OF THE SANDINISTAS

As Honduras fell behind us, Nicaragua loomed on the horizon. The border was a mess. Skirmishes between the two countries had recently plagued the region. Unmarked minefields were abundant, and landslides and floods from Hurricane Mitch had scattered many of the country's landmines, making frontier areas unsafe. At one time blood tests were taken on the border to test travelers for malaria, and prophylactics were administered in the event of positive results, but the practice had reportedly been relaxed; we weren't tested. Accounts of robberies, kidnappings, and extortion committed by armed criminal groups were frequent. Plus, we had heard that drug dealers often served as undercover police agents, so no one could be trusted.

On the Honduran side, men offered rides across the border on makeshift bicycle rickshaws. Each had a double-wide seat and was propelled by a wiry cyclist. Tamara and I opted to walk, along with a crowd of moneychangers who followed behind us with pocket calculators in hand. At immigration, an owlish bureaucrat demanded thirty Honduran lempiras, but let us pass. In the street again, more men persuaded us to ride their bicycle contraptions. We walked instead through the no man's land and across a creaking wooden bridge. The moneychangers claimed that officials required one hundred Nicaraguan córdobas to enter the country, so I exchanged a few dollars. Inside the customs hut, a Nicaraguan official stamped our passports but demanded seven dollars apiece. I handed him the hundred córdobas.

"No," the man said. "We want dollars."

Another guard pointed at the moneychangers standing in the street and indicated I must trade the córdobas back into dollars.

"This is ridiculous," I muttered to Tamara. "We can't even pay the border tax in local currency."

"Is it a tax, or a tip?" she said quietly.

"Good point."

I gave the guard a twenty-dollar bill, and waited for change. After we stepped outside the hut, two border officials stopped us. One handed Tamara's passport back, but both leafed through mine.

"You are perhaps CIA?" one asked, fixing me with a cold stare.

We laughed nervously. "We're on holiday," I said. Their frowns deepened.

"Where do you go?"

"We're traveling across Central America. From Panama, we'll fly to Colombia, or Ecuador."

At this, the men looked us over again and scrutinized my passport more studiously, but eventually let us pass.

"¡Gringos!" a group of lads shouted as we boarded a sweltering bus just inside Nicaragua.

It was soon evident that Nicaraguan roads were in poor repair—dimly lit, frequently narrow, and without shoulders. Many had been severely damaged as a result of Hurricane Mitch, and because most had not been repaired, detours were common. Oxcarts, horses, abandoned autos, and vehicles lacking front or rear lights were everywhere.

Bony cattle grazed mindlessly, gaunt horses ambled aimlessly, and dogs, as thin as bullets with stunted legs, scratched at the dirt. Lining the roadsides were shacks constructed of tin and cast-off cardboard with entire extended families surviving beneath one leaky roof. For miles our bus crawled around gaping potholes.

Along a deserted section of highway we stopped, seemingly for no reason. Locals hurriedly hid boxes under seats and passed items back and forth. A policeman stepped onboard, and everyone on board sat silently. He looked around, walked down the aisle, picked up a box, and passed it to his partner. Then another box, and a bag. Next he swiped a few dozen cans of soda and juice. The passengers' eyes silently followed the policemen as they piled their goods into the trunk of an unmarked car. After the policemen waved us onward, the passengers laughed and shook hands and pulled boxes and bags from hiding places.

"Son malos," said one passenger. *They are bad.*

The bus turned festive. Women prepared tortillas with rice and meat and handed them out. A man passed around sodas. The passengers laughed together, like one happy family.

We pushed forward, pausing at Chinandega, then on again. Gnarled, twisted trees dotted barren fields. Black skies turned violent, with jumbled clouds churning past, until the rain let loose with such fury that we could see only a dozen feet ahead of us. The streets and dirt ditches filled with brown water; fields transformed into gleaming lakes. The driver squinted through the steamy windshield and worn wipers to dodge rain-filled potholes.

He ran late and was not going downtown, so we walked a mile into León. Tethered bony horses chewing cabbage leaves stared blankly at passersby. Downtown, past ancient churches weathered by war and the elements, eateries were sparse. We found a café near the square that served chicken sandwiches. Over a round of Victoria beers I regaled Tamara with the history of how Nicaragua's unsettled nature began with competition over an interoceanic canal that never came to be.

"The idea of connecting the Atlantic to the Pacific had been talked about since the sixteenth century," I said, "and again gathered steam in the 1820s. Nicaragua, Panama, and Mexico's Isthmus of Tehuantepec were all considered."

Regardless of location, the United States wanted total control. When asked by the newly formed Federal Republic of Central America to aid with construction of a canal across Nicaragua, however, officials in Washington balked due to the country's instability. The French decided on Panama, and began digging there. Meanwhile, José Santos Zelaya took control of Nicaragua's Mosquito Coast by military force. His aid to neighboring countries gave European states such as Germany, already in a cold war with the United States, an excuse to intervene to protect financial interests or demand land concessions in lieu of repayment. The United States regarded such actions as threats to its canal ambitions. When the French effort fell into disarray, the United States purchased the failed concession. Santos in turn negotiated with Germany and Japan to build a canal across Nicaragua. Fearful of an alternative effort, the United States labeled Santos a tyrant.

Santos resigned, and when his handpicked successor faced an advance by a United States-backed force, he too resigned. Nationalistic fervor rose amongst the Nicaraguan military, and the Secretary of War rebelled. United States Marines invaded, and for two months battled Nicaraguan rebels. General Benjamín Zeledón assumed command of the rebellion, but was killed. The capture of León–the uprising's last stronghold– marked the rebellion's end. Plans for a Nicaraguan canal were shelved, and two years later, the Panama Canal was completed.

Though the battle in León occurred nearly ninety years before our arrival, the city still held a war-weary tinge. As twilight fell we scurried home, but I lost my bearings in the unmarked streets. We wandered, over and over, past the same, unlit buildings. I wondered what owners of the leery, narrowed eyes that I imagined must be peering at us from the shadows might be thinking, and hurried Tamara along. At long last I stumbled upon the Church of San Francisco, a familiar landmark, and much relieved, found our hotel just as heavy rain drowned the hibiscus blooming beyond our window.

The next morning, near the León bus station, old men sold plastic razors and women peddled mangoes. Our stripped-down local bus twisted and bounced over a ribbon of muddy potholes and rutted monsoon washouts on its way to Managua, the capital city. What was meant to be an hour's journey over a back-road obstacle course stretched into three. Gnarled baobab-like trees dotted brown plains reminiscent of an African savannah. The land turned flatter as we approached Managua's muggy lowland outskirts. We were mindful that armed robberies on crowded buses and in open markets were common, and that carjackings and gang activity were on the rise. Motorists were advised to travel with windows closed and doors locked to prevent purse and jewelry snatchings at stoplights. Robberies, assaults, and stabbings were most prevalent in poorer neighborhoods, but possible anywhere.

Downtown Managua was abandoned. A string of earthquakes–the worst of which in 1972 killed ten thousand people, made fifty thousand homeless, and leveled the city–had left the center a swath of rubble. Portions of the city had never been rebuilt. No city buses ran the downtown route, but taxis went to the central market. Our driver asked where we were from and where we were headed as he negotiated past banana palms, the rusting shells of early model sedans, and street-side ditches running thick with sewage and rainy season overflow. The taxi driver dropped us at the bus terminal beneath a heavy sky and waved goodbye.

"¡Ten cuidado aquí!" he called, as we climbed onto a Granada-bound bus. *Be careful here!*

The rain continued to fall, though the heat remained. In downtown Granada, littered with churches and Spanish colonial architecture dating back to the 1500s, a parade of schoolchildren and a float of the Virgin Mary marched past. A crowd followed behind, walking next to a Datsun with oversize speakers blaring religious rhetoric. At our *hospedaje* we encountered a young Nicaraguan named Ivan selling bags of cashews. Other youths sold cigarettes, Chiclets, and candies. Ivan drew pictures in my notebook: one of the devil, one of the Titanic, and one of Tamara and I. It seemed clear how he felt about foreigners like us.

I couldn't blame him, based on my country's history of involvement in Nicaragua. Conversely, it was for this reason that the country had long captured my imagination. The source of my fascination derived a dozen miles south of our *hospedaje*, in the village where the revolutionary leader Augusto Calderón Sandino was born at the turn of the nineteenth century. As a teenager he had his first taste of imperialism while watching the inert body of General Benjamín Zeledón, killed by United States Marines, roll past on oxcart. The image haunted Calderón for the remainder of his life.

A decade later, when exiled former vice-president Juan Bautista Sacasa staged a coup d'état, Calderón assembled a makeshift, independent peasant army and led a successful opposition effort. His followers were known as Sandinistas—a tribute to Calderón's last name. Bautista's troops were forced by the threat of United States intervention to stand down, and agreed to an accord that kept President Adolfo Díaz, a United States ally, in place but established a new army known as la Guardia Nacional, or the National Guard.

Calderón refused to surrender, and instead waged a guerilla war against the United States. For six years he battled United States Marines who were unable to capture the 'bandit', as he was called. His distinctive uniform of knee-high boots and wide-brimmed cowboy hat became symbols of Sandinista opposition to wealthy imperialist elites and foreign corporate interests. After General Anastasio Somoza García was appointed director of the National Guard, he ambushed and executed Calderón, dismantled the Sandinista army, declared himself president, established an autocratic family dictatorship, and started a dynasty that endured more than forty years.

Though Somoza was eventually assassinated in 1956, his son, Luis Somoza Debayle, succeeded him and ruled as ruthlessly as his father had. Opposition coalesced with formation of the Sandinista National Liberation Front, which saw itself as Calderón's political heir. Supported by students, peasants, communist Cubans, the leftist Panamanian government, and Venezuela, the latter-day Sandinistas were strong enough by the 1970s to launch a military effort against the dictatorship. The Nicaraguan Revolution had commenced. By mid-1979 the Sandinistas controlled everything except the capital. Nicaragua lay in ruins, but the war was not yet over.

In a bid to curb communism, President Reagan supported an anti-Sandinista movement—the *Contrarrevolución*—which was forming along the Honduran border. Reagan cancelled all Nicaraguan aid but signed a directive authorizing covert support to anti-Sandinista forces. Though Congress forbade direct funding to the 'Contras', Reagan officials secretly trained and armed them. In an operation that came to be known as the Iran-Contra Affair, officials covertly sold weapons to Iran, the subject of an arms embargo, and diverted those proceeds to the Contras. Nevertheless, in 1984, a hero of the Sandinista revolution, Daniel Ortega, won the Nicaraguan presidency. The revolution, in essence, had ended.

The aftermath of decades of strife was evident in Nicaragua's shattered economy and infrastructure as Tamara and I made our way through the war-torn nation. Despite government disarmament campaigns, many citizens remained heavily armed. Criminal gangs, some with political agendas, plagued the Atlantic coast and northern mountains. That evening at the *hospedaje* after Ivan had wandered off, I translated recent headlines from a local newspaper for Tamara.

"Two days ago, eleven people in the village of Waspado were machine-gunned to death. Two others were kidnapped and two children seriously wounded. The victims were burned, their heads impaled on stakes, and the whole scene set afire."

"Why?" Tamara asked.

"Seems the vengeance killing was another settling of old scores from the war," I read from the paper, "and one of several attacks against police and the army, which have motivated villagers to beg for relocation."

Twenty years after our visit, little had changed. Sandinista leader Daniel Ortega had lost the presidency in 1990, but won again in 2006. As he grew wealthier and more powerful during his second administration, his anti-democratic tendencies intensified. His allies in the legislature changed the constitution to eliminate presidential term limits. Police and masked gunmen hunted down opposition leaders and protestors. Many were tortured, arrested, killed, or disappeared. Any protests, such as dissent against Ortega's plan to build a Chinese-financed canal across Nicaragua, were met with violence. His Sandinista party controlled the nation.

Ortega's ruthlessness and refusal to step down prompted many to compare the former guerilla commander to the dictator he helped overthrow forty years earlier. Nicaragua had found itself in a position similar to that of 1979: hobbled by an autocratic dictator focused on retaining his power and wealth, whatever the cost to the people. Ortega's Sandinista party had simply replaced the Somoza dynasty.

Nicaragua's successive dynasties reminded me of George Orwell's novel *Animal Farm*, a classic tale about the corrupting influence of power. In my edition, Peter Davison's foreword refers to a letter that Orwell wrote to a friend. Orwell clarified in his letter that though *Animal Farm* was "primarily a satire on the Russian Revolution" it was intended to have a wider application. That kind of revolution, which he defined as "violent conspiratorial revolution, led by unconsciously power-hungry people" could only lead to a change of masters.

Orwell went on: "I meant the moral to be that revolutions only effect a radical improvement when the masses are alert and know how to chuck out their leaders as soon as the latter have done their job."

Like Somoza and all other autocrats, Ortega and the Sandinista party would eventually fall. The question, of course, after eighty years of continuous authoritarian rule, was what the next revolution would bring.

11

RICH COAST

We careened along the lakeshores of Lagos de Nicaragua, past banana trees and encroaching jungle thickets, to the village of Penas Blancas. Though the upcoming border seemed less corrupt than the last, I was still a bundle of nerves. A sign in Spanish claimed that to enter Costa Rica, visitors must produce proof of financial solvency and a return or onward ticket. We had no tickets of any kind, but I surely did not want to return to Managua. At the border, however, the immigration officer glanced at our passports, stamped them, and waved us through. A wave of relief washed over me. Not only were we in, but most of Central America now lay behind us.

Despite being a bastion of stability, relative to the rest of Central America, Costa Rica was not entirely safe. Crime was increasing, and though most incidents were non-violent, including pickpocketing and break-ins, criminals had more recently shown greater willingness to use violence.

The countryside just beyond the border looked much the same as elsewhere, with trash-filled gutters, scattered subsistence farming plots, and decrepit homes lining the roadways. Past Las Cruces, we reached the city of Liberia, near the northwestern coast. A lack of street signs made orientation difficult but in time we eventually found a cozy room. The television only had three channels, all in Spanish—one of which only televised *Baywatch*. In spite of this, Tamara much preferred our little room to the city streets after dark as she had heard that several American women had recently been assaulted at beach resorts on both coasts and in the capital, San Jose. Several foreigners had been kidnapped, and there had been reports of assaults by taxi drivers. We were advised to only use taxis that had working door handles, locks, and working meters—called *marias*—and to not ride in front with the driver.

In spite of such dangers, Costa Rica exemplified the dichotomy between North America and Latin America. Here, in fact, was the exception that proved the rule. Christopher Columbus, or conquistador Gil González Dávila, depending on your source, first dubbed the region "la costa rica," the rich coast, for the gold jewelry that hung from natives' necks. As the conquistadors soon discovered, however, Costa Rica contained no large reserves of gold, silver, or any other precious metals.

Prior to independence in the early 1800s, the Spanish prohibited Costa Rica from trading with its neighbors. With a small indigenous population and no ready labor force, most settlers worked their own land rather than establish plantation-style *haciendas*. The lack of resources, shortage of available workers, and location in a remote mountainous region made Costa Rica isolated and as described by one Spanish governor, "the poorest and most miserable Spanish colony in all America."

Unappreciated and overlooked, Costa Rica was largely left alone by Spain. Without an indigenous, oppressed mestizo, or mixed race class, Costa Rica became more egalitarian than its neighbors, and the lack of often brutal interference by its colonizers allowed Costa Rica to evolve into a rural democracy unlike the dictatorial, authoritative post-colonial regimes that prevailed in most other Latin American nations.

We were roused in the morning by parrots singing in our courtyard. Clouds began building on the horizon and by the time we reached the town of Tilarán later that morning, powerful thunder rumbled across the sky. We stopped for lunch at a *soda*, a small restaurant serving *casados*–meals of rice, beans, fried bananas, cabbage, and stewed meat. We also ordered a delicious *olla de carne*, a soup of beef, plantain, corn, yucca, and *ñampi*, or taro.

Our next destination was the rural village of La Fortuna, which promised the opportunity to see some of Costa Rica's untouched countryside. We rode for hours along rutted and potholed dirt roads skirting lakeshores of Lago Arenal. As we climbed higher, the air grew cooler and the vegetation more luxuriant. Yellow butterflies fluttered past. A young local woman, known as a *tica*, in the seat in front of ours pointed out two howler monkeys hunched in a tree.

Cloud-covered mountains ringed far-off lakeshores. The rain fell, harder and louder, until it became an unending and violent downpour. Rivulets poured down every cliff face. Landslides occasionally covered the road and tumbled into fields. Around each curve, the driver picked his way across washed-out sections of road and brown muddy waters rushing down from unseen heights. The rain intensified as we ploughed through mad, churning currents.

In the valley below the road, an out of control torrent, beyond flood stage, uprooted signs, trees, and rocks. A dirt road running alongside the river completely disappeared, as ours soon would. At La Fortuna, the rain seemed to pour from the heavens with newfound fury. We huddled with a band of locals who were cowering beneath a thatch-roof shelter. One by one they dashed away. Tamara and I finally followed them into the deluge to find accommodations.

When the rains later slackened Volcán Arenal, only a few miles away, suddenly materialized upon the horizon. From the volcano's summit rose great plumes of steam. On some days pumice and lava shot skyward. After *casados* in a thatch-roof *soda* accompanied by a marimba player, we retired to our room, where Tamara settled into her book. Volcano silently steamed, fan gently whirred, pages slowly turned, and rain gently fell. I was feeling philosophical.

"Do you think," I wondered aloud, "that you read as a way to escape?"

Tamara looked up from her book.

"Perhaps," she answered, "but you play with reality like a game, trying different ones out to see what you like."

I thought about this. She was likely right. "I guess everyone needs some kind of distraction," I ventured. I supposed that was why we were here.

"Why do you ask?" Tamara said.

"Just thinking. Some people overeat, some shop, some drink too much, some work late. I like immersing myself in new lands and learning what I can about those places. That's my distraction, I suppose."

"No doubt," she said. "And thank goodness for that."

Thank goodness indeed, I thought. Tamara returned to her book and I noticed that the rain had become gentle enough for us to hear crickets chirping amongst the flowers outside our cabaña window, whereas hours earlier the rainstorm had drowned out every other noise. This striking contrast between soundscapes, I realized, was a significant part of the reason why I traveled. I never knew what to expect from moment to moment, and that uncertainty enthralled me.

In the still of morning, beneath overcast skies, we walked along a rocky track, through rolling uplands towards Catarata de Fortuna–the 'Waterfall of Fortuna'. On either side of the track lay farmed plots and pastures. Clouds crept down from green mountain ridges. Warblers and finches and red-winged blackbirds twittered on the wing. Giant yellow-tailed birds with massive drooping nests squawked from spindly trees.

The dirt path led into a canyon blanketed in thick rainforest. A toucan perched overhead. Small yellow flowers hugging the earth, pink and violet impatiens, scarlet hibiscus, and clusters of magenta leaves growing from skinny stems bloomed all around. Vines hung from every branch; red bromeliads and epiphytes subsisting only on water and air clung to tree limbs. We paused to watch a long line of leaf cutter ants cross our trail.

We heard the waterfall's roar long before reaching the canyon floor. The force of the cascade had gouged a lagoon out of the ground, and midnight blue water boiled up from the cauldron. A few scantily-clad *ticas* swam at the fall's periphery. One tried to swim toward the base, but she could not get closer than twenty feet, the force of the water gushing over the rim was so strong. After exploring downstream we retraced our steps along the rutted track towards La Fortuna.

The next morning, a glimmer of sun brightened the cloud-shrouded eastern horizon. Blue sky peeked from towering masses of cumulonimbus cloud as the bus barreled past banana plantations and row after row of bushy coffee shrubs. Locals filled the aisle from front door to rear as we crossed the lush central highlands of Costa Rica's interior.

We paused only briefly in San José, the capital city. The streets brimmed with olive-skinned denizens flowing past in mini-skirts and tight-fitting shirts. The incessant noise of buses, taxis, and shouting echoed through the night. Before first light, all was a blur of motion beneath our dirt-smudged window. The man behind the desk woke long enough to push a buzzer that unlocked the iron gate and granted our freedom.

Hours later, in the seedy port of Puerto Limón on the Caribbean coast, we stopped for lunch at a *soda* along the square. There was a scurrilous air to the place and the humid atmosphere settled heavily on the land. Even when riding in the bus along the dirt and gravel track separated from sand and surf by a thin screen of coconut palms, sweat had poured down our brows.

"This tastes funny. Here, try it!" Tamara said as she often did to my amusement, when her food tasted strange.

She nibbled on a cold French fry and picked at the chicken fat, bones, and marrow that had been squashed together between two slices of stale white bread. After pulling an intestinal tube from her sandwich, she pushed it all aside in disgust. We sat instead in the shade of a limp palm near the sea. In the few moments that I slipped away to purchase onward bus tickets, men whistled and gestured crudely at Tamara.

"Somewhere near here those two American women were murdered last month," I said when I returned.

"It doesn't surprise me," said Tamara grimly.

We stayed a few nights at Puerto Viejo de Talamanca, a town known for its black sand beaches. At our cabaña on the edge of town, everything was upside down: the fan drew air upward rather than downwards to cool us, and water from the showerhead shot at the ceiling rather than onto us. Gentle waves broke offshore beneath a dark, looming sky. The blazing disc of the sun dropped into the Caribbean. Though on the edge of paradise, not a single tourist, *tico,* or *tica* smiled or gave us more than a stare–the lone exception being a shriveled German oldster at the hotel who gave me a few pointers about getting across the border into Panama.

Despite our lackluster lunch, the specter of recent murders, and the grumpy *ticos* in Talamanca, Costa Rica really was a peaceful place compared to the rest of Central America. This was due to what Costa Rica did *not* have: a history of autocratic leaders. I thought about this as I lay that afternoon beneath the backwards fan. I suspected that leadership cannot be learned from books, and that leaders are not born, rather they evolve into the role. I knew there were different ways of leading, and that the best leaders had mastered each style and could draw upon any as needed. I realized then that leadership is more than something we *do*; it's really an expression of who we *are*. When we lead, we manifest our whole being, because leadership derives from our inner selves–our values, principles, experiences, and true essence.

And I wondered: where does that leave the autocrats who claim absolute authority? They want control, and demand compliance. As world leaders, autocrats often veer towards tyranny. Too often, autocrats become dictators. Obedience is mandatory, individual freedoms squashed.

Autocrats have been the norm throughout most of Latin America for centuries, but not so in Costa Rica. The conquistadors never found the riches in this land that they were seeking, but perhaps the country's true wealth lay in its ability to maintain a government and society free of dictators and authoritarians.

"When I despair," mused Mahatma Gandhi, "I remember that all through history the way of truth and love have always won. There have been tyrants and murderers, and for a time, they can seem invincible, but in the end, they always fall. Think of it—always."

It seemed there was hope, however feeble, for the people of Latin America and others throughout the world who were under the thumb of autocracies and authoritarians. There is a high price to be paid not only in enduring such rule, but also in throwing off the yoke of repression. In every case, I realized, it is leadership that makes the difference.

12

WHERE THE ROAD ENDS

The Pan-American took us to the town of Bibri, then on to the border with Panama, past miles of banana trees held upright with yellow and blue string. On the Costa Rican side we purchased exit stamps, which the official diligently pasted into our passports. There was no road, but a skinny lad guided us up a steep embankment onto a creaking railroad bridge that led across the border. A semi-truck creeping towards us bounced over the blackened wooden ties. Through gaping holes under our feet, where boards had long ago fallen, we spied the brown and muddy currents of the Río Sixaola rushing below.

On the far side of the river, at Guabito, the Panamanian officer stamped our passports but flatly stated we each needed a ten-dollar tourist card, which was only obtainable in Changuinola, ten kilometers farther ahead. A man who had followed us across the bridge led us to a nearby store, where we traded our remaining colónes for Panamanian balboa, but somehow lost ten dollars in the transaction. Outside, hustlers offered expensive taxi rides.

"I think they're all in cahoots," I murmured to Tamara.

Instead, we flagged a bus and left the touts behind. In Changuinola a woman pasted our stamps into place and signed our passports. We were officially in. The road to the coastal city of Almirante carried us past swathes of banana plantations stretching away from the dirt road in all directions. Shoddy wood and tin shacks perched on spindly stilts. Our destination for the day was Bocas del Toro, but the road ended on the edge of Laguna de Chiriquí. The only way across the lagoon was via ferry. The moment our bus paused, touts clambered onboard. Competition between the two ferry companies plying the lagoon waters was fierce. As we entered the decaying dockside office of one company, a competitor ran over.

"Two dollars!" he shouted. "Two dollars each to Bocas!"

The touts indicated with winks and hand gestures that the newcomers were crazy. As I turned back to the woman at the counter, she lowered her price. Falling rain muddled the brown waters as we huddled beneath a tin roof overhang waiting for the ferry. The air and even the docks smelled of stagnant sea. When the ferry arrived we piled aboard; the mate cast off but just as we were pulling away, the pilot swung back around for a late-arriving passenger. As we finally departed, the radio crackled again and the overloaded ferry returned for more.

On the dock at Bocas del Toro a man speaking broken English and Guari-guari—a dialect of Creole English and Spanish with local Guaymí mixed in—led us to a hotel. Weary after a long day traveling, we lay in our room beneath the whirring fan as the afternoon faded into evening and the heat built. Later that evening, seventy-five cent Balboa and Atlas beers then Panama and Soberana beers turned out to be a better bargain in evening hours than the overpriced local fare.

Soon after first light we boarded a water taxi to take us to the far side of the lagoon, and skimmed over smooth Caribbean waters past coconut palm islands, uninhabited but for mangroves and the occasional thatch-roof shack atop rotted pilings. The captain paid far more attention to the local woman in a lime green dress seated next to him than he did to the hazardous-looking, debris-infested waters.

On the far side of the lagoon we found a local bus to take us along a new section of road to David, the capital of Chiriquí Province, on a long though stunning route across the untouched Cordillera Talamanca Mountains. Panama's north-south corridor had just opened, as evidenced by the sparsity of roadside shacks or stalls and the still-virgin rainforest that stretched to the horizon. In David we found a *comida corrida*–inexpensive fast-food menu–of rice and broiled chicken and afterward later relaxed on our hotel balcony, which overlooked the central square. Baby blue birds and twittering green parakeets flitted among the trees. Great burgeoning clouds built in the distance as the sun sank into a murky horizon.

I found it hard to believe that we were already at the conclusion of the Central American leg of our journey. It was as if all the misfortunes to ever plague humanity–earthquakes, hurricanes, volcanoes, mudslides, floods, civil wars, guerilla armies, despots, dictators, corruption, drug-running, disease, poverty, unemployment, deforestation–had clustered in one corner of the world. Yet we had so far survived.

South of the town of Yaviza, the Pan-American Highway ended. The roadless jungle of the Darien Gap–impassable in the wet season with waterlogged trails, swollen rivers, and frequent mudslides–was not recommended at any time of year due to roaming guerilla groups which funded their activities by kidnapping travelers for ransom. We had little choice but to fly over the Isthmus of Panama.

Panama City, the end of the road for us, was typical of all other cities in Central America, with high incidences of armed robberies, rapes, muggings, and petty theft. Upon our arrival I asked our taxi driver about the security situation in San Felipe, the district I intended for us to stay in. Despite his thick Panamanian Spanish, I understood that danger abounded day and night. He stopped at a hotel, where the clerk gave us a three-hour rather than hourly rate.

Pelicans dove into nearby Pacific waters. Tankers on the horizon waited in a long line to cross the Canal. This area has always been a crossroads. Flora and fauna have migrated across the Isthmus of Panama for millennia. The Cueva, Chibchan, and Chocoan people inhabited the region until the arrival of the Spanish, whereupon they fled to the forests and outlying islands and soon succumbed to European diseases against which they had no immunity.

Vasco Nuñez de Balboa's trek from the Atlantic to the Pacific five hundred years ago proved that the Isthmus was the path between the oceans, and present-day Panama became an intersection of Spain's new empire. Gold and silver mined in Peru were shipped to the Isthmus, hauled across, and loaded onto ships on the Caribbean side. Spain controlled the Isthmus for three centuries, until the early 1800s, and even after independence the Isthmus remained part of Colombia. Isthmians' attempts to secede from Colombia all failed.

In time, canal politics became the keystone that gave Panamanians a national identity. Though the United States had considered Nicaragua as an option for construction of a canal between the Pacific and Atlantic, President Theodore Roosevelt had his eye on the flailing French effort already underway across the Isthmus of Panama. After much negotiation a 1903 treaty enabled the United States to lease in perpetuity a six-mile wide strip of land across the Isthmus for ten million dollars plus an annual payment. The United States ratified the treaty, but Colombia's senate did not because many senators felt the payment fell short. The United States refused to renegotiate, and instead gave its political and military support to the Panamanian separatist movement.

Roosevelt implied to Panamanian rebels that if they revolted, his Navy would assist their efforts. A few days before the planned uprising was launched by a group of prominent Panamanian families, the USS Nashville was dispatched. When Panama declared autonomy, the waiting gunship blocked any effort by Colombian troops to interfere. The United States recognized Panama as a sovereign nation, which in turn granted perpetual control of the Canal Zone to the United States. As part of treaty negotiations, the United States bought the French concession.

Having recently completed the Suez Canal, a sea-level effort through sand and desert, the French assumed construction of the Panama Canal would be similar. But Panama's unbroken tropical forests, rampant disease, and the difficulties of digging a channel through rugged mountains that stretched down the spine of the Isthmus proved too much for the French. The Americans understood that mosquitoes spread malaria and yellow fever, and that controlling the insects would reduce fatalities. Further, they abandoned the idea of a sea-level canal and instead dammed the Chagres River to create a lake eighty-five feet above sea level. Engineers built a series of chambers on each end to raise incoming ships to lake level and lower them to sea level before exiting to the ocean. The canal's steel lock gates stood seventy feet tall and weighed nearly eight hundred tons each, yet required only a forty-horsepower motor to open and close.

As a result, after ten years and over five thousand lost lives—in addition to the twenty thousand lives lost under the eight-year French effort—the United States opened the Panama Canal, forever revolutionizing global commerce and shipping and signaling the emergence of the United States as a world power.

Not wanting to miss this modern marvel, Tamara and I made our way to Miraflores, where one of the three locks of the canal is located. A guard let us through, but another one scowling on the edge of the canal approached us.

"How did you get in?" He barked.

We pointed at the other guard.

"¡Mierda!" he cursed. It seemed the viewing platforms were not yet open. "Bien," he conceded grumpily. "You may stay."

We had the place to ourselves, and watched the locks close, fill with water, and push the mammoth tankers up into the sky. Vessels rose, and locks opened and closed, in an unending orchestration.

Panama's politics remained mostly peaceful after secession until a military coup ousted Dr. Arnulfo Arias Madrid, who had won the presidency on the promise that he would end corruption and pave the way for a new Panama. After General Manuel Antonio Noriega Moreno came to power in 1983 he funded his dictatorship with a clandestine drug-and-money laundering economy. Under the supervision of the CIA, Noriega supplied the Nicaraguan Contras and other guerillas with arms. After a massive demonstration in 1987 left over a thousand people injured or detained, President Reagan began a series of sanctions against Noriega's regime. Panamanians voted for the anti-Noriega candidate, but the regime annulled the elections.

When President George H. W. Bush launched an invasion in 1989 to secure the Canal, Noriega was at last unseated. Mireya Moscoso, widow of Dr. Arnulfo Arias Madrid, against whom the initial coup was led, eventually took office. Moscoso handled the transfer of the Canal from the United States to Panama, as earlier negotiated by treaty. After eighty-five years of American control, six months before our arrival, the Canal came under Panamanian control.

Panama remained the perfect country in which to launder money, however. Many of the towering buildings we saw from our seedy hotel window were allegedly fronts for converting illegitimate earnings into official income. First, someone with extra cash bought a hotel or apartment building. Next, they filled the register with fictitious guest or tenant names. Then, they paid themselves an inflated nightly or rental rate. Voila, the cash was clean. The practice continued long after our visit. According to multiple news outlets, many of those who initially bought condos in Donald Trump's seventy-story Ocean Club International Hotel and Tower apparently did so not to live there, but to launder drug cartel, Russian gangster, and people-smuggling money.

Perhaps due to Bush's invasion, the Noriega fiasco, and long-running Canal politics, we found an icy populace in the tropical land. As we strolled back to the hotel from our canal visit, the streets turned slummy. Trash filled the alleyways and ragged clothes hung from the windows of worn, barely habitable high-rise apartments.

"What are you doing?" a voice called after us as we walked. "Where are you going?"

"To our hotel," I replied to the voice, looking around.

"This is a bad area," said an old man from behind a stout iron gate. "You should not walk here. It is dangerous. Take a taxi instead."

We took his advice, caught a cab for the remaining five blocks, and at the hotel packed our gear. We found a bus for the hour's ride through bustling streets to the airport. Fresh rain fell and cooled the air imperceptibly. Unintelligible hand-scrawled words covered the bus's ceiling, walls, and seats. Reggae hip-hop fusion played through the speakers, psychedelic neon stickers covered the black-painted front wall, and a red light twirled whenever the youthful driver slammed his foot on the brakes. The magic bus hurtled us towards South America, a land far larger and more complex than the war-torn nations of Central America. I was reminded of a line from *The Four Million* by O. Henry.

"The true adventurer goes forth aimless and uncalculating to meet and greet unknown fate."

A sense of trepid excitement welled up in me as we walked toward the airport. I could not imagine what unknown fate lay in store for us.

PART II

Why does the guerilla fighter fight? We must come to the inevitable conclusion that the guerilla fighter is a social reformer, that he takes up arms responding to the angry protest of the people against their oppressors, and that he fights in order to change the social system that keeps all his unarmed brothers in ignominy and misery.

- Ernesto "Che" Guevara, *Guerilla Warfare*

13

FINDING A FRAGILE PEACE

For four decades, Colombia topped the list of most dangerous places on the planet. In the year Tamara and I traveled overland across South America, over seven hundred hostages were kidnapped for ransom. There was a greater risk of being abducted in Colombia at that time than in any other country in the world. Violence by narcotraffickers, guerillas, and paramilitary groups affected all corners of the country, urban and rural. Besides kidnappings, domestic airline hijackings and murders were all too common. Unsurprisingly, the Department of State warned United States citizens against all travel to Colombia. We heeded their advice.

The reasons for all this violence could in part be traced back to Colombia's independence from Spain in the early 1800s, which ushered in a century and a half of ideological disparity between Colombia's liberal and conservative parties. Tension between the two factions culminated in *La Violencia*, tragically triggered in 1948 when presidential candidate Jorge Eliécer Gaitán was assassinated. The resulting riots claimed a mind-boggling two hundred thousand lives.

A decade later, the United States sent a team of counterinsurgency experts to investigate Colombia's security situation. Among other recommendations, the team advised that any special aid be covert in nature, in order to shield Colombian and American authorities from interventionist charges. Three years later, a secret report to the Joint Chiefs of Staff encouraged the creation and deployment of a United States-backed force to commit "paramilitary, sabotage and/or terrorist activities against known communist proponents."

During the 1950s, America's anti-communist phobia had whipped itself into a frenzy. Senator Joseph McCarthy spearheaded a campaign that accused hundreds of Americans of being "communists" or "sympathizers" despite inconclusive or questionable evidence. Many government employees, entertainers, and academics lost their jobs; some were imprisoned. Most were not communists. Likewise, American foreign policy was focused on the prevention of communism's spread in other countries. In Colombia, such policies led to creation of a United States-supported paramilitary. Colombian officials recruited civilians into these units, which worked alongside the regular military and served as local intelligence networks that gathered information on guerilla groups including FARC, ELN, EPL, MAQL, and M-19.

Perhaps the most formidable was FARC, a self-labeled 'peasant army' with an agrarian and anti-imperialist political platform that fought for the rights of Colombia's rural poor against the monopolization of natural resources by multi-national corporations, United States political influence, and Colombian paramilitary violence. FARC funded its activities through gold mining, the production and distribution of illegal drugs, and kidnapping for ransom.

These were the guerillas I had heard about as a ten-year-old when my father was preparing to travel to Colombia on business. They were a different breed to Subcomandante Marcos' ragtag band of Mexican revolutionaries. FARC and other Colombian guerilla groups were heavily armed, well-funded, and deadly.

The Sinú River was the reason I had first learned about Colombia. The river originates in the western Andes, and carves out a valley in northwestern Colombia, before flowing into the Caribbean Sea. The Sinú flowed through the heart of the Colombian Conflict, and at the height of violence in 1980, was where my father helicoptered into.

The Colombian government planned to dam the Sinú, and the engineering company hired to assess and design the Urrá hydroelectric project contracted my father's firm for technical assistance. A long-time terrestrial ecologist, he along with an ichthyologist and forester comprised the three-man environmental unit, which replaced a prior team. From Bogotá, Colombia's capital, their rickety plane had swooped over the mountains and seemingly unbroken forest into a primitive airport with barely enough runway for the pilot to touch down and stop.

For the next week the team explored a hundred-mile swath of the Sinú valley by helicopter. They were dropped into the jungle from choppers like American troops in the Vietnam War, usually with a military escort. They motored up and down the river on seventy-foot-long, two-foot-wide handmade dugout canoes tilled by local helmsmen. Smoke from slash-and-burn fires filled the air in places where civilization had crept in. In settlements such as Sinú, near the river's mouth, simple huts dotted the riverbanks and donkey carts transported villagers and goods.

The team found thick forests of the upper Sinú that were filled with mahogany and Colombian ebony. Endangered cattleya orchids, harpy eagles, blue-billed curassows, and two species of tapirs could still be spotted, along with spectacled bear, giant anteaters, jaguars, ocelots, spider monkeys, cotton-top tamarins, and white-lipped peccaries. In the lower reaches puma, crab-eating raccoons, and jaguarondi roamed savannah grasslands. Wetlands served as stopping grounds for migrating songbirds and supported osprey, manatee, and caiman.

Despite the region's biodiversity and fact that indigenous Umbrá and other tribes had inhabited the land for thousands of years, the government planned to flood the entire valley. Controversy over the dam added to the political upheaval and chaos that had plagued the Colombian interior for decades. Loyalties were not always clear. Some Umbrá leaders were murdered for protesting construction of the project. FARC guerillas were supposedly for the people, but sometimes imprisoned and killed villagers. Army soldiers might be in league with the FARC.

The year my father traveled to Bogotá, FARC called for a major strategy shift. Cocaine, the primary drug of Colombia, manufactured from the locally-grown coca leaf, was enjoying a boom in the United States. Whereas most prior fighting was limited to small rural confrontations against military forces, the new injection of drug money allowed FARC to stage large-scale attacks closer to middle-sized cities. Backlash against the United States helped push Colombia into a chaotic war zone.

On one outing my father's team was dropped, as usual, into the rainforest. They were accompanied by an interpreter and a local guide who did not speak English. As they prepared to climb into a canoe to take them down the river, a man paddled to shore with a stretched fox skin to sell. The guide recognized the trader. My father, curious about the species at hand, purchased the hide. After the exchange, the trader continued on his way. As he drifted downstream, the guide conferred with the interpreter. After a few minutes the interpreter turned towards the team.

"That man was just released from prison," the interpreter explained. "He murdered the one who came before him…" and pointed at my father.

Even twenty years later, when Tamara and I traveled overland across the Americas, the risk of being kidnapped was still far too high to travel unaccompanied through Colombia's interior. While narcotics and guerilla-related violence accounted for part of the violence, common criminals were responsible for a large percentage of reported murders. Buses were off-limits due to extortion and kidnapping attempts. At a typical guerilla roadblock, travelers were forced to pay a "war tax," vehicles might be torched or stolen, and people were often kidnapped.

A common example of the kind of violence that plagued the interior was the case of Vigía del Fuerte. The hotly-contested village, located in the northwestern corner of the country along the Atrato River, lay within a major arms and drug smuggling corridor en route to the Caribbean. Twenty-one police officers died while repelling a thirty-six hour FARC assault. Rebel machine-gun fire and wayward homemade missiles destroyed the church, mayor's office, police barracks, and telephone company, not to mention multiple houses. The mayor, two young children, and several villagers were killed.

'Big Fruit' was even caught in the crossfire. During our journey a division of Chiquita Brands International—the powerful entity that created so many Central American banana republics—secretly paid millions to a right-wing paramilitary organization in Colombia in exchange for employee protection within a volatile banana harvesting region. Similar payments went to the left-wing FARC and ELN guerilla groups. The company afterward faced criminal charges and a lawsuit for violating anti-terrorism laws. Chiquita dominated the life and politics of every country it did business in, and served as poster child for the kind of control that multi-national corporations wielded. Yet in Colombia, even Chiquita was held hostage.

Fifteen years after my journey with Tamara I returned to visit the only mainland Latin American nation we had to miss. For this outing I flew to Bogotá, where the murder rate had fallen but muggings were on the rise. After exploring the sprawling city I traveled north to the sixteenth-century colonial village of Villa de Leyva. Centered around the expansive cobblestoned Plaza Mayor, the tranquil village remained largely untouched though weekend day trippers from Bogotá sometimes crowded the plaza.

A twenty-four hour bus journey to the northern coast brought me to Cartagena. The colonial city's heart appeared virtually unchanged since the early 1500s. Cobbled alleyways, balconies covered in bougainvillea, and monumental churches pushed up against the Caribbean Sea. Ramparts of the four hundred-year-old Spanish fortress Castillo San Felipe de Barajas, virtually impregnable due to the wide walls, parapets, and underground tunnels, still overlooked the city.

To the northeast along the Caribbean coast lay Tayrona National Park. Only sandy footpaths and horse trails traversed the coastline where the world's highest coastal mountain range, the Sierra Nevada de Santa Marta, met the sea. Azure waves crashed onto pristine sands and into smooth sun-bleached boulders that lay a few steps from my swaying hammock.

Next, I ventured into the highlands to visit Minca, a mountain village known for its organic coffee and cooler temperatures. I hired Luis and his motorcycle-taxi for forays high into the coastal mountains upon rutted, dirt paths that clung to the side of jungled mountainsides, where waterfalls plunged into hidden pools.

I returned to the lowlands and found myself in the city of Santa Marta. Founded in 1525, this was Colombia's oldest surviving city and South America's second-oldest. Here locals danced in the streets at sunset and swam in the sea, which lapped at the edges of the city. Street vendors sold ice cream and *cervezas* and music filled the air as I walked the waterfront at dusk.

After a few weeks, I circled back to Bogotá. What I had discovered on my travels was a country of stunning scenery, a refreshing lack of tourists, and—despite the violence that had underscored Colombia for decades—an up-and-coming generation with an eye on a new future. I encountered many locals who were quick to smile, hospitable, and eager to share their stories.

One evening in Bogotá I met with a Colombian named Tatiana. Over local beers we discussed her country's history and future. She was open about Colombia's situation. Tatiana had always known violence. At the height of the war, for example, her mother could not wear earrings or any other jewelry in public.

"People had their earlobes ripped off when robbers grabbed their earrings," said Tatiana. "Most of my friends have been robbed. Some were forced to withdraw all their savings from ATM machines. Taxi robberies are very common."

In rural regions, violence still endured. She told of a local village that was coveted by mining interests and paid the price.

"Men with machine guns killed many of the villagers," she said, "and then ran the rest out."

Despite this, in 2016, less than two months after I met with Tatiana, the Colombian government and FARC rebels signed a ceasefire deal to end the fifty-year conflict that had caused over two hundred thousand deaths and displaced more than six million people. Peace deals had already been negotiated with other rebel groups, including Quintin Lamé, M-19, and EPL. A final peace would require approval by the public in a referendum, but a formal end to hostilities with FARC seemed promising.

That October, however, voters narrowly rejected the accord. Though Colombians desired peace, many felt the terms were too lenient towards FARC. Under the proposed agreement, FARC members who confessed to their crimes would be entitled to reduced sentences. Despite the failed referendum, a fragile peace took hold. FARC fighters laid down their weapons, and in November 2016 the Colombian government and FARC signed a revised peace deal, which both houses of Congress ratified rather than send to the people in a second referendum.

There were still ongoing conflicts with other smaller groups and gangs linked to drug trafficking, and stories like Tatiana's continued to unfold. Many Colombians had known only war, and held no memory of what it meant to live in peace. Exhausted by violence, some wanted to leave. Others hoped to build a new Colombia. Though the nation's future was not entirely certain, many seemed optimistic. For Tatiana, and so many other locals, I hoped Colombia's fragile peace would hold.

14

TUNGURAHUA

The flight out of Panama City put Tamara and I into Ecuador after midnight. A man at the airport speaking rapid Spanish warned us to be careful in Quito after dark. Daytime is okay, he said, "pero por la noche hay mucho peligro." *But at night there is much danger.* Wary, we followed a woman to a taxi, then rode with a man through dark neighborhoods before finding a room in Old Town. Quito had seen a sharp increase in not only pickpocketing, burglary, and hotel room theft but also robberies, carjackings, and kidnappings. Thieves increasingly brandished guns or knives. Ecuador's president had, on multiple occasions, declared states of emergency in response to the spiraling crime rate, and at times even imposed curfews.

At daybreak, a light rain drizzled onto the green mist-shrouded mountains ringing the city, and church bells pealed in the distance. As we walked the narrow colonial streets, a Catholic saint atop a flatbed truck led a procession of singers and mournful-sounding musicians. Couples strolled with arms intertwined. Families filing from churches clustered together, boys offered shoe shines, and old women sold ice cream.

Breakfast cost one dollar, our room only four. Local taxis charged a quarter. Yet Quito's low prices came at a high cost. Highland Quechua–indigenous people of the Andes–wearing bright wraps and felt derby hats begged on the streets for money and food. Children holding children motioned to their mouths. Quechua men sold watches and families peddled sunglasses. Other quiteños–residents of Quito–offered small paintings, Chiclets, and candy for sale. One child with a baby swaddled on her back ran up to us. As I reached into my pocket, a dirt-smeared lad clutched Tamara and would not let go. Indigenous people comprised half of Ecuador's population, and most of them lived in poverty. Their plight represented a nation in crisis.

Multiple rebellions, dictatorships, and coups d'état had plagued Ecuador for decades. Sealed-off streets, burning tires, and Molotov cocktails marked sporadic protests against the government's handling of the economy. Angered by high unemployment and land exploitation, protestors sometimes fired handguns into the air and at police; the standard response was with water cannons and tear gas. Such uprisings often blocked highways and disrupted transportation. A growing indigenous movement, instigated by right-wing heavy-handedness and propelled by leftist movements, had steered Ecuador towards collapse.

In January 2020, the unrest culminated with the overthrow of President Jamil Mahuad. Over breakfast soon after our arrival, I shared with Tamara some of the five-month-old newspaper headlines I had clipped for the trip. Erratic El Niño weather had flooded much of the country's crops. Falling oil prices reduced export revenues. The implosion of Asian markets had dealt a final blow.

"Following demonstrations in Quito," I read, "by unions, students, women's groups, African Ecuadorians, and leftist political parties, tens of thousands of indigenous people poured into the city. Even oil workers struck in support. Though thirty thousand troops were deployed to block the protestors' entry, soldiers broke ranks and joined the demonstrations. Units guarding Congress stepped aside. Indigenous leaders announced the president's removal, and welcomed the new 'government of national salvation.'"

Before the celebrations went too far, however, President Bill Clinton condemned the coup d'état and threatened sanctions and an immediate halt to all aid and investment in any military-led government.

"The State Department's top Latin American official warned coup leaders they faced economic isolation akin to Cuba if they persisted," I continued from the clipping. "Indigenous leaders backed down, and Ecuador's vice-president was installed instead as the nation's new president."

"So the United States, in effect, forced a counter-coup against a populist movement," observed Tamara.

"It appears that way."

The resulting turmoil provoked more chaos. Locals warned us to vacate the city streets by dusk. The El Tejar area, where we caught our buses, had grown too dangerous for tourists. Long lines of quiteños stretched outside public buildings and banks. Soldiers stood at the ready. Some were laden with dozens of tear gas canisters in addition to their standard-issue machine guns. Private security and armed guards wielding semi-automatic weapons and bulletproof vests manned nearly every corner. Despite the visible police and army presence, a hyperactive Brit at our hotel claimed he carried an iron pipe in his coat but had still almost got mugged the night prior.

Nor was social unrest Ecuador's only challenge. Malaria, yellow fever, and cholera had reached epidemic levels in outlying regions and in cities such as Guayaquil. As if this were not enough, the Guagua Pinchincha volcano, which towers above Quito like an angry giant, had awoken just before our visit. Intermittent explosions had blanketed Quito in layers of gray volcanic ash, closed schools and the airport, and disrupted power and transportation networks. We were warned that secondary mudflows caused by heavy rains, which often accompanied volcanic events, could bury parts of the city if a major eruption were to occur.

Shafts of sun peeked through choppy cloud, and the day warmed. Though at ten thousand feet, Quito stayed mild year-round thanks to its perch a dozen miles from the equator. We spent the afternoon at Mitad del Mundo, the 'middle of the world'. To the west loomed Guagua Pinchincha's steaming crater. At Mitad del Mundo, inside a museum straddling the equator, we watched a synchronized sunset fall upon a model of Quito's Old Town.

"Since we can't walk in the real city at night," Tamara remarked, "this replica will just have to do."

The next morning, on a street where red and white Especial buses and baby blue regulars churned past, we found one bound for the tranquil working-class town of Latacunga, a couple hours' drive south of Quito. Soaring mountains flanked a verdant patchwork of farms and fields nestled within lush lowlands. Though clouds built atop each other like massive mounds of shaving cream, Cotopaxi's snow-covered summit and the Sur and Norte peaks of the Illinizas stayed clear. In Latacunga, boys offered shoe shines and girls sold lollipops.

"Look at this!" Tamara exclaimed in horror as our bus roared off. Blood covered parts of her rucksack, and one of the zippers was broken.

"Looks like somebody tried to rob you," I said, "but cut themselves prying the lock."

"And no one said a word?" Tamara lamented. "Someone must have seen the guy under the seat fiddling with my bag."

"Maybe," I said. "But either way, we've got to stay vigilant, especially if we can't count on locals to watch our backs."

The next day we took a side trip to Saquisili, a village known for its lively market stocked with hand-woven blankets and shawls. We wandered past stalls selling *cabuya* ropes and cords coiled like snakes. Cow, pig, and sheep parts were piled high upon tables. On the periphery, animal buyers set up small corrals to collect their purchases. Trucks brimmed with red and yellow bananas, reed mats, fans, and baskets. Quechua women hunched beside radishes, mandarin oranges, potatoes, onions, okra, avocados, and tomatoes stacked in pyramids.

The weather turned sour and as the rain fell harder, the air turned colder. We found an unoccupied wooden table at a hole-in-the-wall-eatery. A bulky woman brought hot water, packets of instant coffee, and sugar in a bowl for us to mix together. Locals who wandered in ate plates heaped with rice and chicken and beets. We settled for cheese empanadas. Brown waters flooded the dirt streets and overran the curbs. Locals pulled down their battered tarps and bent wooden poles, and packed their wares into rice bags. Plastic covered the few remaining market stands, which soon closed.

"How are you doing?" I asked Tamara over our empanadas.

"I don't know," she said. "This coffee is awful. I'm wet, cold, and probably homesick. This weather is depressing. I really feel for these people."

"Me too. This market is their livelihood."

As we huddled pensively in our wooden seats, watching the driving rain, thinking about nearly getting robbed and wondering if we soon would, I could not help but think: is it all worth it?

A few days later, we crept up jungle-covered hillsides to Ambato, where Tamara darted into a Gus fast-food eatery and past the surprised cashier in order to relieve her bursting bladder, before descending into a verdurous valley of forest and sculpted pastureland swathed in clinging cloud. In the town of Baños we took a third-floor room with panoramic views overlooking stunning Andean mountains, white church steeples, and ribbons of waterfall.

Baños means *baths*, for which the town was named. Geothermal springs fed the warm, healing waters that tourists typically flocked to. On our arrival, the streets seemed strangely deserted; a low season ebb, we decided. But, climbing the stairs to our room, we froze. A heart-stopping cloud of gray volcanic ash was towering over the green hills that surrounded the town. The growing plume billowed upward, drifted west, and obscured the afternoon sun.

"Ah, muy tranquilo," the hotel staff in Latacunga had said when I inquired about Baños. "Hay muchas turistas."

"It's very quiet there," I had translated for Tamara. "With lots of tourists."

We knew the town had been evacuated a few months earlier when Tungurahua volcano began ejecting huge volumes of ash and incandescent rock, but thought it safe to visit. As we later learned, though much of the population had left when Baños was evacuated, some refused to leave. When news crews caught soldiers looting abandoned homes and businesses, more residents returned. One local was shot and killed in a standoff. Following the recent presidential coup d'état, the army had withdrawn and the government washed its hands of Baños. A handful of locals hung on, hopeful that Tungurahua would settle down. But volcanologists advised that an eruption would occur quickly and with little warning, and likely send pyroclastic flows barreling through Baños and other local villages. I realized why X-shaped masking tape covered most of the town's windows—to reduce the amount of flying glass when the volcano let loose.

When one of the women running our hotel offered a ride to the volcano for a dollar each, we accepted. Be ready by 10pm, she said. That evening we joined an older English couple, the two young Ecuadorian women who helped run the hotel, and the owner, Rodrigo. We piled through the back door of a stripped-down yellow 4x4 with room for six along two makeshift wooden benches.

As we ground slowly forward, red flashes arced through the night sky. Twenty minutes after leaving the hotel, Rodrigo pulled into a muddy turnaround. The sky was black but for billions of brilliant stars. A thundering roar exploded, like surf pounding a rocky coastline during a nor'easter. Red incandescent rocks spewed skyward as Rodrigo handed us cups of tea to ward off the chill. We watched transfixed as magma poured from the crater's rim and glowing rocks burst into the sky and rained onto Tungurahua's upper slopes. Little warning would be possible prior to a major eruption.

"The residents of Baños are like walking ghosts," Tamara murmured.

The next day she and I climbed lower foothills of Tungurahua. Clouds built to the east, but the volcano stood silent. In lower reaches, poinsettia trees shadowed impatiens and hibiscus. Up high, lilies and lupine grew amongst yellow-orange blossoms. The path of future pyroclastic mudflows was easy to trace. I showed Tamara with a sweep of my arm.

"They'll follow the river canyon, barrel across Baños, and carry everything to the Amazon," I said.

Such a fate befell a village in Colombia fifteen years before. The eruption of a snow-capped volcano in the central Andes melted tons of ice that mixed with molten lava to form a mile-wide wall of hot mud, rocks, and trees that traveled downslope at speeds up to thirty miles per hour. Residents were swept through the streets. Thousands were trapped and killed. With the exception of a few houses and the tip of the church steeple, the village of Armero was buried beneath forty feet of mud.

On our descent, I picked up a clump of brown dirt. "Like dark chocolate," said Tamara. Tungurahua provided the rich lava that eroded into fertile soil and nourished life-giving crops for locals, and would one day take it all away.

Around the main square, some Quechua people begged for sucres, Ecuador's currency. Boys sold hand-painted dioramas. A long line of black-shrouded Catholic mourners snaked past abandoned graffiti-covered hotels towards the half-full cemetery. It appeared many bodies had already been relocated.

"Tungurahua...volveremos con mas neque carajo panchos," read the spray-painted slang on one hotel shell. *Tungurahua...we will be back.* On another concrete wall: "Baños no morira jamas." *Baños will never die.*

We crossed a creaking suspension bridge that led over the frothing river and past a zoo filled with green macaws, red-faced parakeets, blue-headed parrots, Andean condors, spider monkeys, ocelots, jaguars, Galapagos tortoises, pumas, and tapirs. Their fates too were precarious. Later, while descending lush hillsides past cascading waterfalls, we passed a young girl sitting on a mule carrying supplies along the footpath. We greeted her in unison.

"Hola," she said.

The thought of her someday being swept away by mudflows unsettled us both. After the mule train plodded past, we noticed pieces of battered shoes amongst the bits of trash lining the trail.

"It's the land of lost shoes," I said.

"No," punned Tamara. "It's the land of lost souls."

That night, we met Rodrigo again at his clapped-out jalopy, the 'Limusina Ecuadorian', as he called it. This time, only Tamara and I crawled onto the wooden benches. We stopped on the volcano's lower flanks. Rodrigo lit a cigarette and listened, but Tungurahua stood silent.

"Más tarde," he said. *Later.*

Rodrigo talked of life before the volcano had woken. There were many tourists then, at least twenty each night in his hotel. He ran a restaurant and *panadería*–bakery–now both closed. He was grateful we had stayed. I asked where he would go when the volcano erupted. Perhaps Ambato, he said, but the army, police, Civil Defense–all said there would be little warning. If lucky he and his family might have time to flee to Puyo in the Amazon jungle, but likely not. I asked what Tungurahua's silence these past few days meant.

"Muy mal," he said. *Very bad.* When erupting a little each day, it is okay, but when silent the pressure builds, and *kaboom*, the big one, he explained.

We listened in the darkness until a long roar echoed across the highlands. Rodrigo led us to some nearby ruins as another rumble rolled through the valley. With flashlight in hand he took us among roofless concrete walls filled four-feet deep with mud. Next door were the skeletal remains of the house where Rodrigo's cousin, the former owner of the mud-filled restaurant, once lived.

Another grumble filled the heavens. Watching fire shoot into the sky on a clear night was an eye-opening experience, but unable to see the volcano and know whether mudflows might be hurtling downslope felt far more eerie. The dirt road we stood upon, which once led to Riobamba, ended in thick layers of fresh mud.

"Es posible," Rodrigo said, referring to the road we had arrived upon, "en la mañana el camino será intransitable." *It's possible the road will be impassable in the morning.*

Raindrops fell as fireflies dotted the darkness and crickets chirped. We bumped back through the evacuation area past signs warning "zona de alto riesgo." *High risk zone.* Rodrigo asked if we had been to the baths. They are only there, he said while squinting through the mud-splattered wiperless windshield, because of the volcano. And the town is there only because of the baths. As with the fertile chocolate soil, the volcano gives and the volcano takes.

We threaded our way past mounds of fresh mud towering on either side of the track. Each day, bulldozers cleared a new path. A few hours after we had passed, mudflows trapped two vehicles until morning. When the volcano blew, the road would be buried dozens of feet deep. Rodrigo explained what would happen then, just as I had told Tamara. Mud and lava would pour down Tungurahua's slopes, fill the river channel, and carry the town away.

"Ten cuidado," I said at the end of the night. "Y buena suerte." *Be careful, and good luck.*

"Gracias," he said, but ran a finger across his neck, indicating his fate was sealed. He would live and likely die, it seemed, in the shadow of Tungurahua.

15

¡GRINGOS...ASESINOS!

Hard rains drumming our corrugated tin roof through the long night sounded eerily similar to Tungurahua's roar. In our dreams the volcano let loose her fury, and we jerked awake whenever the downpour reached a feverish pitch. In the morning a struggling bus carried us up and out of the valley. A lone condor soared past low-lying clouds hugging verdant Andean slopes. Tamara and I each breathed a little easier when we reached higher ground, for we were at last free from Tungurahua's grip.

To reach the town of Riobamba, in the center of Ecuador, our driver turned onto an unpaved track that twisted past farms and fields clinging to near vertical slopes. Wizened farmers clad in bright blue and pink wraps balanced like nimble goats. Hand-cut paths led to mud-walled cliff-side shacks. On the horizon, Tungurahua's plume of gray ash billowed from a thick bank of white cloud. We climbed past washouts and landslides blocking portions of the narrow roadway, which our driver had to negotiate around. The cultivated hillsides yielded to slopes covered by bushy tufts of grass, then brown mountains dotted with pink, white, and yellow alpine flowers fluttering on sharp breezes. Shadows swept across the rounded mountaintops and a patchwork quilt of endless green hues pieced together by hedgerow seams that stretched to the horizon. In the distance, a sweating sheen of fresh fallen snow swathed the flanks of Chimborazo. I pointed at the mountain.

"That's the highest summit on Earth," I said.

"I thought Mt. Everest is the tallest," replied Tamara.

"Actually, Everest is Earth's highest point above sea level."

"What's the difference?"

"Because the centrifugal force of the planet's rotation causes the ocean, land, and atmosphere to bulge outward, a person on the equator juts thirteen miles farther into space than one standing at the North or South Pole. For this reason, the highest point on Earth's surface, as measured from the earth's center, is Chimborazo."

"Okay, smarty pants."

After topping the pass, the bus roared downhill. Thousand-foot cliffs dropped away inches from bald tires. Dark clouds brooding on the horizon began to build. I stared into the emptiness, noticing the crushed remains of a few buses far below, but was yanked back into the present when our driver jammed his brakes. A shepherdess was hurrying her flock of sheep off the roadway. A few raindrops spattered the windows. Heavy rains would turn the dirt track into a treacherous obstacle course, but thankfully we soon dropped into the lowlands and reached Riobamba—a city founded in 1534 and rebuilt in the eighteenth century after being leveled by an earthquake—before the downpours hit.

At dawn, rain still pattered on the windows. Our goal was Cuenca, and lush countryside soon rolled past our bus windows. After half an hour we screeched to a halt. I slowly deciphered the passengers' chattering. Quechua protesters had blocked the only road between Riobamba and Cuenca, and there was no other way forward. Some of the passengers set out on foot. We considered following them until a kindly Ecuadorian cautioned us against the idea.

"The obstruction is many kilometers long," he said in Spanish. "Crossing would be quite dangerous."

So, we returned to Riobamba and checked back into our room. I asked the hotel manager about the current situation.

"No one knows how long this protest will last," she said. "Many people do not have enough money to buy clothes or food. They wait for days in long bank lines for their monthly stipends."

Prices in Ecuador rose daily, while wages—where they existed—remained flat. Angry with the government, indigenous people sometimes blocked the roads as a political statement.

"Many Ecuadorians are desperate, hungry, without hope," the manager added.

We returned to the same corner table of the local bar we had visited the evening before. The waitress walked up to our table and popped two beer bottles open without us saying a word. I paged through newspaper headlines of the day's *El Comercio*. Local shrimp were dying from a viral affliction known as *la cabeza amarilla*, the yellow head disease. Avoid all shellfish, the article warned. I glanced at Tamara, who was gazing contentedly out at the bustling street while sipping on her oversized bottle of beer. Recalling that she had ordered shrimp the night before, I saved the topic for later and pored instead over other headlines.

"Two nights ago," I read aloud, "'sub-machine gunfire mowed down seven people in Guayaquil.' Conditions in Cuenca, our next destination, don't sound much better. Yesterday panic and chaos engulfed the Banco del Progreso, a downtown Cuenca bank. 'Fifty rioting customers burned tires, smashed windows, and stormed the locked premises in a futile effort to retrieve their life savings.'"

As I read, chants echoed through the narrow cobblestone street. A procession carrying banners, lit torches, and hand-painted signs marched past. It turned out that the protestors were not indigenous Ecuadorians, but over a thousand middle-class teachers.

"What are they protesting?" Tamara asked.

"Based on their signs, looks like they are teachers wanting higher wages. Inflation is eroding their standard of living, too, it seems."

"It feels like this country is heading towards anarchy," she mused. "Where will it end?"

"I don't know, but Ecuador is supposed to be one of our safest countries. I can't even imagine what Peru, Bolivia, Brazil, and Venezuela hold in store."

We finished our beers and fell in behind the marchers. Tungurahua billowed in the distance as fiery torches crowded the city streets. We peeled off from the crowd to head into a restaurant we had enjoyed the night before.

"I feel a little guilty," Tamara said, as she savored her ceviche. "At home we own almost nothing, yet we still have far more than the millions around us here who are living in near-poverty."

"Traveler's guilt. I get it too. But at least we're injecting some cash into the local economy."

The desk clerk greeted us on our return to the hotel.

"The road will be blocked tomorrow," she warned. "To the north, maybe okay. But south, impossible. Danger comes. Next week will be very bad."

In the night I dreamt my brother—who in real life does not exist—descended a great mountainside and met me at the bottom. "Dinner is ready," he said. "Mom and Dad are expecting you at the top." As I climbed upward, I righted the heavy wooden structures that were strewn along the steep slope. At the top, I surveyed my backbreaking work. All the structures stood upright, though most leaned and some were on the verge of toppling over. My parents said to help myself, though only a few scraps remained.

I awoke from the dream and stared at the whitewashed ceiling as daylight filled the corners and crevices of the room. At times I felt like a kind of Sisyphus, pushing upward, overcoming obstacles, and usually making it past though not always in the finest form. Trying to keep us safe only magnified the enormity of it all.

I roused Tamara, and we gathered our belongings in the dim light, planning to catch the first bus out of town. The desk clerk thought the road was clear, but called the station to confirm.

"So far," she said, "the road south is open. By mid-morning, it will be blocked. You must hurry."

"Sí," claimed the taxi driver that we hailed. "El camino está abierto." *Yes, the road is open.*

We found seats on the bus with moments to spare, and were soon rambling past the villages of Cajabamba and then Guamote. The sky broke free and patches of blue peeked from thick cloud. Stones, tree branches, and burning debris littered the rough road. We passed an overturned truck lying on its side. Small crowds watched as we skirted by on the narrow shoulder, but no one stopped us. Farther along, the driver negotiated around the charred remains of an automobile. Locals worked the green fields, and others walked the roadway. We gazed upon vistas that stretched miles to cloud-covered horizons and villages connected by centuries-old switchbacks. The madcap driver nearly blew out the tires and broke an axle while bouncing over the rutted highway. When the simple town of Alausi appeared below us we breathed easier, for we knew we were past the danger.

We stopped at Cañar for lunch. Using a long-handled axe, the proprietress hacked a hindquarter from a skinned hog carcass that was hanging from a bloodstained post. She threw the bloody chunks into a kettle over the fire. A scruffy dog licked stray fat specks from the dirt floor while our driver slurped down the lunch of boiled pork and corn.

Hours later, we lurched along dirt tracks snaking through the heart of the Andes and descended from damp clouds into Cuenca. At the station, we caught a taxi for the ride downtown. I inquired with the driver about the protests.

"No problema," he replied, without taking his eyes from the narrow street. Contingents of armed soldiers wearing riot gear and holding bulletproof shields stood at the ready on several street corners.

"This morning and yesterday, many problems," the cabbie said. "This afternoon, okay."

Our room near the square overlooked a bustling flower market. Heavy clouds scuttled past green mountainsides, but the rains held back. Needing cash, we searched for a bank. On our walk we watched women wash clothes in the Río Tomebamba, then pound the brilliant traditional wraps thin upon worn river rocks. Their *thwacks* echoed from stone homes crowding the riverbanks. The women eyed us warily, as most locals along the way did.

"There's one," Tamara said, and pointed.

Half a dozen soldiers in gray and white fatigues guarded the bank entrance. I looked closer.

"That's the Banco del Progreso!" I said. "The one they burned two days ago. Let's keep moving."

We found another bank, carefully counted our cash, and returned to the hotel we had found. I asked the manager whether the streets were dangerous.

"Before 8pm is okay," he said. His smile disappeared. "After that, be *very* careful. After ten, do not go out." He rattled off more warnings in rapid Spanish.

Tamara and I ventured out to a Chinese restaurant on the corner that served *corvina*, sea bass, our new favorite. Only one other eatery in town remained open after half past seven, unlike most other shops across Latin America, which stayed open well into the night.

Resting in our room later that evening, we watched news footage of Ecuadorians weeping while officials shredded bundles of soon to be worthless sucres. As we discovered, much of Ecuador's current unrest revolved around the nation's currency. The sucre's decline began in the 1920s when Ecuador joined the gold standard, which led to sixty percent devaluation. During the 1940s, one United States dollar brought fourteen sucres. By 1990 the rate had fallen to eight hundred. In the months before our arrival, the sucre plummeted to a rate of 25,000 to the dollar. In an attempt to stabilize the currency the rate had been pegged to the dollar, but in many cities annual inflation reached almost one hundred percent. As the dollar grew stronger the purchasing power of the sucre fell, wages dropped, and prices skyrocketed.

Ecuador was heading towards hyperinflation, whereby a government spends or prints money it does not have, and the public loses confidence in its own currency. As Vladimir Lenin once observed, hyperinflation is, "the simplest way to exterminate the very spirit of capitalism." If a country is flooded with high face-value currency untethered to anything of real value, he explained, people will stop coveting money because they discover it will not buy anything. The great illusion of the value and power of money is then destroyed.

Former president Jamil Mahuad had announced a plan to adopt the dollar as Ecuador's new currency. Following the coup that unseated him just before our arrival, his successor Gustavo Noboa vowed to uphold the move. Each week *El Comercio* featured another United States note. Tacked to the wall of every bank and business were government-distributed posters illustrating American bills and coins. For many, the policy amounted to sacrilege, for there is a hugely emotional component to surrendering one's national currency.

And converting to the dollar created new problems. As Ecuadorian banks failed due to bad loans, customers' accounts were frozen and many saw a lifetime of savings shrink by ten times in a few weeks. Ecuadorians wanted what was left of their cash, which led to attacks on the Banco del Progreso and other banks. Even if they got their cash, exchanging useless sucres to US dollars meant the loss of more wealth. With triple digit devaluation and inflation, eighty percent poverty, rising crime, and fact that the sucre was being replaced by the currency of the same government that recently thwarted a popular revolution—we felt little wonder that locals eyed us with disdain.

The writing was on the wall in Cuenca. "Dolarización = mas miseria" read the graffiti on one building. *Converting to the dollar means more misery.* "Revolución avanca." *The revolution progresses.* And "¡Gringos...asesinos!" *Foreigners...murderers!*

16

VALLEY OF LONGEVITY

South of Cuenca, the road was clear. Villagers in their distinctive pink and blue wraps walked the roadsides amidst Andean highlands worn smooth by wind and weather. Atop the passes, a swirling whiteness surrounded us. At each checkpoint, machine gun-toting soldiers ordered all local males from our bus. The soldiers lined the men up and frisked them one at a time. During such checks, tension filled the air, though some women managed a weak smile when the men boarded.

Two peasant girls slept on Tamara's shoulder. A Quechua woman with coarse black hair tied in two thick braids beneath a tilted derby sat motionless beside me. The infant swaddled to her back by maroon blanket, and another daughter nestled in her lap both slept soundlessly.

At Loja, the passengers poured from our bus. Tamara and I followed them and found a basic room within the seedy city. An Australian couple joined us for beers and a dinner of *corvina*. We swapped stories and savored conversation in our native tongue, though to our American ears their Aussie slang almost comprised a language all its own.

Denise despised the filth of Central and South America. Her eyebrows rose when Tamara pulled out a bottle of hand sanitizer. When I mentioned that Tamara brought her own pillowcase with BACKSIDE written in magic marker on the bottom, Denise bubbled with excitement. Steve rolled his eyes.

"The bathrooms are the bloody worst," Denise said. "I hate the pubes on the shower floors, and I never sit on the dunny. Sometimes the pong is just awful."

"Pong?" I asked.

"The stink. And no one washes the blankets! Plus there are heaps of bugs and cockroaches. Even more than in the bush."

"What has the rest of your experience been like?" I asked.

"No worries, mate," said Steve. "Some bludger pinched my camera. I'd like to give that bloke a punch in the goolies! And a few villages have been a bit iffy. But mostly this trip has been a real beauty."

"Seems like the people are really struggling," Tamara said.

"Crikey!" Denise said. "Bloody oath."

"I think part of the issue is that Ecuador relies too heavily on oil revenue," Tamara theorized. "And when oil prices drop, the government runs short on funds, which usually means cuts to social programs or some kind of austerity. And then, the people protest."

"Defo," agreed Steve. "Seems pretty fair dinkum. It's a real problem."

In the morning, midnight-blue clouds roiled overhead. Long lines of dour-faced locals snaked away from the entrance of every bank. Mist rose from nearby hills, and eucalyptus trees ringing the central park moaned with each breath of wind. I scanned an *El Comercio*, noticing the newspaper's price had risen two thousand sucres in two days. I learned that hours after we departed Cuenca, a band of thugs had robbed a bank two blocks from our hotel.

After breakfast, Tamara and I left Loja behind aboard a microbus that followed an unpaved road into a lush valley surrounded by fog-shrouded mountain ridges. Cypress, eucalyptus gum, and monkey puzzle trees interspersed podocarpus, Ecuador's sole native conifer, and hid mountain tapir, giant armadillos, northern pudu deer, spectacled bear, and jaguar. Olive and yellow-scarfed tanagers and bay-vented cotinga were rarely seen elsewhere. Bearded guan, golden-plumed parakeets, and red-faced parrots flitted amongst the canopy of Ecuador's only undisturbed montane forest.

At the village of Vilcabamba, a Frenchwoman and the driver of a battered Chevy Blazer swept us up and to their hostel. High walls hid a travelers' paradise, of sorts: in-ground pool, Jacuzzi, Turkish steam bath, pool tables, table tennis, e-mail, videos, cable TV, library, music in each room, breakfast, and dinner included; massages and horse rides cost extra.

While they cleaned our room, we shot a game of 8-ball using the warped blunt-tipped cue sticks. On the other table a contingent of Israelis yelling in Hebrew glared at us. They left the room a shambles. Young Euros drank beer by the pool and watched videos. Though each room had cable, every television broadcast the same channel. All other *hosterias* in town were closed and vacant. Though overbooked, the hostel staff raced to the bus station to drive foreigners in, and placed mattresses on the video room floor to accommodate any overflow. They seemed to have monopolized the flow of tourists into the village and driven all competitors out of business.

We walked past the downtown park, which was adorned with poinsettia and impatiens, and ordered beers from an empty restaurant on the tranquil main square. A sinking sun lit the green mountainsides afire. Clouds hued with magenta and hints of carnation drifted silently. The sun set behind a fiery horizon as darkness tinged with the aroma of bougainvillea and hibiscus settled into the valley. Little wonder some locals within this so-called 'Valley of Longevity' reputedly lived more than a hundred years.

As the Southern Cross rose over the Río Chamba flowing down from mountain heights, we turned the corner into our hostel. An unexpected sight lay before us. Dozens of people were feasting hungrily at cafeteria-style tables laden with soup, hummus, pâté, beef, and gravy. We decided to join the throng.

During the night, Tamara dreamed of a white Chinese globe lantern hanging from a wooden ceiling. She had seen one like it many years before. In my dreams, Tungurahua erupted. My hometown rather than Baños was evacuated, and my grandmother's stone farmhouse stood in peril as the orange glow of approaching magma shimmered nearby.

After breakfast, in search of waterfalls, we walked a dirt path that followed the Río Chamba and wound among farmers' shacks. Giant spiders waited in webs two-feet-wide, giant beetles lay on the trail, and hundreds of yellow, black, baby blue, copper, and orange butterflies fluttered by, as Tamara said, "like flying flowers."

We encountered a cluster of tourist cabañas perched upon a hillside. The main cabin was made of traditional wattle and daub, a *bareque* built of sticks and mud, with a sleeping loft upstairs and fireplace and cooking utensils below. We had a look inside one cabaña, and there hung a white Chinese globe lantern, exactly as Tamara had dreamt.

Near the cabañas, river water rushed past boulders and cotton cumulus clouds drifted by. Away from the rushing river, all was silent. A lark dashed onto a branch covered by bromeliads and white and lime-green lichen. The scent of lemon and orange permeated the air. Coleus, walnuts, and sugar cane grew in the valley floor, prickly pear cacti and yucca filled the thickets, and afternoon sun played over distant peaks.

After walking back to Vilcabamba we found a quiet, deserted open-air coffee bar with second floor tables overlooking the jade-green Andes. Mules trudged past unaccompanied dragging twenty-foot sugar cane poles to the mill. The owners of the bar were happy to have us and brought warm popcorn flavored with spicy chili sauce. They played vintage American music and we sang Olivia Newton John songs as afternoon faded into evening.

Back at our hostel, the cafeteria bustled. Dinner had already started, and an Englishwoman asked whether we were ever on time. The enterprise seemed to turn otherwise independent travelers into automatons. We escaped to a quiet bar where

Gavin from New Zealand touted his horse business and offered three-day rides into the hills.

"Travel is about finding a place you like and sticking there a while," Gavin said. When he came to the Valley of Longevity seventeen years before, the mountains reminded him of New Zealand's South Island. "Vilcabamba is warmer, jobs at home are scarce, and sheep there outnumber Kiwis," he said, "so I stayed."

In the morning, no one could go anywhere. Striking teachers and Quechua protestors had blocked every major road in Ecuador. Locals hurled rocks at any passing vehicles. No buses were running, even back to Loja. The nation was paralyzed. We decided to leave the hostel, packed our bags, and left the panicked Euros and the chaos behind.

We walked the dirt path back into the hills, heading towards the cabañas we had seen the day before. Roosters tied to wooden stakes scratched for bugs, wiry dogs lay in the dirt, and passing locals called out "buenas" or "hola." We climbed alongside the rushing stream past salmon-colored impatiens and banana and lemon trees. Tamara, weakened from a long sleepless night with diarrhea, struggled on the hour-long walk but stoically endured, as always.

At the cabañas, the local woman's slight daughter led us, unbidden, to the cabin with the white Chinese lantern. It seemed we had been prophesied to stay here. The lilt of a flute drifted across the valley. Darkness fell, and the chitter of insects filled our cabin. I later wrote near the fire, as crickets whirred in the shadows and the full moon slipped behind a veil of cloud. I too had become sick, thanks to the hostel. Tamara talked feverishly in her sleep through the long night.

"Are you all right in there?" she asked repeatedly, thinking I was in the bathroom, though I lay beside her.

The next few days were spent talking with Gavin at our favorite open-air second-floor coffee bar, eating meat tamales and maize *humitas*, walking along the Río Chamba, and relaxing in our cabaña as soothing sounds of the night poured in. Sometimes we hiked the muddy path to the top of the ridge through pockets of lush cloud forest past vine, bromeliad, and orchid-covered trees. Clouds always roiled the hilltops.

We had left our laundry with the local woman when we first moved into the cabaña. After four days our clothes were still not ready, but we heard the roads might be open, so I had the girl bring our laundry up. Not only were the garments still wet, but also they smelled worse than when we left them.

"The bad weather has not let them dry," she apologized.

The next morning Sarah, the English co-owner of the cabañas, gave us a ride to town in her battered pick-up truck. We were going to try to get out, if we could. As we bounced over the rutted road, Sarah bemoaned the hostel's monopoly that slowly ruined her business.

"I'm not one to wait at bus stops and chivy after customers," she explained.

"What do you think about conversion to the dollar?" Tamara asked.

"Dollarization is aces in my mind," she responded, "because inflation and devaluation are so bad. Most Ecuadorians don't realize the extent of United States involvement down here, or know the whole country is corrupt, or that dodgy businesspeople have their hands in politics and pocket huge sums on the side."

"What can be done?" I asked.

"I don't know, but the situation is getting serious. I was in Quito a few years ago when I was surprised by a whole movement that erupted out of nowhere—I think it started because the president had announced an end to utility and fuel subsidies. Overnight, the price of petrol doubled. Indigenous people from across the country flooded into Quito. Roads were blocked, government offices taken over, and the country, like now, shut down."

"Were you trapped there?"

"Yes. Everything went all to pot," she recalled. "Black smoke from burning cars and trash fires filled the sky. Helicopters circled overhead. In Old Town it felt like the end of the world. It was madness. Police in riot gear shot canisters of tear gas at demonstrators carrying sticks, two-by-fours, metal pipes, whatever they could find."

"Was it mostly indigenous people?" asked Tamara.

"Oh no, everyone was there. Students, transit workers, farmers, Quechua women wearing their bowler hats, religious organizations, women's groups, and lots of other wankers...everyone was on edge."

"What did they want?"

"People here are frustrated. The poverty is real. One thing they wanted then was the president ousted. '¡Queremos tu cabeza!' I remember people shouting. *We want your head!* Two weeks later, he was out."

"How did things go for you?" I asked.

"The whole thing was a real cock-up. A curfew went into effect, of course. A few people were killed. I couldn't go anywhere until the roads reopened. I didn't want a brick through my windscreen. So, I was in Quito nearly a week, before I was able to get out."

Sarah pulled up to Vilcabamba's main square, and Tamara and I grabbed our gear.

"Thanks for the lift," I said. "Good luck to you."

"Cheers," she responded. "I hope you make it out."

"Me too," said Tamara.

"If not," I said, "we'll be back!"

17

THE ROAD TO PASTORURI

Before venturing to the bus station, Tamara wanted to call her
parents to let them know we were safe. The lines at the kiosk
in Vilcabamba were down, so we tried an Internet phone. The
connection was poor and the lag time long.

"What?" Tamara said into the phone. "Can you hear me?
What? Are you there? Mom? Hello?"

After a dozen minutes she gave up, unsatisfied and
unhappy. Afternoon sun lit the hills ablaze and shadows of
cloud played over the mountainsides as we plodded up and out
of the Valley of Longevity. At Loja's chaotic bus terminal, the
air was thick with exhaust. I listened for our bus while Tamara
read. The roads were indeed clear, at least for the moment.
Hours later, at four in the morning, we walked the hundred
yards from Macará into Peru and waited with a half dozen
Ecuadorians for a sleepy, unhurried official to stamp our forms
in triplicate. Someone then sputtered at us in Spanish and
pointed to a squat one-story building across the road. Inside, a
guard signed the visas that were stamped into our passports. I
asked him where to trade money.

"I will change!" the guard said. "I am your bank. How much soles do you want?" Feeling uncertain about the legitimacy of this proposal, we opted to wait.

The day dawned over a flat, barren desert. On our bus to Piura, thorny scrub fences held skittish goats. Every so often we swerved around sand dunes that had encroached upon the road. Three-wheeled motorcycle rickshaws whirled along rural dirt streets. The few cars we saw were ragged early-model imports with missing bumpers, fenders, and hoods. Desolate, boxy homes of mud brick or crude adobe with tattered thatch roofs huddled on the arid plains. Piles of trash cluttered the landscape, and a pungent haze of burning refuse filled the air. Flocks of buzzards circled over mangy teat-dragging dogs, which nosed amongst the scraps.

Such apocalyptic scenes filled me with distress, and I wondered whether we were prepared for the political strife of Peru lying ahead on the Pan-American. I expected poverty, but not devastation. Ecuador, though sliding into chaos with coups, volcanic eruptions, rampant inflation, and civil unrest, at least bore a tidy façade that lent the impression, however superficial, of relative safety. The infrastructure in northern Peru, where it existed, was crumbling into dust.

Since Peru lacked central bus stations, every company maintained a private office somewhere within the maze of each city's unmarked streets. We reached the town of Piura, our first stop after the border, too early in the morning. To avoid a mugging, and to keep moving, I bought two tickets to Chiclayo, which lay two hundred kilometers to the south. While we waited, some locals nearby shooed away a withered beggar woman. I handed her a few Ecuadorian coins, figuring she might find some way to use them. She inspected them closely, muttered darkly, and threw the coins into the street. The locals laughed. The views from our next bus revealed yet more of the litter-strewn landscape.

"It's like the countryside was destroyed by an earthquake or a war," Tamara commented, "and then abandoned."

The outskirts of Chiclayo resembled tenement slums, and I

worried for our safety. Street corner moneychangers with rigged calculators flashed wads of cash. Rebar poked skyward from half-finished or ruined buildings. Trash and car parts littered the streets, and small fires burned in the road.

Our bus wove through a flowing stream of beeping taxis, buses, and motorcycle rickshaws. At our hotel, Tamara wanted to try her parents again and I thought I should call mine too. The phone in our room had no dial tone, but at a corner shop an old man inside a glass booth said our card should work in the blue pay phone. A young woman selling pastries from behind a tall counter tried to help. She punched in the numbers I gave her. Nothing. Then she handed me the phone.

"Hello," said a crackly voice. "Who is this?"

"Yes, I'm trying to call America."

"Is this some kind of joke?"

"I'm trying to reach the international operator..."

"Son, is that you?"

The young woman had somehow dialed direct.

"How is every..." my father said, just as the line went dead.

We were able to reconnect and while Tamara spoke with her parents I stood outside on the corner. Women selling candies and snacks from wooden boxes asked where we came from and where we were going.

"¿Por qué no está casado?" one asked. *Why aren't you married?*

"No sé," I responded. *I don't know.*

"Deberías estar," another said. *You should be.*

Three teenage girls stopped to watch. Since you're not married, teased one lady as she gestured towards the girls, why not consider a Peruvian girlfriend? The girls laughed.

In the morning, more decrepit shacks of mud and stone lined the roadsides. Our plan was to continue south along the coastline, thereby avoiding disputed border zones and the guerrilla-controlled coca-growing valleys of the interior. Brown, barren desert again surrounded us, though in the distance, the arid foothills of the Andes appeared through morning mist. One of the passengers entertained us with magic tricks. He poured water from a glass into rolled up newspaper, then held each sheet up to show they were dry. He rolled the sheets together again and poured water from the rolled up newspapers back into the glass. Next he tore a pile of paper into small pieces and crumpled them into a ball. When he opened his fist, the paper was whole again. In another trick he had two passengers in different seats each hold a rolled-up newspaper. The magician dropped a red cardboard tube into one. The red tube emerged from the second newspaper roll, while the first was empty. Back and forth went the red tube. We were impressed.

From Trujillo, a *colectivo* took us to the coastal resort town of Huanchaco. A peculiar quirk of the fixed-route minibus *colectivos* was that drivers punched blue cards in numerous 1950s-style time clocks located in the hole of some wall or abandoned storefront. The conductor raced out, punched the card, then walked slowly back to the *colectivo* while examining the marks. The driver also studied the marks, and safeguarded the card until the next stop, where the conductor again raced to the punch clock.

We took a room at an otherwise empty oceanfront hotel in Huanchaco. From our terrace we watched lines of brown pelicans skim over crashing waves. Surfers rode two-meter-high South Pacific breakers beneath a stiff offshore breeze. The true surfer hangout, Puerto Chicamea seventy kilometers to the north, boasted the longest left-hand point break in the world. Narrow boats made of totora reed stood stacked along the beach. Fishermen rode the narrow pointed craft like surfboards. Young men on the beach were building more of these *caballitos*, little horses, just as their indigenous Moche ancestors did two millennia before.

As evening approached we strolled along the deserted *malecón*–jetty–and then drank beers on the sand. At dawn, a lad arrived at our seaside terrace with a tray filled with warm bread, eggs, and Nescafé. Flocks of blue-footed boobies flew beyond the breakers while fishermen balanced upon their narrow reed *caballitos* paddled out to sea.

"I feel like a wealthy European," said Tamara wryly.

"Yes, except we had no electricity or water yesterday. And for some unexplainable reason the staff hauled our television away. Much to your dismay."

"Good point. Maybe not so much wealthy," she mused, while gazing over the crashing waves, "as privileged."

"It's true, we do have a kind of freedom that few, if any, locals are able to experience."

Such feelings of disparity always intensified on my travels when disabled or sick individuals gave long speeches on buses and then collected coins from sympathetic passengers. Or, when coming across places like Chimbote, which we arrived at the following day, where block after city block was virtually in ruins.

"This is bad," said Tamara, looking concernedly out of the bus window. She pulled her shirt over her nose, for even on the outskirts the stench of fish processing saturated the air.

"Here are the notes I have on this city," I said. "'Chimbote is a thoroughly unsafe and unpleasant city, and many travelers are attacked and robbed here. All visitors should take extensive precautions, always use taxis from bus stations to their hotel, and not venture out at night.'"

"Great."

Loudspeakers, frequent firecrackers sounding like gunfire, and perhaps actual gunshots punctuated the night. At eight the next morning we slipped back into the streets, and found our small battered bus in far worse condition than any of the others.

"I hope this thing makes it," I muttered to Tamara.

We crawled along the Pan-American, past Pacific waters lapping bare brown beaches. Breaks in the clouds drifting inland revealed patterns of gold upon barren, sand-covered mountainsides. At Chazma, dwellings with half-completed walls, partial roofs of corrugated tin or tattered thatch, missing windowpanes, sagging doors, crumbling walls, and dirt floors cluttered the roadside. We climbed upward, into the barren Cordillera Negra mountains. Barrel cacti and scrubby shrubs dotted sparse foothills. In the middle of desolate nowhere, we stopped long enough for the driver and his assistant to pull a bald tire from the roof rack and replace the flat. From the pass, we saw the snow-shrouded mountains of the Cordillera Blanca, named for the white peaks that shimmered on the horizon. Huascarán, the highest mountain in Peru, pierced a blanket of cloud.

Afternoon sun played over patchwork slopes leading downhill past weathered Andean villages. Quechua people bundled in thick sweaters tended goats, prepared evening meals, and carried firewood and water. A stiff wind bent rows of oats and blew dust through the open bus windows. Lavender clouds drifted past the towering peaks of Huandoy and San Cristóbal. In the shadows far below nestled the city of Huaraz.

A cataclysmic earthquake destroyed Huaraz in 1970, and much of the city has been rebuilt. The nearby town of Yungay was permanently buried when a portion of one of Huascarán's glaciers pried loose, and started a massive mudslide. Only a handful of residents who happened to be visiting an old cemetery upon a hill survived. Around two hundred minor earthquakes rattle Peru every year, and every six years or so a major one strikes. Homes of adobe or mud, of which there are many, are particularly vulnerable. During the 1970 earthquake alone, over 100,000 people were killed.

At sunrise the western hills gleamed golden. Sun peeking round the Cordillera Blanca bathed Huaraz in a soothing softness and turned the purple dawn clouds cotton white. As it was Sunday morning, schoolchildren swarmed the Plaza de Armas and drew colorful patterns and images in the streets. They used flower petals and sawdust dyed red, blue, brown, and yellow to fill in outlines of Jesus, Mary, and create slogans such as *God is Love, Yesterday, Tomorrow,* and *Always.*

Tamara and I wanted a taste of the Andean high country, but no public transport went there so we reluctantly signed onto a tour, our first. After waiting to board the *colectivo,* we crisscrossed the city to pick up locals at their homes. Some of them still needed to rent hiking boots. One woman's hair was still wet, so she told us to return later. The rest were simply unhurried. After over an hour we returned to the tour agency where we had started. A Japanese couple joined us.

"We're done," I told the guide. "Too much waiting. We want our money back."

"¡No, no!" he said. "We leave soon. ¡Prometo!" *I promise!*

We grumpily got back into the *colectivo*. When we at last had everyone aboard and hit the road, we followed the Rió Santa, which separates the gleaming Cordillera Blanca from the barren Cordillera Negra, flows north then west through the spectacular Cañon del Pato, and empties into the Pacific.

At a wayside restaurant we drank coca leaf tea to cope with the altitude. Indigenous Andeans have long chewed the leaves to relieve hunger, fatigue, and pain. Visitors were advised to drink the brewed leaves to relieve nausea, breathlessness, headache, and other symptoms of altitude sickness.

"Are we going very high?" Tamara asked the guide.

"Oh, somewhat," he said.

"Higher than fourteen thousand feet?"

"Oh, no, señora."

At the bubbling Aguas Gasificadas de Pumapampa, a gasified natural spring, locals dipped dirty cups into the mineral waters to drink up the healing powers. Near El Ojo de Agua de Pumashimi, a deep brilliant blue cold water spring, stalks of Puya Raymondi bromeliads towered overhead.

"These are very rare," said our guide. "Each one lives a hundred years before sending up a thirty-foot spike covered with twenty thousand flowers. After this, the plant dies."

Cumulus clouds drifted through cobalt skies. The snow-covered summit of nearly six thousand-meter Mururaju loomed in the distance. At well over sixteen thousand feet, we finally stopped. Tamara and I ventured down a side path leading to the Pastoruri Glacier, stopping every few minutes to catch our breath. We crawled into a thirty-foot-deep ice cave, and marveled at blue light filtering through the overhead ice. We had found ourselves at one of the highest road-accessible points in the Andes, and what a journey it had been to get here. We paused to relish the moment. Here was a place I had not even known existed the day before. I was exhilarated, for this was why I traveled.

At such an altitude, without proper acclimatization, symptoms of altitude sickness arise quickly. Tamara's headache suddenly exploded. Our silent celebration over, we returned to the *colectivo*. The Peruvians and Japanese sat inside looking haggard and spent. I felt fine until, as we descended the mountainside, my head too felt like it was on the receiving end of a rogue jackhammer. We stopped at a roadside restaurant for coca leaf tea and giant bowls of soup, and could do little else but wait for our rapidly intensifying headaches to subside. Despite the agony, I could not have been happier.

18

PERU'S DIRTY WAR

Tamara wrinkled her nose, then pinched it shut. "It smells on here," she mentioned twice. We had just boarded the overnight bus to Lima, Peru's capital city. Since we had crammed one rucksack between us and wedged the other under our feet, we crawled over each other so she could be near the window. Shaky and pale, she huddled in her seat during a frigid ride over high mountain passes. A nauseating aroma, like sewage mixed with stale wine, stayed with us through the long night.

Where the Andes met the sea, the Humboldt Current–a cold ocean current flowing north along the coast–formed a fog that drifted inland and condensed on the desert landscape. The dew sustained fog meadows called *loma*, which supported Raimondi's yellow finches, thick-billed miners, and cattle that were driven down by farmers from the highlands each autumn.

In early morning hours, after passing through the *loma,* we reached the squalid outskirts of Lima. Founded by conquistador Francisco Pizarro in 1535, for a time few cities in the New or Old Worlds rivaled Lima's wealth. Pizarro had joined Balboa in 1513 during his crossing of the Isthmus of

Panama, when they became the first Europeans to reach the Pacific. After two failed expeditions to Peru, Pizarro convinced the Spanish king to grant him permission for a third. Pizarro afterward founded the first Spanish settlement in Peru, conquered the Incan capital of Cusco, and executed the Incan emperor. Two years later he founded Lima, which he considered his greatest achievement.

The earthquake of 1746 undid the city's opulence. Of three thousand houses, just twenty-five remained standing. During reconstruction, only second floors built in bamboo, not adobe brick, were allowed. Though Lima never recovered her glory, the city remained the center of Spanish South America until Peru's independence.

Since 1746, descriptions of Lima have tended towards the unfavorable. Prussian naturalist Alexander von Humboldt said "the filthiness of the streets, strewn with dead dog and donkeys, and the unevenness of the ground make it impossible to enjoy." Charles Darwin during his trip aboard the Beagle in 1835 described the city as "in a wretched state of decay, the streets are nearly unpaved and heaps of filth are piled up in all directions where black vultures pick up bits of carrion."

Little seemed to have changed. Mile upon mile of litter-strewn streets and half-finished concrete dwellings comprised shanty settlement suburbs known as *Pueblos Jóvenes*. Decrepit slums such as Villa El Salvador, a self-governing squatter camp populated by over 350,000 people, crowded every hillside. Carjackings, assaults, and armed robberies were common throughout Lima, as were short-term armed kidnappings during which criminals forcibly withdrew funds from victims' accounts at ATMs.

I shook off the dystopian visions and nudged Tamara awake; she blinked sleepily at the city unfolding beyond our window. Our bus finally pulled into a secure terminal and we settled down to wait for morning in a filthy waiting room alongside a few Lima residents—known as *limeños*—who were dozing in cracked plastic seats. The *garúa*, a blanket of smoggy haze that smothered the city from spring until winter, prolonged the dawn. While we waited, a Peruvian student named Cristian introduced himself. I asked where he grew up.

"Ayacucho," he responded.

I remembered that this was where Sendero Luminoso, better known as Shining Path, got its start. The Marxist-Maoist guerilla group, founded by a communist philosophy professor named Abimael Guzmán, had launched a war against the military government in hopes of overthrowing the state, establishing a proletariat-style dictatorship, and sparking a world revolution.

"What was it like growing up during the war?" I asked.

"That was a very difficult time," Cristian replied. "Because Sendero Luminoso was based in Ayacucho, my people had no rights. The government sent Sinchis after us, who killed any peasants they believed might be part of Sendero Luminoso."

"Sinchis?" Tamara asked.

"Sí. These were very dangerous men, a special police force, sent to fight the rebels. Some say they were trained by the United States."

"That sounds scary," said Tamara.

"¡Claro!" *Of course!* "In some places the military trained peasants to fight against Sendero Luminoso. These men were called *ronderos*. I knew a man who became a commander in Sendero Luminoso. The *ronderos* found him, stabbed him, set him on fire, and then shot him."

Tamara and I glanced at each other.

"Sendero Luminoso leaders were very angry about this. They killed seventy peasants in Huanca Santos, and fifty more in Tambo in retaliation. Many others were killed and they forced peasants to farm and grow coca and live in labor camps. Anybody who tried to escape was murdered."

"I can't even imagine what life was like for you," I said.

"It was terrible in many ways," he said. "And sometimes aterrador." *Terrifying.* "Sendero Luminoso kidnapped children, too, and forced them to fight. This is what happened to my cousin, Diego. He was twelve when they took him."

"I'm so sorry, Cristian," Tamara said.

"It is okay. Things are better now."

"You go to the university here in Lima?" I asked.

Cristian nodded. "I am studying to be a doctor. I want to help people."

"¡Ayacucho!" someone yelled.

"Is that your bus?" I asked.

Cristian smiled. "Sí. I am going to visit mi madre. It has been too long."

"Good luck, Cristian," Tamara said.

"Gracias," he said. "May God be with you."

At six, Tamara and I ventured outside the bus terminal to inquire about the train to the village of Huancayo, which we were heading straight to rather than stay in Lima.

"No hay," a man claimed. *There isn't one.*

Apparently the world's highest train line would carry only freight until further notice. Instead, we decided to take a bus to Huancayo and followed a man who said he was a taxi driver to a battered, unmarked automobile without even a "taxi" sticker in the windshield. As block after block slipped past, the driver admitted he did not know where the Huancayo bus station was. He stopped and quizzed various pedestrians as we wound our way through Lima at daybreak. Every vehicle we saw was battered and smashed. Heavy chains secured side mirrors, spare tires, and anything not bolted to the frame. Some city buses had no taillights, and one was missing every window. At last, our driver found the near-deserted bus terminal, and someone pulled the tall iron gates open to let us in.

From Lima, we climbed the Cordillera Negra to sixteen thousand feet before dropping down into Huancayo, a village known for *papa a la huancaína*–boiled potato topped with white cheese sauce, milk, hot pepper, butter, and olives–which we hungrily tucked into as soon as we arrived and washed down with cold beers. A passenger train service out of Huancayo did still operate, and before first light we boarded the morning express. A guard led to the buffet class car, a basic carriage with rickety folding tables between wooden seats. Once the diesel train lurched forth a young Peruvian woman came around and offered us soup or chicken with rice. We opted for the latter and settled back as the sun, cresting eastern ridgelines, revealed patches of gold on shadow-covered hillsides.

Whenever the train paused, as it often did, the cars jumped forward. At one stop a girl's entire breakfast clattered to the floor. We held tight to our coffees and swayed with the tracks. Tamara recalled a holiday in England when she was four years old. Her family had traveled into the countryside by train.

"Dad held his tea, just like this, without spilling a drop," she recalled, balancing her coffee in one hand. "Mom was so proud. Until I knocked his cup out of his hand and spilled hot tea all over the table. Mom wasn't so proud then!" she laughed.

When the young woman came around again she brought sickly sweet yellow Inca Kolas, which tasted more like bubble gum than soda, and we sipped them while passing through farmland interspersed with mud brick and red tile-roofed homes. Villagers wearing thick wool sweaters, derby hats, and colorful skirts over knee-high stockings trod the footpaths. Dirt-smudged children waved and watched us pass.

We climbed out of the Mantaro Valley, followed the river towards its headwaters, and passed sheer cliffs inches away. Crystal clear river waters riffled over bone white boulders. The land warmed and the blue sky yawned overhead. In the early afternoon we called at Huancavelica, an indigenous Andean village perched at twelve thousand feet and marked by sixteenth and seventeenth-century colonial churches and tidy daisy-filled parks. The locals stared at us in surprise as we wandered about.

Huancavelica, along with Cristian's home Ayacucho, had long been a base of operation for Shining Path. In order to root out the guerrillas, President Alberto Fujimori dissolved Congress in 1992, abolished the Peruvian Constitution, and established an "iron fist" policy. He sent military personnel wearing black ski masks into villages that arrested, tortured, interrogated, and on occasion massacred their occupants. The government's record of "disappeared" citizens had earned Peru multiple "Country with the Highest Number of Missing Detainees" honors.

As Shining Path lost ground to the military and *ronderos*, it launched a bombing campaign that led to the capture of Abimael Guzmán, the group's founder. Though the fighting had been mostly contained by the time we arrived, roadblocks, village raids, and armed confrontations between Shining Path units and army patrols had again erupted near Huancayo and elsewhere. The Shining Path had even shot down a Peruvian Army helicopter. A 2001-2002 Truth and Reconciliation Commission found that some seventy thousand Peruvians— mostly indigenous peasants—were killed or "forcibly disappeared" in what became known as the Dirty War.

Huancavelica had only recently been brought under military control after having been closed to visitors for nearly two decades. Many locals wanted to talk with us. Proud old men asked where we were from. Not one individual passed without smiling, stopping, or staring in our direction. The Quechua from whom we purchased hand-knit alpaca wool sweaters, scarves, gloves, and hats in anticipation of the Andean passes ahead gawped at us in open-mouthed amazement.

As evening fell, black and white televisions in every open store, barbershop, and restaurant were tuned to the Peru versus Ecuador *fútbol* match. Rapt crowds of men gathered around any available screen. At a sparse eatery, Tamara and I devoured *salpicón de carne*—a heavily seasoned shredded beef salad—followed by *caldo de cordero*—meat broth soup—and finally *carapulcra*—a stew of boiled lamb, peppers, garlic, and potato.

Afterward, we headed inside a local bar, where we found walls adorned with posters of half-naked women, and a few drunken locals sitting at wooden benches. Before them sat pitchers of potent yellow *caña*—a rum-like liquor fermented with sugar. Every few minutes they shouted *"¡Salud!"* and downed another shot.

Tamara needed to use the bathroom, which consisted of a white-tiled, men-only porcelain trough. A five-foot-high non-locking door stood between her and the shot-drinkers.

Through some trick of contortionism, she managed to use the stall, her bemused eyes just clearing the top of the door, without complaint.

When she returned, a local man asked us endless questions in slurred Spanish before making a nuisance of himself. The barmaid ran him out, though not before he danced a jig for us.

"That morning in Baltimore, when we left for Mexico, I thought I'd never see my father again," Tamara confided, as the barmaid guided the man outside.

"What do you mean?"

"I didn't think I'd make it home again. I thought I was going to die in South America."

"Really? No wonder you seemed so sad. I thought you might quit after the roach hotel in San Luis Potosí."

"I thought about it. I was afraid you'd continue by yourself and get hurt, or worse, and I'd always regret not sticking it out in case I could've changed the outcome somehow."

"Are you enjoying yourself now?"

A smile crossed her lips. "Did you see me in that bathroom stall? I'm figuring it out. I'm liking this place."

After a second day in Huancavelica, we ventured deeper into the Andes, the bus making its way along a lone, rutted road leading to the sea. Temperatures plummeted as we climbed higher and darkness fell. Barren grass-covered slopes rolled upwards towards not-so-distant snow-capped peaks. Alpine snowfields reflected light long after sundown. It was the first of July and the height of winter in the Southern Hemisphere. Frigid air poured through the cracked windows and even with our new woolen sweaters our teeth chattered. The Southern Cross appeared near an upside down Big Dipper. For miles, and sometimes hours, no villages, traffic, or signs of life were to be seen. On occasion, the driver blared his horn as we roared past unlit roadside mud brick huts. Sometime in the night we crested the last of the high passes, and began a gradual descent towards the coast.

We reached the Pan-American and then, in early morning hours the dark, deserted streets of Pisco. The bus dropped us off at an empty, debris-strewn courtyard rather than at a bus station. In the street, a toothless wrinkled taxi driver led us to yet another battered, nondescript vehicle. We stopped, unsure. A woman looked through an open window.

"Está bien," she said. *It's okay.*

We rode with the cabbie to the central Plaza de Armas.

"We want Hostal Pisco," I said.

"No hay," he said. *That doesn't exist.*

On the plaza I asked a couple of idle taxi drivers nearby where the Hostal Pisco was. One pointed to an unmarked door set within a plain building. We rang the bell, and a tiny door opened.

"Lleno," said the eyeball. *Full.*

I asked the taxi man to take us to another place. Other cabbies laughed and teased when his car didn't start. When it eventually came alive we moved through dark, narrow alleyways. The streets turned rougher and darker as the driver continuously turned partway round and asked questions before finally slowing to a halt on a broken dirt street far from any light or human activity.

This is it, I thought. We're finished.

He moved forward a few more feet, still asking questions, and stopped again. We appeared to be in front of a *hostal*.

"¡Estamos aquí!" he proclaimed. *We're here!*

It seemed our driver was no more than a curious cabbie. Much relieved, I paid the taxi man, the hotel proprietor led to our room, and at last we crawled into an actual bed and fell into a deep sleep.

19

EGYPT OF THE AMERICAS

Christened San Clemente de Macera by the Spanish, the town of Pisco later took its name from the grape brandy that the region became famous for. Local grape cultivation began with importation of vine stalks from the Canary Islands; Peru's favorable climate soon spurred the spread of wineries around Cusco and Ayacucho. Though deemed a threat to the Spanish wine industry, and despite royal bans seeking a halt to local vineyard expansion, Peru's pisco market surged in the sixteenth and seventeenth centuries.

Production thrived into the modern era. Upon our arrival, small traditional wineries still crushed grapes by foot to the beat of a drum, and emptied fermented grape juice into stills called *falcas*–critical for a true pisco. Wood from the slow-burning carob tree yielded a consistent source of heat as well as a finer flavor. The unscented Quebranta grape brought over by the Spanish lent characteristics unique to pure piscos. Bodegas also sold fragrant piscos made from the Muscatel and Albilla variety of grape as well as a creole pisco, and green piscos using partially fermented grape juice.

Pisco held a second claim to fame: the Ballestas Islands. At six in the morning our hotel proprietor banged on the door and, what seemed like minutes later, we were whisked to the edge of Reserva Nacional de Paracas by a harried microbus driver. At the jetty, we boarded a motorboat and ducked the spray as we cruised beyond the mouth of Paracas Bay and into the South Pacific. Paracas was the wind that whipped up the waves each afternoon. The Ballestas Islands were named for the myriad wave-carved caves strung along their perimeter.

Thousands of Peruvian boobies perched upon the steep slopes of the islands and countless Guanay cormorants flew overhead in tidy formations. Petite Humboldt penguins waddled on the rocky beaches. Peruvian penguins fed on fish, as did hundreds of sea lions swimming in nearby swells or resting on cliffs. These were the poor man's Galapagos, although they seemed quite rich to us, and Pisco was their gateway. The reason for such an abundance of wildlife was due to the Humboldt Current, which swept microscopic plankton towards the islands, and upon which schools of anchovy fed. In turn, birds attracted to the anchovies covered every slope and filled the skies like a scene out of Hitchcock's *The Birds*.

For thousands of years bands of nomadic hunter-gatherers fished these waters and roamed the coasts of present-day Peru. The abundant sea life, a reliable source of protein-rich food, boosted their populations, and enabled settlements and the domestication of llamas, alpacas, and guinea pigs. Climatic change dried up the *loma*–Andean fog meadows–around four thousand years ago and drove the anchovy shoals into deeper waters, so indigenous people eventually turned towards farming. Their communities spread along the river valleys and across the highlands.

During the next two millennia the first signs of Andean high culture emerged. Farmers still lived in simple adobe or rough stone houses, but began building larger and more complex ceremonial centers. Innovations in pottery led to trade and links with outlying areas. The cultures that followed– Paracas, Moche, Chimu, Nazca, and finally Inca–rose and fell but all were initially made possible by the wealth of life pushed inland by the Humboldt Current. The legacies and abandoned cities left by these civilizations provided Peru with the apt nickname "Egypt of the Americas."

In the north, the militaristic Moche people built an empire that stretched from Piura to Chimbote. They harnessed rivers spilling down from the Andes and channeled them into a network of irrigation canals that watered the arid coastal valleys. Lush fields and bountiful fishing gave the Moche a robust diet and ample leisure time for creating masterful clay pottery depicting animal and plant life, deities and demons, hunting and fishing scenes, rituals, and ceremonies. As they had no written language, it was their pottery that told the story of Moche culture. The Pyramids of the Sun and Moon enhanced this story. While in Trujillo, we had hailed a cab to the area where buses departed for the pyramids.

"Come," a man said, approaching us. We followed him into a still seedier neighborhood of boarded-up storefronts and litter and rock-strewn side streets.

"¿Es peligroso aquí?" I asked. *Is it dangerous here?*

"Sí, pero conmigo, está bien," he said. *Yes, but with me, it's fine.* We walked past women selling fruits and vegetables.

"Peru, pobre," he said. *Peru, poor.* He pointed to a battered early model Plymouth with a wide dusty rear seat. Tamara and I looked at each other, then at him.

"Hay un autobus?" I asked. *Is there a bus?*

"Ah," he said, and pointed to a minibus across the street.

At the pyramids a Peruvian guide led us up a ramp towards Huaca de la Luna, the Pyramid of the Moon, past intricate geometric patterns and yellow, white, red, and black friezes depicting fearsome feline deities. The Moche temple consisted of six levels built upon the other over six centuries. Priests and kings from each one hundred-year dynasty were buried in their respective layer with earthly possessions needed for the afterlife. The nearby Huaca del Sol, the Pyramid of the Sun, was the largest human-made structure in the Western Hemisphere until sixteenth-century Spanish conquistadors diverted a nearby river and washed half of it away in a vain search for gold.

The Moche in time yielded to the Chimu, a despotic state which thrived on wars of conquest. Power rested with the great lords, although urban courtiers held some sway. Peasants and slaves filled the bottom ranks. Chan Chan, the capital city of Chimu culture, was once the largest pre-Inca city in Peru and is still today the largest adobe city ever built anywhere. To get there from Trujillo, our hired driver Fernando drove us along a dirt road leading to Tschudi Palace. Crumbled ruins lined both sides of the road, and friezes of birds and fish adorned some of the walls. Fernando pointed to the ruins spreading in all directions.

"There are bad men with guns out there," he said. "Car...safe. Walking...no."

Tamara and I stayed close but wandered alone amongst the mud walls that were once temples, canals, workshops, and funerary mounds. The sound of the surf pounding the nearby shoreline echoed faintly; otherwise, silence filled the air. Tall walls once surrounded nine great compounds, sacred enclosures, and rows of storerooms containing grain and food. Huge walk-in wells tapped into the groundwater that had been channeled from higher in the valley. Despite such provisions, the Chimu had no choice but to surrender to the increasingly powerful Inca after an eleven-year siege.

Back in Pisco, after our last night in town, we continued south to Ica, where sidewalks pulsed with pedestrians and vendors selling bread, beverages, and trinkets. There was barely room to squeeze between the throngs and the auto-rickshaws streaming past. It was here that the Paracas culture thrived nearly three thousand years ago. Their colorful *mantos*–large cloths woven with geometric, zoomorphic, and anthropomorphic designs–are among the world's finest. Mummified bodies discovered on the slopes of nearby Cerro Colorado reveal that the Paracas elongated the skulls of the living and practiced trepanning, a brain surgery technique that replaced sections of skull with metal plates.

The Nazca people replaced the Paracas. The monumental "lines" and abstract designs that the Nazca scratched into the barren desert surface, near the town of Nazca, are their most famous legacy, often called the Eighth Wonder of the World. While in Nazca, we spotted a sign along the Plaza de Armas advertising flights over the lines for twenty-five dollars. A half hour later a rickety six-seat Cessna taxied up a potholed runway. After lifting off, our pilot banked hard over lines depicting a monkey, spider, hummingbird, orca whale, astronaut-like figure, and other extraordinary designs. The Nazca created the lines by removing reddish-brown iron oxide-coated pebbles on the desert floor to expose a light-colored lime-rich clay layer beneath, which then hardened and protected the markings from wind and time. Some believe the outlines served as an astronomical calendar, others as a means to communicate with the gods. Their true purpose might never be known.

Included in our flight cost was a visit to Chauchilla Cemetery. Rodrigo drove us there in his battered taxi. Grave robbing *guaqueros* had ransacked the tombs through the centuries, and vertebrae, femurs, and ulna bones littered the sands. More tombs were evident from sandy depressions filled by the Paracas winds. Rodrigo explained that the tombs were discovered in 1901 by a German archaeologist. He repeated that the Nazca believed in and prepared their dead for Nueva Vida. *A new life.*

"Atención," he said again. *Attention.* "The Nazca believed in a new life."

Having seen a slice of the cultural remnants left by the Paracas, Moche, Chimu, and Nazca, only the last and greatest of the ancient Peruvian empires remained: the Inca. To witness their legacy required an arduous journey through the Andes. First, a long and bitterly cold ride across the mountains brought us to Ayacucho, Cristian's hometown, before dawn. We waited on the bus in icy darkness for morning to arrive. Huddled locals wrapped in thick woolen blankets slept around us. When I reopened my eyes a pink glow tinged the eastern horizon. Tamara was sleeping with her rucksack still strapped to her back and her head slumped on the seat in front of her.

It was in Ayacucho during the Peruvian War of Independence that Spanish rule came to an end, in 1824. The residents of Ayacucho celebrated freedom before any others in Peru. Perhaps for that symbolic reason the Shining Path later used Ayacucho as a base in the 1980s and early 1990s. Tourism vanished, and only recently had a handful of diehard travelers begun passing through. Unlike in Huancavelica, the locals in Ayacucho regarded us with indifference.

A few weeks before our arrival, demonstrations protesting autocratic president Alberto Fujimori's fraudulent third term election victory over leftist rival Alejandro Toledo topped international headlines. The Lima-born son of Japanese immigrants and the Southern Hemisphere's longest-serving democratically elected president, Fujimori achieved peace with Ecuador, stamped out Shining Path, and moved towards a free market economy, but eventually resorted to beatings, torture, and killings to control the masses. Peru's rewritten constitution limited presidents to two terms, but Fujimori claimed the restriction did not apply to him because the rewrite happened after he had come to power. Fujimori's win over Toledo—a Harvard professor, Stanford doctoral graduate, and son of impoverished Andean peasants, turned World Bank economist—despite fraud, tampering, and rumors of vanishing ink, led to protests and rioting in Lima. The United States also failed to recognize the election result.

"I think locals around here want Fujimori in power because he rid the countryside of terrorism," theorized Tamara.

She was likely right. When Fujimori won the presidency, he promised a new era of progress for Peru. His social programs, pro-business policies, and anti-crime initiatives aimed mainly at Shining Path rebels made him popular with many Peruvians.

To our surprise, a few months after our visit, Fujimori faxed in his resignation and fled to Japan. He was afterward captured and extradited to Lima, where he was sentenced to twenty-five years in prison for human rights abuses, corruption, and the sanctioning of death squads. Two decades later Fujimori was still serving time for his role in the killings of twenty-five people, including an eight-year-old boy. Still, plenty of Peruvians were willing to forgive his crimes because they believed he had brought peace and stability to Peru.

From Ayacucho's cobblestoned streets we continued into golden hills and barren Andes beneath a burning sun. The eastern sky was lit with purple and gold clouds. Fields of corn, lush highland meadows, and groves of eucalyptus, alder, and willow interspersed rolling hills and deep canyons. Mud brick homes comprised Uripa, Chincheros, and other mountainside villages.

When we stopped at a police checkpoint, Tamara slept hard and never budged. The soldier glanced at her and asked me for our passports. I kept them buried beneath layers of clothes, preferring not to dig them out in full view, and instead handed over tattered photocopies. He wanted the originals and ordered me off the bus. An officer pulled out a thick stack of notebooks filled with signatures and stamps. He showed me where to sign.

"¿Cuántos días son sus visas?" he barked. *How many days are your visas?* I could not remember.

"¿Noventa, tal vez?" I guessed. *Ninety, maybe?* The bus engine revved as the officer studied the passports.

"Apurémonos esto," another man commanded. *Let's hurry this up.* The bus inched forward. "¡Apúrate!" he yelled. *Hurry!*

The first officer waved me away. I climbed onto the bus as it jerked forward, and slipped into my seat as we roared off. Tamara still slept soundly.

We reached Andahuaylas at dusk and collapsed, exhausted, into bed in a simple hotel. Up at five the next morning, we walked through still-dark streets. In the cramped bus terminal, two men sitting behind a wooden counter started at a black and white television. When a small bus at last pulled to the curb, the driver climbed to the roof and unhurriedly unknotted the tangled ropes in order to tie produce and luggage down, and on occasion stared into the distance. A few Peruvians stood to the side with worn rice sacks, waiting. Feeling guilty for dragging Tamara out of bed so early, I called to the driver:

"¡Vámanos!" *Let's go!* He didn't notice.

When the driver was finally ready we puttered off, the bus laden with every seat and the entire aisle filled with villagers. Thick clouds filled the valley bottoms, but on the horizon jagged snow-capped peaks jutted through the morning cloud. The dark-bladed silhouette of a condor knifed past. Below the passes, villagers tending cliff-side plots and hand-breaking the rocky earth with crude wooden implements paused to watch us rumble by. Llamas and sheep skittered out of the bus's path. Another condor disappeared into the mist.

An hour and a half of rutted switchbacks and unpaved zig-zags brought us to Abancay. I went straight into the nearest bus company, then hesitated. I had awoken Tamara at five the past several mornings. She had only eaten a bowl of soup and a square of chocolate in the past twenty-four hours, was recovering from a bad cold, and suffering from multiple symptoms of altitude sickness—headache, restless sleep, diminished appetite, constipation, nausea, and moodiness.

"Just buy the tickets," she said.

"We don't have to go…"

"You want to go, and I don't care. So let's go before we miss the bus."

The men by the bus motioned that we had better board if we wanted to make Cusco, but the woman behind the counter seemed in no hurry.

"Let's go!" said Tamara crossly.

The engine revved. *The bus is ready to leave*, someone said in Spanish. The lady finally tore off a ticket, but had no change. A man ushered us outside and onto the bus.

"We need our change!" Tamara hollered to an idle bystander. As the bus jumped forward the woman rushed outside and shoved some bills through our window.

Afternoon sun lit the mountainsides aflame and glinted from red corrugated roofs that dotted the hillsides. At last we entered the Sacred Valley and Cusco itself, once the great capital of the Inca Empire. Five hundred-year-old colonial cathedrals surrounded Cusco's grand Plaza de Armas. Painted wooden balconies overhung white stucco and stone walls that fronted cobbled streets. Shops piled high with paintings, gilded frames, and artisanal silverwork lined the narrow street of Cuesta San Blas.

The origins of the Inca Empire are shrouded in myth. The story goes that the sun god created Manco Cápac and Mama Huaca, his sister-wife or mother depending on legend, who arose from Lake Titicaca as divine founders of a chosen race. Their small tribe centered around the city of Cusco and over three hundred years grew into the largest empire the Americas had ever seen. By the 1400s, the Incan aristocracy controlled the "Tahuantinsuyo," or Empire of the Four Regions, which included present-day Colombia, Ecuador, Peru, Bolivia, and parts of Chile.

Our grueling four-day journey had finally brought us to this age-old Incan capital of tapered stone walls and archways sculpted by perhaps the finest stonemasons in history. At a balcony restaurant, we blithely indulged in pisco sours and nacho chips with fresh guacamole while an old man plucked magical sounds from his massive arpa, an Andean version of a harp.

Bars and cafes crowded the streets, flowers and fountains filled the plazas, and amber-hued lights lit church facades. We felt like we were in Europe, without the high prices or heavy crowds. And Tamara was in her element.

"I am so happy," she said, "I could almost cry."

After recuperating for a few days, we felt ready to take a side trip. Cusco faded into the distance as our train climbed mountainside switchbacks. Mist clung to valley bottoms until sun warmed the chilled earth. Of the many broad pampas grasslands in Peru, those around Anta were among the most famous as the site of a vicious battle between a young Incan prince and the Chancas people. Thousands of Incan soldiers disguised as stones hid in trenches lightly covered by dirt. The warriors leapt from hiding and surprised the Chancas, who thought the sun god had turned the stones into soldiers.

After the village of Izcuchaca, our train continued past fields of potato, corn, lima beans and groves of peach, apple, and pear. Beyond Pachar we followed the Vilcanota River, a tributary of the Amazon feared by the Inca for her unpredictable rainy season floodwaters. Snow-capped mountains rose to the north, including the nearly six thousand-meter La Veronica. Beyond the village of Chillca we entered a narrow gorge that grew ever deeper. Orchids and ferns covered the hillsides and mountainous fringes of the Amazon known as the eyebrow of the jungle.

At Aguas Calientes, the train stopped. The teeming ramshackle, frontier-style settlement felt to me like a nineteenth-century outpost in the American West. People of all sizes, shapes, and colors milled about. Above Aguas Calientes loomed Macchu Picchu, meaning "Old Peak" in Quechua. And nestled below this peak was the ancient stone city of the same name. This was our destination.

We spent the night at Aguas Calientes and, at dawn, we watched as rays of sun splayed out from the towering peak, and crept towards the ruined city. We climbed higher for a better vantage. To the west stood snow-covered peaks and, far below, the Urubamba River rushed. Light bathed the stones in warm green and yellow hues as the sun cleared the stoic mountaintop and lit the edges of the peak on fire. Swallows twittered, but all else was quiet as the morning air took on the aroma of an awakening jungle. Before us stood perhaps the most iconic sight in all of South America.

No one knew why the Inca built the city or what had happened to its residents. Perched upon a rock shelf over the Urubamba River among vertical cliffs would have provided a natural defense against enemies; perhaps it was a religious center or temple honoring the Andes.

Whatever political misfortunes that might befall Peru, this cultural centerpiece of the continent would likely always draw tourists from around the world. Though the Inca had been conquered by the Spaniards half a millennium ago, their stone legacies served as indelible reminders of past glories.

I was not generally drawn to places where tourists congregated. Crouching in the ice cave of Pastoruri Glacier high in the Andes a few weeks ago was a moment I could never have imagined, but wandering amongst the stone ruins of Macchu Picchu at dawn was an experience I had long dreamed of. In such moments, the question I asked myself a month ago while huddled in the rain in the Ecuadorian market town of Saquisili was easily answered. Yes, I thought while gazing upon the scenes before me. This is absolutely worth it.

20

¡VIVA LA PAZ!

Morning sun rose over the rust-colored barren plains and hills of the Altiplano—a tableland plateau in the Andes intersecting Peru, Bolivia, and Argentina, and the highest plateau on Earth outside Tibet. On Lake Titicaca, the world's highest navigable lake, islanders paddled handmade totora reed boats across midnight blue waters. From Puno, we rode past the villages of Chucuito, Acora, and Ilave to the border town of Yunguyo, where we stood in a long snaking immigration line of impatient Peruvians, before walking into Bolivia.

In the village of Copacabana, along the shores of Lake Titicaca, ice lay in shadows along the dirt streets. On the plaza, bundled-up locals sold reed baskets, woolen sweaters, and heavy shawls. Every *residencial* was rough and dirty. We settled upon a shabby, basic room with shared bathroom and full-size *matrimonial* bed—Tamara's preference when sleeping mid-winter in rooms without heat at elevations of twelve thousand feet. Excrement filled the toilet, which did not flush.

"The water is off," the proprietor explained, "but should be back in an hour."

Hot water would not be available until sometime the next day. Thin asparagus soup and fried fish at an outdoor café did little to warm us. A man offering rowboat rides on Lake Titicaca waved us towards his boat, so we climbed aboard. After pushing off, he pointed to the oars. He was only along for the ride, it seemed. I rowed hard across the deep blue waters. A light breeze blew out of the northwest and waves lapped the shoreline, but the feeble sunshine managed to thaw a little of the ice in our veins.

As darkness descended, orange and purple clouds cast a brilliant backdrop to fishing boat silhouettes moored offshore, and a nearly full moon rose. It was from nearby Isla de la Luna (the Island of the Moon) that Incas believed their creator commanded the rising of the moon. At the "rock of the puma" on the tip of another nearby island, the Isla del Sol (Island of the Sun), they believed the sun was born. There, the first Incas–Manco Cápac and Mama Huaca–mythically transpired.

In the age of the Inca, citizens worked four months each year in public service under a tribute system called *mit'a*. All males aged fifteen to fifty had to work in mines, build roads, and erect monuments, so long as they could still care for their families and crops. After the Spanish colonized Bolivia, the number of mandated months in the mines remained constant, but conditions became abysmal. Low earnings and high taxes left workers in ongoing debt. Since a man could not leave the mine until he paid his debts, children often mined in the place of fathers who had died. As able-bodied workers died and fled, and communities succumbed to European diseases, the amount of food available fell and famines struck.

In 1781 an indigenous rebellion laid siege to the city of La Paz for nearly two hundred days. Though unsuccessful, opposition to colonial rule grew. The first cry of freedom in Latin America arose from La Plata, in Alto Peru, as Bolivia was then known. Revolutionaries rang the bell of the main cathedral nearly to the breaking point. From there, the ensuing Spanish American wars of independence raged across the continent. Alto Peru was at last liberated when Antonio José de Sucre swept in to join Simón Bolívar, and together they defeated the Spanish. Sucre created a new nation, which he called the Republic of Bolivar. La Plata was renamed Sucre. A congressman from the fledgling Bolivian republic observed that, "if from Romulus comes Rome, then from Bolívar comes Bolivia." Both place names stuck, and today in the Quechua language their nation is known as *Buliwya*.

To reach La Paz, we had to cross the bridgeless Straits of Tiquina, so we followed Lake Titicaca's dark waters deeper into Bolivia. When the bus stopped at water's edge a uniformed man motioned for Tamara and I to step aside, and while armed guards scrutinized our passports, the bus inched onto a wobbly barge only large enough for one vehicle. After all other passengers had stepped onto the ferry, we were allowed to board. A cloud of smoke trailed behind the ferry as we puttered past our bobbing bus.

Hours later, we negotiated the jam-packed streets of La Paz. At an elevation of nearly twelve thousand feet above sea level, this was the highest capital in the world. Triple-peaked Illimani, a perpetually snow-capped mountain, towered over a broad canyon filled rim to rim with half-finished brick and concrete structures. Autos and microbuses followed few rules and darted in any direction they pleased. We were growing accustomed to the high altitude and had definitely arrived in La Paz the right way. Those flying directly into the city without acclimatizing to the lack of oxygen were likely to suffer from multiple symptoms of altitude sickness, yet options were limited for any newcomers requiring evacuation since most ambulance services couldn't fly into the city due to the thin air.

We had also been warned about La Paz's particular brand of mugging. In a typical scenario, the victim was grabbed from behind in a chokehold, while an accomplice collected passport, money, and valuables. Often victims were rendered unconscious. Such occurrences were most common after sunset but entirely possible at any time.

Our first project was to call Tamara's parents—never an easy task. Parades, marching bands, and floats celebrating Virgen del Carmen, patron saint of La Paz and the Armed Forces, crowded the narrow streets and every plaza. I dumped coins into a sidewalk phone, which ate the change. I tried again, to no avail. Near the main square we purchased a phone card from a street vendor. Music blared as I dialed.

"¿Hola, habla inglés?" I hollered at the international operator. *Hello, do you speak English?*

The operator couldn't hear me and hung up. We tried another phone, with the same result. We continued along the street, trying each phone, but none worked. I asked a woman at a kiosk how the cards worked. There should be no problem, she said. We tried again, without success.

Teeming mobs and lines of parade floats blocked further progress along the boulevard. Nor could we return to the hotel, so we clawed our way to a restaurant and there drank liters of draught beer while waiting out the throngs. Thousands of torch-bearing Bolivianos sang anthems and chanted "¡Viva La Paz!" while streaming towards the main square. Military bands played and parades kept filing by as a full moon climbed through the sky and booming fireworks burst overhead.

In the years preceding our arrival, military rebellions, fraudulent elections, coups d'état, and counter-coups plagued Bolivia. Efforts to stop coca leaf production, a primary source of income for many farmers, instigated frequent and sometimes violent protests in La Paz and the coca-growing regions. Living conditions for indigenous people, the majority of Bolivians, had reached a nadir.

The festival celebrations, thick crowds, and bustling activity surrounding us closely resembled the civil unrest that frequently erupted in Bolivia's largest cities. Celebration could easily spill over into confrontation. In fact, just prior to our arrival, major protests had spread across La Paz and the city of Cochabamba.

"Is this what it was like here last month?" I asked our waiter, Luis, who had taken an interest in us.

"Sí, señor. Mucha gente. Y mucho ruido." *Yes, sir. Many people. And much noise.*

"People were angry about water?"

"Sí. For many years *campesinos* shared the cost of the wells. When I was a boy I carried water home from the village well in metal cans. My grandfather still struggles each day to carry water from the well. For many, it is not easy. Sometimes the water is the color of coffee, but at least everyone can afford it because the law in Bolivia is that water cannot be sold. Yes, the people want clean water, but no, they cannot afford to pay more. So when an international company came to Bolivia and took over the wells and doubled the price, the people rose up."

"What happened?" asked Tamara.

"The president sent police into the streets. Men and women carried sticks and threw rocks. Here it was muy loco." *Very crazy.* "Smoke from fires and tear gas filled the streets. Some people were shot with rubber bullets. In Cochabamba, they carried one man through the streets after he was killed."

"Was it mostly indigenous people protesting?" I asked.

"Oh, no," said Luis. "Many were farmers angry because they were not allowed to grow coca anymore. But there were also teachers who wanted more pay. Many were students. Even firemen wanted more wages."

"How did it end?"

"The international company left. This was a victory! But really, everything is the same. The people are still poor and unhappy. This has not changed."

Luis moved on to attend to another table. I gazed at the crowds surrounding us.

"It seems to be the same story everywhere down here," I reflected. "People struggle, reach a breaking point, rise up, and afterward life is the same again. Nothing really changes."

"I suppose it's the story of the ages."

"I wish there were another way."

"There have probably always been haves and have-nots," she philosophized. "The haves try to keep what they have, and the have-nots envy what the haves have. The tension between these two has probably always triggered conflict. I doubt that will ever be different."

21

JUNGLE JOURNEY

In the morning I asked the old man at the front desk about the hotel phones, hoping to be able to try Tamara's family again, but he brushed me aside. I tried an outdoor phone and this time managed to get through to an English-speaking operator, but she couldn't hear me and hung up. In this era before cell phones, there was no easy or affordable way to talk with loved ones abroad. It seemed Tamara would have to wait yet another day to phone home.

I hurried back to the hotel as more festival celebrants gathered to march. Tamara and I hailed a taxi, which burst through the crowds and into the bus yard just as the parades began filling the streets.

We climbed aboard our battered Coroico-bound bus and over sacks of rice and grain filling the aisle. Women selling bread and oranges yelled through the windows. We rode higher onto the cold, barren Altiplano towards snow-covered peaks. Beyond the highest pass, hints of green dotted the brown and white landscape. At a police checkpoint, uniformed soldiers looked us over but this time did not demand our documents.

The driver turned from the macadam onto a narrow, twisting dirt track that led through thick jungle and then plunged towards the valley floor. Beyond the steep, vertical edge that dropped inches away from our bus tires there was only a sea of white cloud. There were no barriers to prevent a careless turn of the wheel from sending us into a thousand-foot free fall. Though tarred highways connected the primary population centers, less than five percent of all roads in Bolivia were paved. Potholes covered most routes and many roads and bridges were completely washed out during rainy season. On blind curves our driver honked to warn any trucks approaching from the opposite direction. Sometimes we had to jam to a screeching stop and reverse to let one pass. Waterfalls raining onto the muddy track added to the peril by making everything dangerously slick. We dropped ten thousand feet in fifty miles before descending, white-knuckled, from the thick cloud.

At Coroico, hundreds of Bolivianos filled the town for the holiday festival weekend. We still owed Tamara's parents a call, but learned that local phones did not allow collect calls. Of the few locals willing to help, every one said "no es posible." *It's not possible.* We finally connected by calling direct. Tamara's mother wasn't in the best way. It turned out that her son had just wrecked his motorcycle, her brother had been diagnosed with cancer, and her only daughter was somewhere in the heart of Bolivia.

At every eatery we tried, the staff seemed not to care whether we stayed or left. Even when we tried to make simple purchases, they wanted nothing to do with us. It became something of a joke. At one restaurant we asked for *el menú del día*, the set meal of the day, but the proprietress said no, without explanation, and walked away. We had a beer in another place but were treated like nuisances. We returned to the first place, but the woman ignored us and as we left she pulled the shed door partway down. We settled on the hotel restaurant. There, the brusque waitress brought us a local dish of Argentinean beef, peppers, onions, tomatoes, cheese, and sausage, and at the end we both felt strange. I felt dizzy and all

I could see were shades of yellow and orange swimming in front of my eyes. The room began swirling around me, so I dashed upstairs. Tamara paid and then ran after me. During the night we both hovered around the toilet.

A mob of shouting Bolivians crowded around the desk at the bus stop the next morning. It turned out they had been there all morning and the evening before–they were waiting impatiently and angrily for passage back to La Paz, but there were not enough buses. It seemed our best option was to delve deeper into the jungle. To catch a Rurrenabaque-bound bus, we were told we must catch a ride down the mountainside to Yolosa, and from there await a *flota*–long-distance bus–passing through from La Paz.

We were directed to the open-air bed of an idling pick-up truck, laden with a dozen indigenous travelers, and we climbed in with them. Thick morning fog canvassed the town, and clouds whisked past verdant valleys as we got on our way. We rode standing up, like the locals, for the half-hour downhill ride. After an hour's wait in Yolosa, a *flota* with a windscreen placard reading *Rurre* blared its horn. Tamara and I hustled onboard and crammed ourselves into two tiny seats, mentally preparing for the long ride ahead.

Hours passed with only one brief village stop just long enough for Tamara to dash into a restroom. As dusk fell, the jungle–amongst the most stunning countryside we had yet seen–turned still more lush. The road was rough, merely a dirt path barely wide enough for one vehicle to snake through the jungle carpet. As evening fell, the track turned muddier and though it was the dry season, in places it was barely passable. When a truck or occasional bus approached we stopped and reversed up the track to the cliff edge. Once, with the gleaming headlights of an advancing truck probing the darkness, we inched slowly backwards, farther and farther, until our right rear wheel slipped completely over the edge. Our bus leaned towards the precipice as the truck inched past. Then the driver hit the gas, we lurched forward, bounced side to side, and slowly slid back onto the road.

Farther on, at a cluster of restaurants lining the roadside, we waited in the muck while a man clad in mud- and grease-covered overalls loosened the dozen lug nuts from the rear wheel. For an hour, he and another man hammered at the tire with a rusted pick and assortment of sharp tools that looked to be doing more harm than good. Eventually they managed to mend the leaky tube, refitted the wheel, and the engine roared to life once again. We continued through the inky blackness over rocks and ruts; stopping, backing up, and inching forward through foot-deep mud and across bridgeless rivers until, after eighteen hours, we reached the bustling, haphazard Amazonian frontier town of Rurrenabaque.

The eastern horizon was lit up in an orange blaze above mist-covered pampas of grass and palm. Motorcycles buzzed through Rurrenabaque's dirt streets. Jungled mountains loomed to the north. Red hibiscus and pink impatiens awaited the deluge promised by clouds that were filling the sky. Children kept chinchilla monkeys and lemurs as pets; roaming dogs ran free. Tamara stroked each monkey she saw, having always wanted one. A girl sat by the road with a juvenile three-toed sloth draped about her neck. Another youngster fed banana bits to green macaws perched in a tree. One tot was sitting on the side of the street with a bag of bottle caps. He handed me one gleefully, took it back, and handed me another. We played while Tamara petted the stray monkeys.

At dusk, we walked to the Río Beni. Silent, swirling river waters reflected lavender and orange cloud. Dugout canoes drifted downstream and motored against the current, while a worn wooden ferry carried passengers across the river to San Buenaventura. Though most of Brazil's accessible rainforest had succumbed to development and overpopulation, much of Bolivia's remained intact. To go deeper into the jungle, however, we would need a guide.

Raul seemed competent, though being in the jungle held no guarantees. Some female tourists had recently reported being drugged and raped by their guides in Rurrenabaque, and we had been warned to choose wisely.

At dawn, stiff breezes ruffled the trees beneath a roiling sky. "We must leave soon," said Raul, "for the rains will soon fall and the river may swell."

Sure enough, a cold rain pattered the river's surface as we climbed into the dugout canoe that was to take us to a jungle encampment, from where excursions deeper into the rainforest would be possible. Behind us loomed mountains of the Alto Madido. Raul motored downstream past palmetto-lined banks, tree trunks, and debris washed down from the highlands during the rainy season floods. We huddled against the wind and rain. On occasion the sun peeked forth, but mostly clouds and mist-covered mountains accompanied us.

After three hours, Raul cut the motor and the dugout drifted towards a chunk of mud bank at the forest's edge. We formed a human chain and unloaded our rucksacks along with crates of bananas, eggs, fruit, and other provisions for the encampment. Rain fell in a steady pitter-patter onto the leaves as we marched along a footpath leading away from the river, under logs and through muddy mires. Red flowers sometimes dotted the green understory; gargantuan black and white spiders waited in massive webs spanning the trail. After half an hour we reached camp on the edge of a broad lake where two smiling women cooked lunch over a fire. They brought bowls of cold potatoes, olives, and cucumbers to the mess tent. As we ate, another guide entered.

"Someone is sick," he said. "You must help."

We walked outside to find two guides carrying an immobile woman into camp upon a makeshift stretcher comprised of a hammock slung under a tree branch. She vomited by the fire, and again when they carried her into the sleeping tent. The two guides and I took turns ferrying her through the forest to the river, where we loaded her into the dugout. Her companions, two Englishmen, wore grim expressions as they climbed in.

After they had motored off, a guide named Juárez led Tamara and I from the path into the lush, overgrown understory. We climbed over the broad buttressed roots of massive five hundred-year-old trees as parakeets chattered overhead. We tracked a troupe of yellow monkeys leaping from branch to branch in the canopy high above. Towering termite nests littered the forest. The rain stopped and clouds parted enough for a bit of sun to shine through. A foot-wide blue and black butterfly danced in the sunlight. Juárez sought tarantulas, and thick webs and white patches on the trees betrayed their hiding places. Each time he found one he kicked off his sandals and scurried up the tree to dig at the spot with his machete. Inch-long venomous ants emerged from the base of one of the trees we rested against. When we grew thirsty Juárez chopped a vine and water from deep underground poured forth.

In camp again, after a dinner of meat and rice, we climbed into a long wooden dugout for a moonlit paddle across the lake. Juárez propelled us across. The nearly full moon hiding somewhere in the overcast sky lent an ethereal glow. A black line of jungle separated the smooth gray sky and the gray water. From amidst a cluster of totora reeds a baby alligator suddenly leapt into the canoe. Juárez picked it up by the neck and handed it to Tamara. She gave it a look-over then tossed it overboard. We continued poking amongst the shallows. Another one leapt in. And another. The red eyes of the parents of the babies leaping into the dugout glared at us. Caymans and crocodiles also patrolled these waters. We drifted back to camp and fell asleep under thick shrouds of mosquito netting, until the otherworldly cry of a howler monkey echoing through the forest awakened us before the dawn.

The river returned us to Rurrenabaque, and from there, only mud tracks stretched into the jungle. We bumped and rattled over rutted roads and rushing streams on our way to a cluster of shacks at an unmarked junction. There we waited for a ride to San Borja. A man driving a Nissan pick-up bound for the village stopped. He offered us a ride, and twenty minutes later motioned us into the bed of his truck. He circled slowly through the village, ran inside a building, and returned us to where we had started. After more waiting, he drove us to the petrol station, where two small children appeared.

"¡Papá!" they yelled.

Five minutes later, a rumpled, languid man turned the corner. He bypassed the dry pumps and used a plastic hose to siphon fuel from a large drum into a small can, which our driver poured into his tank. After another slow circle we eventually followed the dirt road to San Borja.

Jungled hills to the north glowed in the afternoon light. Lavender clouds skimmed across an immense cobalt sky. Grasslands interspersed with canopied trees stretched to the horizons, and occasional wood and thatch-roof dwellings fronted woodlands and open fields. Naked brown boys bathed in chocolate-colored swimming holes. Goats scampered along the roadsides and cattle sometimes grazed, but mostly the savannah lay open and empty. We bounced along the dirt track until a family flagged us down. They tossed sacks of grain in beside us, and climbed aboard. A little further on, another group waved. This continued until the truck bed was filled, but still more piled in with bags of apples and live chickens tied together with string until there were twenty of us crowded together. A band of orange settled beneath cerulean clouds as the sun nestled on the horizon. Tiny bugs hopped on and off us. Darkness fell. Grasslands yielded to village outskirts, and dust to concrete. We took a room at a frighteningly dirty *alojamiento* on San Borja's plaza, the finest accommodation in town, and crawled, fully clothed and exhausted, into our beds.

In the morning, we hopped onto the back of two motorcycle-taxis and clung tight for the ride to the bus terminal, where we would catch a bus to Trinidad and continue our jungle journey. A battered minibus filled with boxes and sacks appeared. After they tied the cargo onto the roof, we climbed inside. The sun roasted us as we ground our way over tortured dirt roads scratched into the pampas and jungle. Dust streamed through the open windows and covered our ears, mouths, clothes, and gear in a fine layer of grit. Again, the sky was immense yet barely contained the billowing cumulus clouds that towered overhead. A brief lunch stop somewhere past Ignacio de Moxos provided nothing but biscuits and stale strawberry wafers. We pushed on, across wetlands teeming with herons, storks, cranes, condors, and kingfishers. Alligators lay in the sun beside their favorite waterholes.

At a bridgeless river, everyone clambered off. A wooden plank-bottomed barge propelled by a sputtering outboard lashed to the gunwale ferried us and our bus across. On the opposite shore, we climbed off the ferry, back onto the bus, the driver gunned the engine, and we steadily crawled up the muddy embankment. After five minutes we piled off the bus again for another crossing. Raindrops pattered the river. At the third river crossing, sitting in the bow of the ferry, a pink freshwater dolphin broke the surface. The rain fell harder and the air cooled as we approached the sewer-lined streets of Trinidad. At the station, one of the men asked if we were bound for Santa Cruz.

"Yes," I responded.

"Only tonight," he said. "There are no buses tomorrow, or the next day."

The other men nodded. I glanced at Tamara. We needed to rest, but neither of us felt eager to spend the next few days in the rough jungle outpost of Trinidad. Tamara nodded, and I reluctantly bought two tickets for Santa Cruz. The only place to wash our dusty faces was a skanky open-water pit that someone pointed us towards. We hungrily ate a few sizzling meat kebabs before stepping aboard. Lightning flickered, and moments later the clouds let loose. At our only roadside stop we ate cheese-filled empanadas while the wind blew and the rain fell in sheets.

Hours later, I awoke on the bus to utter silence. We were only a few hours into the twelve-hour run to Santa Cruz, but there was no movement, no tinkling of tools that would explain a breakdown, no traffic noise. The darkness was so complete that I could not see my hand held at arm's length. I groped my way forward.

"We sit until morning," the driver said.

I felt my way back, hoping to crawl into the correct seat. Morning grew into afternoon and we still sat. I wondered whether the mud track had collapsed, or flooded. We had hoped to reach Santa Cruz by dawn to get money, bathe, eat, drink coffee...instead we peed into the rain-saturated roadside muck and ate the last of our biscuits and stale strawberry wafers. Every hour or so we inched forward ten or twenty feet, once managing nearly half a mile. The thick mud stood a foot deep, and sucked buses and trucks in like quicksand. There were more than one hundred fifty miles to go, which at this pace would take days to cover.

In the late afternoon the pattern repeated itself: we moved forward again, paused again, and moved a bit farther until getting mired in the mud. The driver rocked the bus back and forth, gained a few feet, and edged slowly forward through the slop. We inched around buses filled with bleary-eyed Bolivianos, trucks packed with white cattle, and dozens of immobilized vehicles.

We crossed our fingers. Whenever the bus paused we grew a bit anxious, but each time the driver pushed forward. The mud lessened a bit, and we wondered if the worst was behind us. We watched as empty green countryside began to roll past. After several hours, we stopped at a village. Locals stared at us as we devoured fried empanadas and a kebab with yucca. Afternoon slid into night, and after twenty-eight hours we reached the outskirts of Santa Cruz. It had been a full thirty-six hours since we left San Borja.

We found a clean *residencial* near a cluster of *alojamientos*. Karaoke bars and chicken restaurants lined the boulevard. At a fast-food burger joint called Toby's we ordered two specials and, with four cans of cold Paceña beer also in hand, we collapsed gratefully into our sanctuary.

22

ACROSS THE ALTIPLANO

During the all-night ride to Sucre, bumping along beneath star-studded skies, we engaged in conversation with Sérgio. He was bound for his hometown of La Higuera, better known as the village where Argentine revolutionary Ernesto "Che" Guevara was taken following his capture by CIA-supported Bolivian forces on 8 October 1967 and executed the following day. Che Guevara played a prominent role in the Cuban Revolution. Following the Cuban Revolution and a failed campaign in Africa, Fidel Castro decided Che's next project should be a Marxist revolution in Bolivia.

"I remember when I first met him," recalled Sérgio. "He had dyed his hair gray, part of his disguise when he first came to Bolivia, but I could see he was younger than he appeared."

"You knew Che?" I exclaimed. "What was he like?"

"He was quiet," reminisced Sérgio. "Thoughtful. Proud. Very idealistic, I realize now. But I admired him greatly."

"What was he doing in Bolivia?" asked Tamara.

"He was trying to build an army. Which took time. He hoped to overthrow the military government. Eventually there were more than fifty of us fighting with him."

"How old were you then?"

"I was twenty. My family was poor, and I wanted a different life for them. I believed in his vision for Bolivia's future."

"So you decided to fight with him?" I asked.

"Yes. In the beginning we had some victories, but then the Bolivian Army took out two of our units. The shortwave radios Che brought with him from Cuba never worked, so he could not ask for help from Havana. Many peasants turned against us. We found ourselves alone and low on supplies. We were losing the war."

"What happened?" asked Tamara.

"Someone, an informant, told the army where we were camped. I was away, collecting firewood, when the soldiers came. They wounded Che and took him to La Higuera. The next day, a soldier shot him. They buried him in a mass grave, but no one knew where until three years ago, when an archaeologist found his body and a few revolutionaries that the army had buried alongside him."

"I never knew that," said Tamara. "What happened to you?"

"When I saw the soldiers I ran away. I knew they had found us, and I did not return. I went to La Paz, and heard that Che had been murdered. I did not come home for nearly a year."

"That must have been hard."

"Yes. Che was a good man. And I missed my family. After I returned to La Higuera I met *la maestra*, the schoolteacher, whom Che spoke with before he was killed. She told me he said it was wrong that government officials drove Mercedes cars, while students were taught in a dilapidated mud schoolhouse. 'That's what we are fighting against,' he told her."

"That's what he believed," Tamara said.

"I once heard him say he saw death as a promise of rebirth. Not until much later did I realize he was right. He became a symbol against oppression and tyranny. For a long time I believed we had fought for nothing. Now, his face is everywhere. People believe in what he fought for."

"He really was reborn," Tamara nodded.

"Yes. And our fight was not for nothing."

Sometime in the night, Sérgio got off the bus, bound for La Higuera, and by mid-morning Tamara and I reached Sucre. Here, the first cry for freedom in Latin America erupted in the early 1800s. At the turn of the twentieth century La Paz became the de facto–in practice but not by law–seat of government, while Sucre remained Bolivia's constitutionally-recognized and judiciary capital.

A single bulb hung from the ceiling of our basic room, but the wooden door, armoire, and floors lent a quaint charm. As the city was renowned for chocolate, we indulged ourselves along with glasses of orange juice squeezed fresh by cart vendors. Sun drifted behind the palm trees as Bolivians sat glued to a televised *fútbol* match versus Venezuela. We downed beers while overlooking the plaza, then splurged on balcony seats at the movie theater. The kindly popcorn seller gave us two sweets for free, and an old man handed us two opened bottles of banana-flavored soda. Besides two Bolivians, we were the only patrons.

The luxuries we enjoyed in Sucre were not to last. Turquoise sky complemented the ochre hills and valleys of the arid Altiplano as we rode through vast, unspoiled countryside on the way to Potosí. Situated at over thirteen thousand feet, Potosí is one of the highest cities in the world. The abundance of silver ore found here underwrote the Spanish economy in the sixteenth century and funded the monarchy's extravagance. By the eighteenth century, thanks to millions of forced laborers, many of whom succumbed to accidents and disease such as silicosis pneumonia, Potosí was among the wealthiest cities in Latin America.

Potosí marked a return to the Bolivia we were more familiar with. The first hotel we found had one cramped room but the woman had no interest in renting to us. The second had only singles. The next two were full. The last place had one dirty double, which we took. When we returned later that afternoon for our change, a different woman said the room cost twice as much as the first had quoted. While huddling in our room, we facetiously conspired against the hotel staff.

"Let's cut the lamp wires," suggested Tamara. "Or steal some ashtrays." Freezing mid-winter temperatures and the thirteen thousand-foot elevation had sapped our patience.

"Or, we could 'borrow' a blanket for our upcoming bus rides," I proposed.

"Yes, I like that idea!" laughed Tamara.

Our next task was to find our way into northern Chile, but few connections linked the two countries. We heard there might be a rail line running out of Uyuni with a train or two per week. We walked past ice-lined fountains, sorting our plans, and attempted to change a wad of Bolivian bolivianos into Argentinean pesos. The exchanges along with the *librerías* and *pastelarías*–bookstores and pastry shops–had shut for siesta. Instead, we browsed a local market selling toiletries, leather belts, socks, shoestrings, pans, and butchered sheep heads, drank *mate de coca*–coca leaf tea–to cope with the altitude, and wrote a satirical song about Bolivia's backwardness.

Later that afternoon, we took a pile of Tamara's finished books to the university. In order to satisfy her penchant for reading, once she finished a book we always tried to find a book exchange, which proved harder than expected. In Baños, the few shops with books printed in English had only traded or rented; none bought or sold.

"Muy delgado," said the man at one store when Tamara had offered her F. Scott Fitzgerald paperback in exchange for a thick Stephen King novel. *Too thin.*

"Un libro es un libro," I responded. *A book is a book.* "El tamaño no importa." *Size doesn't matter.*

He shook his head. "No trade."

In Vilcabamba we had tried to trade but the shop owner wouldn't take Tamara's fiction for a non-fiction; he liked to keep everything the same, he said. We had limited success in Peru, where Tamara picked up a monstrous collection of Jane Austen classics, but here in Potosí, the young woman at the hotel directed us only to slums and *comedors*–food stalls.

On the day we left, still miffed at the rude hotel staff for the pricing snafu and other slights, we actually did stuff a blanket into Tamara's rucksack. The hotel matron ran after us as we briskly walked towards a taxi.

"¡Frazada!" the woman yelled. "¡Frazada!" *Blanket! Blanket!*

As I climbed into the cab the woman grabbed Tamara's arm. Her shouts attracted a green uniformed police officer.

"¡Vámanos!" I told the taxi man. *Let's go!*

Instead, the driver turned the motor off and turned to watch events unfold. I somberly remembered the State Department's warning about Bolivia's legal system.

Incarcerated persons can expect to wait longer than two years before being sentenced. Prison conditions are very primitive and prisoners are expected to pay for their own room and board. It often takes years to reach a decision in Bolivian legal cases, whether involving property disputes, civil, or criminal matters. The court sometimes orders a defendant held in jail for the duration of the case.

We sat stupidly and denied everything. Horns honked and pedestrians stared as the woman yanked the *frazada* out of Tamara's rucksack. Tamara held her hand in the air like a disgraced celebrity deflecting paparazzi flashbulbs. The green uniformed police officer gave us a menacing look, but allowed our taxi to ease through the crowd towards the bus station.

From Potosí we traveled through still more desolate and breathtaking landscapes, over dirt and rock-strewn desert sands as the sun drifted into a purple horizon. I worried about how we would get into Chile, and what we would do if there wasn't actually a train going across the border. My thoughts were interrupted when the French couple in the seat behind us suddenly realized they had been robbed in Potosí of their credit cards and cash.

"Yikes," I remarked to Tamara. "It could always be worse. And at least we're not sitting in a Bolivian jail cell."

We reached windy Uyuni in freezing darkness. At the rail station, a man sitting behind a typewriter said the train departed at eight the next morning, and that we could buy tickets starting at seven.

A kindly one-eyed woman at the hotel across the street showed us three rooms before we settled on one with six blankets. Beyond Bolivia lay the continent's Southern Cone, and the start of a new phase of our journey, but to get there we would have to endure a jaunt across the desert where temperatures often plummeted to zero degrees Fahrenheit. In the meantime, we crawled under the mound of covers to find warmth and await the morning train.

PART III

The attitude in the White House seemed to be, 'If in the wake of Vietnam I can no longer send in the Marines, then I will send in the CIA.'

- Senator Frank Church, *The Secret Government:*
The Constitution in Crisis

23

ENDS OF THE EARTH

At first light, Gustav chipped away the ice from a wooden tub in the unheated hotel lobby so we could rinse our faces. We had met the Dutchman the evening before. The proprietor, wearing a ski mask against the bitter chill, had opened a padlocked door to let us into his drafty eatery, and we had afterward struck up a conversation with Gustav while sipping on hot soup and tea. Like Tamara and I, he was in Uyuni to catch the once-weekly train to Chile.

In the morning, we walked to the station, where locals slept beneath thick woolen blankets amongst towering heaps of bags and boxes. Gustav and an Irishman named Dave arrived soon after us. When the window opened we purchased tickets for the four remaining seats. Tamara and I dashed back into the frigid streets to spend the last of our bolivianos, and returned to a madhouse. Locals were pushing fifteen or twenty bags each onto the train through the lone door. When we tried to board they blocked us from entering, so we had to force our way on. I removed half a dozen bags from our seats, and squeezed our rucksacks into the overhead rack.

More bags and locals crowded on board behind us. An older woman thrust her flanks in our faces while arranging boxes of baby shoes and pulling in other wares that people passed her through the open window. She tried to convince Gustav and another passenger to carry cartons of cigarettes across the border for her. Under every seat were bags and boxes, the seats themselves were piled high, Dave had to stretch his feet into the aisle, and blocking mine were gallon jugs of oil wrapped in stained blankets. Baggage even filled the toilets. Another woman again began moving our rucksacks. Gustav argued with her.

"Ustedes son mala gente," she scolded. *You are bad people.*

The train jerked forward and after passing the steam locomotive graveyard, found open empty desert. Bone-white salt flats stretched to the horizon. The town of Uyuni lay, bitterly cold and unprotected, on a plain at the edge of a broad salt lake in the heart of the Atacama. The world's driest desert, the Atacama was a stark land shaped by wind and time. Unmarked tracks led into nothingness. Mountains floated mirage-like in the distance. When dry, the salt crust was as blinding as an empty snowfield. If it did rain, sky and water merged into one and to be in the middle was like standing on a mirror. Between Uyuni and the outpost of Río Mulatos, the deep sand was passable only with four-wheel drive; from Uyuni to San Pedro de Atacama there was no petrol and little hope of help in event of a breakdown. Where roads existed, they must never be forsaken. The nearby crust might take a person's weight, but a vehicle would break through into the soft mud beneath.

After several hours, the train stopped and the locomotive uncoupled. Ancient wooden boxcars on an abandoned siding slowly bleached beneath the blistering sun. A volcano smoked nearby. Empty desert surrounded us.

Once we had cleared Bolivian immigration, Gustav suggested we bide our time in the makeshift dining car. He ordered a round and we sipped beer in the afternoon sunshine while exchanging our stories.

"I'm from Holland originally," Gustav explained, "but moved to Australia a decade ago. Last year I sold my restaurant in Perth. Now I travel half the year."

"Have you been to a lot of countries?" I asked.

"A fair number," he said. "Chile will be my eighty-fourth."

Gustav's interest in politics led us into a discussion about America's involvement in Chilean history.

"During the 1950s and '60s," he began, "the CIA covertly spent millions funding political campaigns and opposing leftist presidential candidates like Salvador Allende, who had close ties to communist Cuba. Allende won, eventually. But fearing another Cuba, President Nixon cut off all aid to encourage Allende's overthrow or defeat."

Worse was a CIA operation overseen by Henry Kissinger. His goal was a full-blown coup. The first step was to find army officers willing to participate. The second was removal of their commander, an anti-coup constitutionalist. The CIA provided cash, a satchel of tear gas, and three submachine guns, the latter by diplomatic pouch. When the officers approached the commander, he drew a gun in self-defense. They shot and killed him.

"Soon after," continued Gustav, "the army attacked the presidential palace. They found Allende's body in the rubble. Kissinger told Nixon the United States had 'helped' the coup. The new military junta, led by Pinochet, controlled Chile for seventeen years. It was a dark time. During his regime, thousands of people went dead or missing, tens of thousands were tortured–including children–and more than eighty thousand were imprisoned. It took an economic collapse and mass protests to get him out."

Though the United States' admission of interference in Chilean affairs during the Allende and Pinochet era had been inconsistent, three months after Tamara and I visited, a White House press release acknowledged that, "actions approved by the U.S. government during this period aggravated political polarization and affected Chile's long tradition of democratic elections."

Chile regained its luster after Pinochet but, twenty years after our visit, protests and marches coalesced into the worst unrest the country had seen since its transition to democracy. Chile's president invoked a state of emergency, declared war on the protestors, and cracked down as repressively as Pinochet had. I later wondered how Latin America's most prosperous country, and one of its most stable, had fallen so far. The answer seemed to be that the roots of Chile's former dictatorship had never been routed out. And Chile was not alone. When most Latin American countries transitioned to democracy, outgoing dictators and their inner circles rarely left politics. Many authoritarian-era elites—including former dictators, junta members, and party officials—retained high-level posts in government and continued to wield serious influence.

The Pinochet dictatorship went a step farther by enshrining its political and economic agenda in an authoritarian constitution that continued to benefit allies of the old regime. As a result, Chile became one of Latin America's most unequal countries. Even a successful economy could not placate Chileans when there was such a wide gap between the haves and have-nots, especially when many of the haves obtained their riches through ties to the dictatorial past.

In 2019 and into 2020, protesters wanted a new constitution. After weeks of confrontation, the president agreed to a rewrite. Waves of protests in other countries across Latin America, from Brazil to Bolivia to Colombia, served as a warning that change might be postponed but could not be avoided forever.

While we talked, another locomotive shunted us across the border into Chile, then decoupled and disappeared. Again we waited. Locals pulled their bags and belongings from the train and piled them into grand clusters for inspection. Uniformed guards patrolling the perimeter watched the piles grow. We battled our way outside. The rumor was that the train might not leave for two hours, and then would take eight more to reach the city of Calama, the first city inside Chile.

"A bus soon leaves," the Chilean guard said, "and only takes four hours to Calama. Are you on it?"

We were not aware that a road even existed, and had bought tickets for the full journey. Dave stayed with the train, but Tamara and I joined Gustav on the bus after waiting another hour for the customs official to arrive and a border guard to search our bags.

Aboard the bus, I watched the lonely rail cars fall behind; the desert's immensity seemed to swallow them. Afternoon sun lit polychrome peaks aflame. Volcanoes puffed in the distance. Lavender and purple tones were painted across the western horizon. A few puddles amidst the salt plains had remained when prehistoric lake waters of Salar de Uyuni evaporated. Magenta peaks now reflected from these shallow pools, and bright pink Chilean flamingos waded in the midnight-blue oasis waters. We watched silent as a surreal kaleidoscope of form and color passed our dust-covered windows.

"A hundred years ago," Gustav said, "this desert belonged to Bolivia..."

He explained how, in the early 1800s, American President James Madison sent special agent Joel Roberts Poinsett to Chile and Argentina to investigate the nations' readiness for independence from Spain. Poinsett's main adversary turned out to be the Peruvian government in Lima, which was loyal to Spain. The capture of a whaler and ten other American ships by the Peruvians prompted Chile to declare war. Poinsett joined the Chilean army to aid their effort. With his help, the Peruvian royalists were defeated, and newly independent Chile emerged as a stable authoritarian republic.

"Yet another example of foreign meddling," noted Tamara.

The War of the Pacific later erupted between Chile and a united Bolivia and Peru. The United States tried to intervene, but couldn't match Chilean naval power and backed down. Chile won the war and increased in size by nearly a third. Peru ceded two territories. Bolivia lost Antofagasta, the northern Atacama, and access to the sea, becoming landlocked. Bolivia's ongoing quest to reclaim ocean access remained unresolved even during our visit, a hundred years later, since the two countries had cut diplomatic ties over the issue.

Long after night fell we rattled into Calama, an oasis of light amidst the desolation. The next morning, I stood in line with Gustav at the lone *casa de cambio* to trade dollars for Chilean pesos. Dave suddenly appeared with his gear still strapped to his back. The train had just arrived, and weary locals were unloading their bevies of bags and boxes. After sitting at the border for ten hours, the train had taken another eight to reach Calama, amounting to a twenty-four hour journey.

"I'm glad we took the bus," Tamara confided to me. "Sleeping on that train would have been impossible."

She and I continued south from Calama through slender string bean-shaped Chile towards the heart of the continent's Southern Cone. Comprised of Chile, Argentina, Uruguay, and Paraguay, the Southern Cone's high life expectancy and standard of living marked the region as the most prosperous in Latin America. Though the root of Chile's name is not certain, some theories claim it derives from the indigenous Mapuche word *chilli*, meaning "where the land ends" or "ends of the earth." This, in fact, was our aptly named goal: the southern tip of South America.

We changed buses at the port city of Antofagasta later that evening. I admired the silver crescent moon hanging overhead and the Southern Cross twinkling from cobalt blue heavens, until the steward yanked the curtains shut, snapped them tightly together, brought out warm blankets, and fluffed every pillow. We watched dumbfounded as he served sandwiches and juice, and then passed out Bingo boards. We threw ourselves into the surreal act of playing Bingo on a moving bus, with me translating the numerals to Tamara, until the man behind us won a yellow mug. When the lights dimmed, the steward helped us fold down padded boards for our feet. In early morning hours the luxuries continued. The steward opened the curtains and wiped condensation from each window. Green shrubs and lavender flowers dotting desert sands flashed past, and Pacific waves lapped at western shores.

Breakfast sandwiches and coffee soon followed. Later, from some corner of the bus, our steward miraculously served a lunch of meat, potatoes, and custard.

At Santiago, we entered a world unlike any we had seen since even before Baltimore. For forty cents the metro carried us uptown, past clean, efficient, fully functioning stations. Every time I consulted the map someone stopped to help: first two ladies, then an elderly gentleman, and later a young man. Santiago smelled of the earth awakening. It was early August, and spring was just unfolding. Brasil Park burst with the aroma of fresh-planted pansies and budding trees and shrubberies. Palm trees stood proudly against white snow-capped mountains looming on the horizon. Throngs of businesspeople crowded pedestrian alleys and plazas. Crowds watched mimes and buskers and artists. As in most cities, street crime was a problem–thieves targeted shoppers and riders on the metro and public transport, but levels were far below what we had grown used to.

Inside a *schopería* serving oversize dollar mugs of *schop*, draught beer, we chatted with the ultra-friendly owners. After a feast of fresh fish accompanied by smooth Chilean cabernet in another neighborhood of the European-flavored capital, the waiter shook our hands, and waved us a cheerful goodbye. Outside, a policeman in green uniform warned us to be careful. I asked if there was danger afoot.

"Después, sí," he said. *Later, yes.* Then he shook my hand and kissed Tamara on the cheek. We were loving the Chilean warmth and welcoming spirit.

After two days in Santiago, we continued south, towards the end of the earth. As we made our way to Chile's Lake District the rain fell, as it had for days, onto water-soaked fields laced with broad puddles and overflowing streams. Slowly dawning daylight revealed massive clouds piled atop both sides of the verdant valley. A double rainbow arced overhead as the sun climbed above the cloud-shrouded mountains. The air was cool, but not as frigid as we had been warned it would be. At Puerto Montt, gateway to Patagonia, we discovered that no buses were leaving for Punta Arenas—the capital city of Chile's southernmost region, Magallanes and Antartica Chilena—for three days, which mattered little. Tamara was nearly ecstatic in Chile, compared to our time in Bolivia. We happily spent the next three days in Puerto Montt—I took long walks on the *malecón,* past deep blue lake waters. She relaxed by soaking up the television in our warm, roach-free room. Sometimes the sun peeked forth until fast moving clouds rolled past and the rain again fell.

The cool, wet weather, dour faces of the people, continental flavor, and lack of tourists reminded me of an Eastern European winter. But, although stable and prosperous, Chile was not the culinary capital of the continent. On lazy mornings, I brought small lidless Styrofoam cups of instant Nescafé, our only option, to the room, before wisely buying a tin of granules from the grocery which we then mixed with hot tap water. At lunchtime, we bought fresh bread, ham, and cheese for inexpensive sandwiches, and sometimes indulged in cheese and *lomito*—meat—empanadas. Once, we labored over an oily soup of chicken, potato, and peas.

In the evenings, we found *schop* shops where men crowded around televisions watched *fútbol* matches, drank liter draughts of Cristal beer, and barraged us with slurred questions. Despite the amenities, we felt far removed from our loved ones as we hunkered at the bottom of the Americas. After receiving news from home, we felt even more isolated.

"The world does not stop simply because we are sequestered in some far-off corner of the globe," Tamara observed. The lives of our families and friends were continuing, with or without us.

24

PERONISM'S PERSISTENCY

To reach the bottom of the Americas we had to cross Argentina because, below Chile's jewel-like Lake District, the continent narrowed and the road ended in a jumble of impassable watery fjords and jagged mountains. A broad rainbow graced rippling lake waters on our way to the border. After border control, we rode past giant ferns, lush vines, and odd Precambrian-like trees crowding roadside conifers. The traces of snow gathered along the shoulders of the road grew deeper as we climbed higher into the mountains. At an unmarked pass, driving snow blanketed the surrounding rocks and trees. A half-buried sign marked the continental divide, and our entry into Argentina. On the downward slope, the drifts lessened, and deep blue rivers flowed beneath the rough road. The black soil mixed with plowed snow reminded me of Oreo cookie vanilla ice cream.

On the Argentine side, mountains balancing on the horizons fringed placid waters. Billowing clouds took on orange and amber hues cast by the sun's last rays. We passed through a Swiss alpine-style town of log timber A-framed chalets before continuing into the darkness. The steward distributed sweet black coffee before the first of three wretched action movies with distorted graphics flickered across the television screen.

At first light, the land was black, and the horizon a single unbroken line. Clouds hinted of purple and lavender. We had left the Andes behind, and entered instead the vast windswept expanse of Argentine Patagonia. As dawn broke, we drove through a flat brown desert-like prairie that stretched to both horizons. Gaucho cowboys wearing wool ponchos and leather Wellington-style boots rode saddleback across the plains. Occasionally, we passed a thick wooly sheep grazing or spied a hawk taking flight; otherwise, little disturbed the gray skies and flat lakes and frosty grasslands.

Tamara finished one book, and started another. Our highlight was a breakfast of ham sandwiches and apple crumb slices. Later, in the midst of endless treeless plains at an out-of-the-way restaurant we managed a bowl of bone and potato soup, which was dreadful but better than *lomito* sandwiches, before the bus roared off again.

In the evening we turned southwest along the Strait of Magellan, which separates the southern edge of the continent from the archipelago of Tierra del Fuego. A half-moon hung overhead. Gray waters lapped russet-tinged shores a dozen feet from the road. Fresh snow topped the rolling hills, and pockets of frozen water dotted the landscape. On occasion, a few faded yellow and red shacks of corrugated tin accentuated the desolation. We caught sight of two rusted ship hulls lying half-buried on a lonely beach.

As on the opposite end of the Americas twenty thousand miles away, on the North Slope of Alaska along the Beaufort Sea, the sky was oversized and the clouds endless. There, musk oxen and caribou roamed free, and no buses traveled to the Arctic. Otherwise, to my surprise, each end of the landmass strongly resembled the other.

When we arrived at Punta Arenas that night, a swarm of people surrounded the bus. Some handed out bits of paper with directions to their *hospedajes*. We chose a *residencial* on a corner not far from the bus station. Winds howled through the night, as they did in a nor'easter, and we burrowed deep beneath the covers. Before dawn, a metallic orange fire lit the clouds. We dressed in the frozen darkness. The first five *colectivos* heading towards the port were filled, but the sixth brought us to outskirts of town where workers took their time boarding a few cars onto a rusted red ferry for the journey across the stormy Strait of Magellan. We rode over dark blue choppy seas to Tierra del Fuego. White mountains lined up like mismatched soldiers in the distance, and carnation-blue lenticular clouds skimmed across the sky.

On the far side of the strait, at the edge of the village of Porvenir, a few green, yellow, and blue shacks topped by corrugated tin roofs fronted a single tidy dock. Puffins, cormorants, and oystercatchers dotted the deserted shoreline. We found the only restaurant that was open and settled into a table. On our one hundredth day since leaving Baltimore we savored bowls of mushroom soup, bread, and two bottles of Austral beer at the brown and barren end of the world; not chilled white wine with Chilean sea bass, as we had imagined, but close enough.

Beyond Tierra del Fuego were only the roiling Pacific waves and the unpopulated continent of Antarctica, seven hundred miles to the south. We toasted our success. We had found our way to a place that once seemed impossibly far away; places once merely names on a map were now infused with memory and familiarity. Meeting a goal usually inspires a sense of accomplishment, pride perhaps, fulfillment even. Sometimes, however, a sort of melancholy also seeps in. Porvenir marked the end of the earth for us, and our pivot north towards home. I was struck with a sudden sadness, a kind of mourning for that portion of our journey which could never be relived and which would forever more reside only in the recesses of our minds.

Yet our journey was far from over. I soon remembered that thousands of miles lay between Porvenir and Caracas, the

Venezuelan city at the northern edge of the continent, which was to be our next goal. We had much to sort out before reaching this country on the Caribbean, which itself now seemed impossibly far away. Our first task was to reach the Argentine city of Río Gallegos. A ferry from Porvenir brought us back to the mainland as afternoon faded beneath a brilliant magenta sunset. Pools of water reflected scarlet and lavender clouds. Unending plains held a golden hue and the sky a surreal shade of cerulean. At Río Gallegos, mud flats and decayed wooden boats lined the river, which meandered through town.

To reach our next destination, the fashion-conscious cosmopolitan capital of Buenos Aires, we endured a thousand-mile, forty-hour double-decker bus journey across the plains of Argentine Patagonia. The place name *Argentina* derives from *argentum*, the Latin lexeme for silver. Though rumors of silver-filled mountains drew the first Spanish prospectors, no precious metals were ever found. Settlers from Peru, Chile, and Paraguay later trickled into the region. Following independence in 1816, a century of war and struggle underscored Argentina's attempts to establish itself as a sovereign power. By the eve of the twentieth century the country had emerged as one of the ten richest in the world. Market speculation, excessive money printing, and the Great Depression, however, led to the turbulent 'Infamous Decade', which endured until the president, Ramón Castillo, was overthrown in a military coup, known as the *Revolution of '43*.

The European-style architecture and skyline of Buenos Aires filled the horizon beneath a pale gray sky as we approached. *Porteños*, as residents of Buenos Aires are known, scurried through city streets. All seemed thin, attractive, and trendy. Beyond the tall clock tower at San Martin Plaza, we found a not-so-bad room with a balcony. Prices were far higher than we expected, and with our funds running low, we smoked cigarettes to stave off the hunger. We watched the rain falling and waves of *porteños* flowing past from our balcony while playing cards and sipping cheap boxed wine. At dinnertime, we found a no-frills restaurant around the corner.

"I was twelve when Juan Perón first became president," said Tomas, the older gentleman at the next table after introducing himself. We had expressed our interest in one of Argentina's most enduring political legacies. "The people loved him. The army hated him. The navy tried to kill him, by bombing the Plaza de Mayo. After that he resigned and left the country. But Peronism remained."

"Why was he so popular?" Tamara asked.

"He was for the people," Tomas mused. "He wanted better working conditions for the poor. He wanted a better Argentina. I remember once, when he was arrested, thousands of people filled the streets. The army had no choice but to release him."

"What actually is Peronism?" I asked.

"It's a movement, really, that has long outlived Perón. It means different things to different people, but at its heart it is for Argentines, for the workers. Peronism is about a government that works for the people. The cause is alive and well today."

"Perón later returned to Argentina?" asked Tamara, referring to his exile after the attempt to assassinate him.

"Yes. He came out of exile and became president a third time. He died soon after. His second wife, Evita, had died many years earlier. So his third wife, Isabel, became the new president, until yet another military coup took over the country. This is when Montoneros and the People's Revolutionary Army gained strength."

"These were political groups?"

"Political groups which also waged war. Kidnappings, assassinations, bombings...these things happened almost weekly. The military fought back by killing many activists, militants, Peronists, trade unionists, dissidents, students, journalists, Marxists...anyone it considered on the left, really. This was the Dirty War."

"I've read about that," said Tamara, nodding. "Many cases were never documented, and commissions that were supposed to make sense of what happened often didn't count those who were forgotten or whose records were destroyed. Something like thirty thousand Argentines were abducted, killed, and 'disappeared' during that time, is that right?"

"Yes," nodded Tomas. "They were *los desaparecidos*, the vanished ones. Some were pushed from airplanes on death flights, *los vuelos de la muerte*. Newborns were taken from their mothers because the government believed subversive parents would raise subversive children. Thousands were murdered in hundreds of concentration camps. It was a terrible time."

The junta stayed in power until invading the British-occupied territory of the Falkland Islands in 1982. The regime hoped the United States would back Argentina, which instead aligned with Britain. Some American politicians preferred to support authoritarian regimes around the world so long as they abided by Washington's aims, believing they could be led into democracy by example. Jeane Kirkpatrick, one of Ronald Reagan's chief foreign policy advisors, believed that, "traditional authoritarian governments are less repressive than revolutionary autocracies." In this case, however, Reagan supported the British Prime Minister Margaret Thatcher.

The junta's belief that the United States would support it probably derived from the existence of the United States-backed Operation Charly, a program tasked with exporting right-wing military methods to Central American dictatorships to quash left-wing activism. The junta considered itself an ally of the United States in the struggle against communism. Argentina's defeat in the Falklands War also marked the end of the Dirty War; when we visited there were no known active guerilla groups, but acts of anti-American violence were still possible, given the existence of extremist terrorists along the Triple Frontier, where the borders of Argentina, Paraguay, and Brazil converged. In Buenos Aires, other dangers abounded. Armed invasions of restaurants and residences even in the fashionable suburbs were on the rise. Pickpocketing, aggravated robbery, and shootings had grown commonplace, and passengers were increasingly targeted while riding in false taxicabs.

After saying goodbye to Tomas, Tamara and I took a stroll along the sidewalks, past nineteenth-century buildings fronted with elegant wrought-iron railings, to Casa Rosada, the pink presidential palace, where Juan and Evita Perón had stood on their balcony in the 1940s to speak to *porteños* massed upon the Plaza de Mayo. Works such as the Andrew Lloyd Weber and Tim Rice musical *Evita* later glamorized their lives. As the story goes, fifteen-year-old María Eva Duarte convinced her tango-singing lover to take her with him to Buenos Aires. Once there, she left him behind to seek her dream of being a model, radio star, and actress. In parallel, ambitious military colonel Juan Perón climbed the Argentine political ladder and came to power through a right-wing coup d'état in 1943.

Following a powerful earthquake the next year, Perón organized a charity concert, where he met Evita. During a secret rendezvous, she hinted that she could aid his ambitions. He introduced her to the upper classes and to the Argentine Army, which both disdained her. Nevertheless, when Perón launched his presidential bid, Evita organized the rallies where the people came out in droves to show their support. The second act of *Evita* opens with Perón's sweeping victory, and the two standing on the balcony of the pink presidential palace. Perón addresses his *descamisados*, the 'shirtless ones', and Evita sings to her adoring supporters.

*Don't cry for me Argentina…*she serenades.
The truth is I never left you.
And as for fortune and as for fame,
I never invited them in.
They're not the solutions they promise to be.
The answer was here all the time.

Tamara and I happened to arrive during a prosperous phase in Argentina's boom and bust history. After our visit, the country's economy rose and fell, prices dropped and skyrocketed again, and Evita's legend grew, but politics never strayed far from Peronism.

Before returning to Argentina from exile, Juan Perón remarked, "It is not that we were good, but those who came after us were so bad that they made us look good."

After he died in office in July 1974, his controversial legacy and loosely populist movement embedded itself in Argentine political culture. Allegiance to Peronism became an unwritten requirement for any president wanting to complete a full term. Two decades after our visit, the first non-Peronist leader to govern the country since its return to democracy and also complete a full term was swept out of office after four complex years in an election that shifted Argentina firmly to the left and back into the hands of Peronists. The ongoing question on the mind of most Argentines seemed not to be whether Peronism's persistent populism and policies would prevail, but when and in what manner it would reoccur.

25

OPERATION CONDOR

Ferries daily departed Buenos Aires on the Argentine side of the Río de la Plata basin. Half-sunk rusted tugs and trawlers lined rotting wharfs on the city's outskirts. After three hours, outlying tree-covered islands and a lone lighthouse foreshadowed our arrival in Uruguay and the city of Colonia del Sacramento. The Portuguese were the first Europeans to sail these waters, in 1512. Four years later, the Spaniard Juan Díaz de Solís sailed through on his ill-fated search for a passage between the Atlantic and Pacific. Before losing his life to attacking Charrúa, a small tribe driven south by the Guaraní people, he named these broad waters Mar Dulce–sweet sea.

The Portuguese navigator Ferdinand Magellan also briefly visited in the course of his circumnavigation around the world. Sebastian Cabot, for one, stayed a while. During the late 1520s the Venetian explorer traveled along the Paraguay and Uruguay rivers, ascended the Paraná River as far as present-day Asunción, and traded with the local Guaraní people for silver trinkets. The Mar Dulce was renamed Río de la Plata, river of silver, for the trinkets that Cabot traded for.

The river basin forms an estuary that begins where the Paraná River–one of the longest in the world–meets the Uruguay River–which forms the border between Argentina and Uruguay. A mile wide at this confluence, the mouth of the basin broadens and at its widest measures one hundred and forty miles across. Rainfall in Bolivia, Brazil, Argentina, most of Uruguay and all of Paraguay empties into the Río de la Plata. In South America, only the Amazon pushes more water into the ocean. Fresh rainwater slides atop the denser waters of the salty Atlantic, and the two layers do not intermingle until well out at sea.

Unlike much of Latin America, habitation on the Uruguayan side of the basin remained sparse until Portugal established Colonia del Sacramento in 1680. Strong resistance by the Charrúa tribe and a lack of gold and silver had previously made the area a low priority for the Spanish, but after the Portuguese built a fortress, Spain ramped up its own colonization efforts in order to limit its competitor's expansion. The town changed hands between the two nations nearly a dozen times until Uruguay finally won its independence in 1824.

Soon after independence, Uruguay split in two: the conservative Whites, *Blancos*, represented rural agricultural interests, and the liberal Reds, *Colorados*, favored businesses in the capital of Montevideo. Each aligned with comparable Argentine factions. Uruguay's *Blanco* president was a close friend of the Argentine president; *Colorados* favored exiled dissidents who had taken refuge in Montevideo. Ideological differences between the two factions led to the Guerra Grande, Great War, which began in 1839.

After thirteen years of conflict the economy rebounded, exports exploded, Montevideo evolved into an economic center, and immigrants from Italy and Spain flooded in. This European influence remained embedded in Uruguay, and we found the locals spoke rapid Spanish with a powerful continental-tinged accent, so different to the countries we had traveled through previously.

From the ferry we stumbled, half-starved, into a corner restaurant near the port. After filling our bellies I handed over the pesos I had acquired in Santiago. I awaited my change, but learned that rather than seventy pesos we owed nearly two hundred because they charged per item rather than a flat *menú del día* price. This would not be the last time I misunderstood what rapid-tongued Uruguayans were firing at us.

At the downtown plaza, fountains shot pink and blue water into the sky and, along the sparkling waterfront, palms and evergreens surrounded seventeenth-century colonial homes. Model T Fords from the 1920s, 1930s Plymouths, and an assortment of antique Depression-era automobiles interspersed by a few boxy Fiats puttered through time-warped sycamore-lined cobblestone streets.

As the evening sun drifted into the Río de la Plata, Uruguayans gathered along the shore. They sipped caffeine-rich yerba mate from hollowed-out calabash gourds through metal straws called *bombillas*. The infused beverage was made from the leaves of a particular holly tree, a tradition begun by the indigenous Guaraní and Tupí peoples. Rare was the Uruguayan not holding a mate in one hand and a thermos of hot water in the other. Wisps of orange and pink cloud hovered above the horizon. The lights of Buenos Aires twinkled across the dark waters of the river, while a lighthouse perched on a rocky outcrop beaconed to passing ships. As we strolled uptown in search of dinner, a full moon rose over the stucco colonial buildings.

Over dinner, we discussed Uruguay's recent history. "The unrest seems to have started in the early 1960s," said Tamara. "Tupamaros was a Robin Hood-style guerilla group, which robbed banks and gave stolen money and food to the poor. When the government banned their political activities, the Tupamaros went to war."

"Sounds like a familiar story," I commented.

"It's so true," she said. "As in many Latin American countries, the military arrested and 'disappeared' any suspects. After Tupamoros joined together with other left-wing guerilla groups across the Southern Cone, a number of regimes began a collaborative counter-insurgency campaign called Operation Condor."

"I've heard of this," I said. "Most of the ruling dictatorships in the southern part of South America came together to fight communism and consolidate their power."

"Yep," she nodded. "Alfredo Stroessner took control of Paraguay in 1954. The Brazilian military overthrew their president ten years later. A dictatorship took power in Bolivia through a series of coups. The bombing of the Chilean presidential palace in 1973 killed Allende and put Pinochet in power. That same year, the Uruguayan military also established its regime. And Argentina's military took power three years after that. The CIA helped bring all these regimes together by coordinating death squad meetings."

"Argentina's Dirty War that Tomas talked about in Buenos Aires was part of this, correct?"

"It was. Thousands of Argentines thought to have leftist leanings went missing and were killed."

Like Argentina's Dirty War, Operation Condor ended following Argentina's failed invasion of the Falklands and the country's ousting of its military dictatorship. By the time we arrived, Uruguay had become among the most affluent nations in Latin America. Similar to Argentina, however, soon after our visit a recession and unemployment spike led to an explosion in the number of poverty-stricken Uruguayans. In Latin America, stability never seemed to endure for long.

The next day, as morning stars still blinked in the sky and the full moon set, we walked in chill darkness towards the plaza to find a northbound bus. Tamara would have preferred to stay in Colonia del Sacramento a bit longer; but the miles before us spurred me forward. I promised her an affordable respite somewhere ahead. We rode together along the highway that wound picturesquely along the Río Uruguay. In the villages of Fray Bentos, Paysandú, and Salto, it was as if time stood still: parks and houses fronted the river and vintage cars motored through the streets. Horse-drawn carts clopped down dirt side roads. Deciduous trees were bare and the meadows brown, as it was still early spring. Where the land grew flatter, cattle and sheep ranches grew more common. Large ostrich-like flightless birds, called rhea, raced across the rolling wheat fields of the pastoral heartland.

As evening approached we reached the border with Brazil in the northwest corner of the country. No hotels or restaurants were to be seen. The first few Uruguayans we came across barely understood me as I inquired about a place to stay, possibly because Portuguese-speaking Brazil lay only a few miles away. They gestured vaguely in different directions. I poked my head inside one boutique, and a lady pointed down the street. We found an unmarked building serving as a hotel and took a basic room. The only automobiles in town were three vintage cars driving slowly down the street, all blaring music from massive speakers mounted on their roofs.

The closest we found to a restaurant, after locals pointed to the plaza, was a hotdog stand and an eatery stall serving meat on a spit. We ended up sitting on two plastic chairs perched on the edge of a sidewalk outside a convenience store, sipping liter beers. Passing locals turned to stare, including one guy on a three-wheel bicycle carting an oversize speaker. Those not walking rode past on motor scooters. Everyone sipped their mates.

Our journey seemed to be slipping past too quickly now. The comforts of the Southern Cone had replaced the chilly nights and logistical challenges of the Andean nations. This change pleased Tamara. Though relieved to be on a northern tack, I admittedly missed the mountains, Quechua culture, and uncertainty of Ecuador, Peru, and Bolivia. Yet my pining was short-lived for, as I would soon learn, there was plenty of instability in store in the countries ahead.

26

THE STROESSNER SAGA

The full moon still hung in the night sky when, again, our alarm shattered the darkness before dawn. Pinkish hues soon streaked across the horizon. We hopped aboard a bus idling near the dark plaza. Our goal for the day was to reach Paraguay, but to do so meant crossing three borders–into Brazil, across a corner of Argentina, and finally into Paraguay.

We first passed over a tributary of the Río Uruguay, lined on both banks with decrepit wooden shacks, and then entered Brazil. At our request the driver stopped. In a leap of faith we left our rucksacks aboard and ran to the border to get our passports stamped. The customs office was closed, but a man sitting nearby claimed that entry stamps were unnecessary since we only intended to visit Brazil for the day.

Our driver had waited. At the bus station he told us to be wary, and to safeguard our valuables. I bought tickets for the town of Uruguaiana from inside a dank, hollow building on a dead-end street. With time to spare, we accepted an invitation from a kindly Palestinian who owned a furniture shop to share some sweet black tea, which he drank from a thermos. His primary language was Arabic, but he also spoke Portuguese, Spanish, and English. We chatted as the morning unfolded.

"You go to Paraguay?" he asked. We nodded.

"The politics there...so crazy!" he said, tapping the side of his head.

He told us about the first real election in forty years, which had been held a few years before. At last, someone not from the military was elected but, of course, an army general soon tried to overthrow him.

"This time, the people said 'no!' so the army general, *he* ran for president. But he was arrested for attempting the coup, and not allowed to run. The general's running mate was elected, who of course dropped all charges against the general. Then the vice-president–a rival of the general–was murdered! By the general, they say. Students protesting the government were killed, by the general's people, I think. You see? Crazy! This is what happens in Paraguay. The leaders there are very corrupt."

"From what I have read it sounds like Paraguayans are really struggling," observed Tamara.

"Oh, yes," nodded the Palestinian. "A few people own most of the land and earn most of the income. The poorest? They earn next to nothing. The rest only get by. This is why there are so many robberies, burglaries, muggings. You must be careful!"

Our departure time neared so, after thanking the Palestinian for his hospitality, we headed back to the station. The bus lumbered along a rough road that led through rolling hills and farmland. Horse-drawn carts pattered past. At the bus station in Uruguaiana the attendants spoke only Portuguese, but I gleaned from a man pointing outside that we must stand at the corner to catch a bus going to the next border. A few minutes later one chanced past. This carried us out of Brazil, across the Río Uruguay, and into Argentina's Mesopotamia region. As the Argentine official brusquely stamped our passports our bus began moving past us, but paused long enough for us to run after and leap aboard.

At the first town past the Argentine border we found

another bus, this one to the town of Posadas. Old women offered stale baked goods for sale and children sold toy guns. We rode through the afternoon past the villages of Yapeyú and Santo Tomé and Apóstoles. Cowboys with wide-brimmed gaucho hats and elaborately decked-out horses stood by the roadsides. We reached Posadas in darkness, crossed the Río Paraná, and stepped onto Paraguayan soil.

When the bus stopped at the final checkpoint a tall young woman came up to Tamara.

"You must hurry," she said. "The driver, he will not wait."

We ran across the street and stood in line for our visa stamps. After I cleared immigration I hustled to the bus and stood in the glare of the headlights until Tamara had returned and boarded. After another hour we reached Encarnación, and took the first room the curt clerk offered.

The Paraguay River runs north to south through the core of the country and drains heartily into the Paraná. Paraguay's central South American location earned it the nickname Corazón de América, the *Heart of America*. A population blend of German Mennonites, indigenous peoples of the Chaco, and Japanese immigrants–most speaking Guaraní before Spanish– made for a diverse atmosphere. The semi-nomadic indigenous Guaraní, among other tribes, had occupied present-day Paraguay for at least a thousand years before the sixteenth-century arrival of the Spanish. Explorer Juan de Salazar de Espinosa founded the colonial settlement of Asunción at a bay on the Paraguay River in 1537. Early in the seventeen century, Jesuit missionaries consolidated the indigenous inhabitants into settlements called *reducciónes* to protect them from Spanish enslavement and also to encourage their conversion to Christianity. As Paraguayan Catholicism embraced elements of native culture, it evolved into its own brand. The *reducciónes* flourished until 1767, when the Jesuits were expelled from the Americas by order of the Spanish king, Charles III.

On the morning after our arrival, we explored the massive deserted stone ruins of nearby Trinidad, one of several seventeenth-century Jesuit *reducción* missionaries, in awed silence. Afterwards, feeling ravenous, we walked along the dirt road and flagged a bus back to Encarnación. The two restaurants I had read about no longer existed. A soup place had *pescado almuerzo*, fish lunch, but the mushy, bony, musty fish and moldy-tasting rolls comprised our worst meal since the oily soup in Chile. The local grocery store stocked only mildewed, shriveled vegetables and packets of weeks-old cheese and ham. There was the sense, as if in some communist-era Soviet rationing program, that food and basic commodities frequently ran in short supply.

A century of turmoil, oppression, and dictatorial regimes in Paraguay had led to this. We discussed this over dinner, with Tamara explaining that the nation's isolationism began soon after independence from Spain. In the early 1800s, dictator José Gaspar Rodríguez de Francia isolated Paraguay and ruled with almost no outside contact. His goal was a utopian society based on Jean-Jacques Rousseau's *The Social Contract*. In reality, Gaspar's dystopian creation in no way resembled Rousseau's vision.

"For one thing, Gaspar wanted a mestizo society, one solely of mixed blood, so he encouraged miscegenation," Tamara explained.

"Meaning?"

"He only allowed white colonials to marry mulattoes, black Africans, or indigenous people, and he didn't permit whites to marry each other. He became an absolute ruler, cut ties between Paraguay and the rest of South America, and eliminated most personal freedoms. Military leaders brash enough to plan his overthrow paid with their lives."

"Sounds pretty grim."

Life didn't get much better after that. After Gaspar died, his nephew declared himself dictator. Power was then transferred to his eldest son, Francisco Solano López, who led the country into the Paraguayan War, South America's deadliest conflict. Paraguay lost major chunks of territory to Brazil and Argentina, and hundreds of thousands of lives. Of those who survived, less than thirty thousand were men.

"It's hard to imagine," Tamara said.

The twentieth century saw few improvements. In the 1950s, following the Paraguayan Civil War of 1922-23, army officer Alfredo Stroessner took control of the country. The number of crimes committed under his dictatorship is too numerous to count. Police tortured citizens. Political opponents disappeared. High-ranking officials sexually enslaved young girls. Indigenous people faced a level of violence akin to genocide. This went on for over three decades. Stroessner ruled longer than any other South American leader. Paraguay descended into a sort of living nightmare. A truth commission later found that thousands of Paraguayans were forced into exile, nearly twenty thousand were tortured, and thousands more likely murdered. I couldn't believe only a handful of people were ever prosecuted. Paraguay's first dictator, Gaspar, had imbued the country with a tradition of autocratic rule that lasted, with only a few breaks, from the early 1800s until 1989.

Stroessner's conservative Colorado party held onto the Paraguayan presidency for twenty-five years after the start of free elections in 1993. Legislators loyal to his party blocked attempts to label his era as a dictatorship. Even the educational system was complicit. Students were not taught about the past. Tamara read that the typical Paraguayan teenager didn't even know Stroessner existed.

"I think a lot of Paraguayans don't understand the lessons to be learned from their own history," she said as we headed through darkened streets to our hotel.

An enduring legacy of the Stroessner era was the inequity of land ownership in Paraguay, an issue which grew worse following our visit. As the Palestinian furniture-seller had indicated, nearly ninety percent of the land was owned by less than three percent of the people. Stroessner had illegally distributed land to his cronies, and post-dictatorship governments had done little to recover these lands for small-scale farmers or indigenous people. Paraguayans did not protest as openly as Chileans, Ecuadorians, and Bolivians, but change was coming.

For decades, some Paraguayans celebrated *fecha feliz*, 'the happy date', an annual commemoration of Stroessner's military dictatorship. He so successfully wove this nationwide birthday party into his propagandized personality cult that *fecha feliz* survived long after his death in 2006. It was not until many years after his tenure, once many supporters of the regime had gradually died off, that most of the better-known pro-Stroessner celebrations disappeared. Despite subtle signs of change, Paraguay had yet to fully embrace the legacy of Stroessner's rule. Like Chile, the authoritarian past weighed heavily on the psyches of many Paraguayans.

As a result, the Paraguay we found felt a bit like a tinderbox needing only a spark to explode. Tourist facilities were scant in the major cities, and almost nonexistent in remote areas. To complicate matters for us, I found the dialects that many Paraguayans spoke nearly impossible to understand. While waiting in morning sunshine for a bus that would take us from Encarnación to Ciudad del Este, a young girl selling breath mints named Lucille befriended Tamara. Though eager to communicate, Lucille's Guaraní, mixed with Portuguese-tinged Spanish, made conversation a challenge.

When our bus arrived, she sat with us in one of the bus's broken seats while we waited to leave.

"¿De dónde eres?" she asked. *Where are you from?*

"De los Estados Unidos," I replied.

"¡Ah!" she exclaimed. "Muy lejos." *Very far.*

"Ask her about Stroessner," Tamara said to me.

"¿Sabes sobre Alfredo Stroessner?" I asked Lucille. "¿De la escuela?" *Do you know about Alfredo Stroessner? From school?*

She shook her head slowly. "No sé," she said.

"¿Dónde están tus padres?" *Where are your parents?*

"¿Quién sabe? En el centro, tal vez. *Who knows? Downtown, maybe.*

When the bus driver revved the engine, Lucille smiled and walked to the door of the bus.

"Adiós," she said cheerfully, before returning to the business of selling breath mints.

The bus soon passed through a region of sub-tropical palm savannah en route to Ciudad del Este, near the border with Brazil. Though a few roads in Paraguay's capital were tarred, rough cobblestone comprised most urban streets while the roads outside the cities and towns were unpaved and nearly impassable during rainy season. At Ciudad del Este, the broken windows, rubble, and trash-littered streets made me think of war zone news footage. Most of the few people in sight were stern, grim-faced men wielding large guns who guarded banks and businesses. The nearby city of Foz do Iguaçu, where we were headed next across the border in Brazil, was reputedly even worse.

We found only one restaurant that was open, ordered beers, and tried to sort out possible reasons why this city held such a hard edge. When the proprietor returned with a second round, Tamara asked him whether the streets were dangerous.

"Sí, señora. This is because the big business in Ciudad del Este is...how you say in English...contraband. Yes? Cocaine, arms trafficking, money laundering...all are big business here." He pointed towards the upper stories of several nearby buildings. "You see those lights, señora?" The rooms above many of the stores were clearly lit, though darkness had not yet fallen. Tamara nodded. "Many fake parts come here from Asia. They are put together in those factories up there." He pointed again towards the rooms above the stores. "¿Comprende?"

Many goods sold in Ciudad del Este arrived in pieces, it seemed, and were assembled in clandestine plants just upstairs from the retail stores. Phony brand-name labels were slapped on, and the counterfeit items sold in outdoor markets.

"No one tries to stop this?" Tamara asked.

"The chief of police? He says the mobsters own the judges, so nothing can be done. You can buy anything here, but almost all of it is fake." He shrugged. "This is how it is."

Afterward, Tamara and I perused the hodgepodge of metal stands, shacks, and shopping warrens crowding the city's sidewalks and streets. It was not always easy to know which items were counterfeit, but prices often gave them away. Fake

Motorola cell-phone batteries, identical to real ones, sold for a fraction of market value. Bootlegged video games went for three bucks instead of ninety. CDs cost a dollar or two.

As we walked back to our hotel in the early evening we noticed several buses and vans with Brazilian license plates passing by on their way to the nearby border bridge. Passengers had packed the roofs with televisions, stereos, recorders, appliances, records, compact discs, tapes, perfumes, copycat sneakers, and cigarettes. Now, at sunset, the buses were heading back to Brazil with everyone onboard hoping to not be searched at the border.

For many Paraguayans and Brazilians, smuggling meant survival. As we walked the broken streets of Ciudad del Este, I thought of Lucille. I wondered what her parents and grandparents had endured under the Stroessner regime. Though she had never heard of him, did the past still haunt her family? What kind of future did Paraguay promise for a kid like Lucille? As with Francisco and Gaby and all the other young people we had met on our journey, I could only wonder what kind of life lay in store for them.

27

RED LIKE AN EMBER

"Brazil is truly a land of superlatives," I remarked to Tamara as we walked the cobblestone streets of old Curitiba. A few days earlier we had crossed the border into southern Brazil, and made our way into the heart of Paraná state. "The United States is the world's fourth largest country thanks to Alaska, even though the state is located thousands of miles from the mainland. Much of Canada, the second largest country, is comprised of islands. So, Brazil is the largest contiguous territory in the Americas, the largest country in the Southern Hemisphere, and the fifth largest in the world!"

"Impressive," said Tamara, smiling.

Despite having no sizeable lakes, Brazil holds one fifth of the world's fresh water. The Amazon carries more water into the ocean than any other river in the world, and can be navigated by oceangoing vessels as far west as Peru.

"Sounds like we have a lot of ground to cover," remarked Tamara. "What's our plan?"

"From Curitiba we'll continue north past São Paulo–largest city in the Americas–to Rio de Janeiro. From there we'll head northeast, into the Atlantic Bulge. This poverty-stricken area is sometimes called the Bangladesh of Brazil. Then we'll travel across the Amazon Basin, the least populated part of the country. From Manaus, we'll try to get into Venezuela."

"Sounds daunting," responded Tamara, "but exciting!"

Having been colonized by settlers from Portugal in the 1500s, Brazil naturally held more Lusophones–those speaking Portuguese–than any other nation. History, culture, and Portuguese linguistic links are the threads that tie together so many disparate regions with few railroads–and even some areas still relying upon rivers to get around–into a single unified territory. Unfortunately, neither of us spoke Portuguese.

"Communication is going to be a challenge," I noted dryly. "My other concern is crime."

We stayed alert while strolling the cobblestones of Curitiba amidst graffiti-covered nineteenth-century buildings. We had been told that, if we were robbed–a common occurrence in Brazil–we should yell "¡ladrão!" or "thief!" and give chase if we thought safe to do so. Locals would likely join the pursuit and beat the thief down if caught.

A regular occurrence near banks was so-called 'quicknappings', where criminals abducted victims for a short time in order to receive a quick payoff from the victim's family or ATM card. Some people had been beaten and raped. Good Samaritan scams were also common, in which a tourist looking lost or having trouble communicating was helped by a seemingly innocent bystander, whose real intent was to commit robbery.

In Curitiba, seductively clad women plying the city sidewalks rarely failed to turn heads. Street signs looked like they were written in Spanish, which would make orientation possible, but the words turned out to make no sense. Meeting Erik in the hotel lobby thus seemed a mixed blessing. We were unsure what to make of this hand-trembling, eye contact-adverse man when we first came across him. After introductions, he invited us to visit some friends of his across town, and we accepted.

"My wife is Peruvian," Erik said, as we walked through an evening market. "And I have a little girl. They're both at home."

"How long have you been in Brazil?" Tamara asked.

"Four months."

In the market we passed an abundance of produce: beans, fish, vegetables, breadfruits, kumquats, and array of fruits that we had never before seen. After a half hour walk, we arrived at his friends' house.

"Olá," said Lourdes, who was of Italian descent, when we arrived. "Bem-vinda!" *Welcome!*

Her Japanese husband smiled and gestured for us to come inside. We did not stay long, as neither of the two spoke English. They gave us handfuls of cashews on our way out, and told us in Portuguese to not be strangers. Afterward we asked Erik to join us for a few beers. He hemmed and hawed.

"Well, maybe, if you buy. My wife should be wiring me money tomorrow."

We settled into a place around the corner. We bought a round and Erik borrowed a cigarette before spilling a potted version of his story.

"I lived in Brazil until I was twelve, then moved to the States with my mother. I joined the Air Force, and later National Security Agency, where I gathered intelligence and decoded ship-to-shore transmissions. I'm a sort of spy," he confided.

As if on cue, Erik glanced around, downed his beer, and then looked at his watch.

"I must go. I have a previous engagement. If you do nothing else, you absolutely must visit Ilha do Mel," he said. "The Island of Honey. I'll tell you more about it tomorrow." With that he was gone, leaving Tamara and I curious as to what his actual story was.

The next morning Erik knocked at our door. I followed him to his room, where he gave me information about Ilha do Mel. Stuffed piranhas, pressed framed flowers, wooden popsicle stick boats, and other bric-a-brac cluttered his room.

"I'm hoping to sell all of that on eBay," Erik explained, which did not quite align with his spy story.

On our last morning, Erik knocked again.

"Today is my birthday," he said.

After several cups of sweetened coffee we found a *churrasco* restaurant with prime cuts of all-you-could-eat Brazilian beef and an endless salad bar. Erik threw back half a dozen 151-proof shots included with the buffet, handed us another item about Ilha do Mel, and saw us to the station. Tamara and I were left wondering what this odd fellow was all about.

The early afternoon train descended rainforest-covered slopes and lush mountainsides en route to the sub-tropical coastal lowlands. At Paranaguá's waterfront dock Tamara and I boarded a passenger ferry to Ilha do Mel. Some of the Brazilians onboard were dark and exotic looking; others paler than us. The sole pilot spoke some Spanish and invited us to the bridge. He let us each take the helm, and we took turns playing tag with a gargantuan Chinese tanker while bouncing over the rough seas.

The modern world quickly fell behind. No cars or vehicles existed on the Island of Honey. Sandy footpaths led to thatch roof *pousadas*–lodgings–dotted amongst vine and epiphyte-draped trees. Pink blossoms and abandoned wooden boats were scattered on the beaches. A white lighthouse perched atop a lush southern cliff. That evening, we drank beers by the Atlantic and shot billiards to the sultry sounds of Brazilian reggae. At first light, only a few chirping birds stirred. Wading egrets and herons fished for breakfast. The sandy beach took on a fiery glow as the sea sparkled in morning sunlight. We walked north beneath increasingly overcast skies, past the aptly named beach of Praia da Fortaleza, where stone remains of the eighteenth-century Fortress of Our Lady of Prazeres overlooked the ocean and untouched forest.

But for the few *pousadas* and the near-deserted fortress, Ilha do Mel differed little from the day Portuguese explorer Pedro Álvares Cabral arrived in 1500. The nation now known as Brazil then teemed with semi-nomadic peoples and over two thousand hunter, fisher, and gatherer tribal nations. Early pottery found in the Amazon basin dates back eight thousand years, though indigenous tribes thrived long before that. The Guaraní, Gês, Arawak, and Tupí–themselves divided into Tupiniquin and Tupinambá–composed the first tribal nations.

The Portuguese viewed the warlike native people as 'noble savages' and aspired to 'civilize' them. Their real motive was commercialization. Rich red dyes derived from the brazilwood tree were in vogue in the sixteenth century and highly sought after by the European garment industry. Plentiful along the coast, massive amounts of brazilwood harvested by indigenous peoples comprised Brazil's first export. European sailors and merchants knew the area as Terra do Brasil, the *Land of Brazil*. Named for the brazilwood tree, Brasil in Portuguese means *red like an ember* and derives from the Latin for ember, *brasa*.

Prior to Álvares' arrival, Pope Alexander VI had attempted to avert conflicts between Spain and Portugal by splitting South America into an eastern Portuguese portion and a western Spanish one. The strategy had little impact in Brazil. For the next two centuries, indigenous tribes and European settlers waged constant warfare. The Fortress of Our Lady of Prazeres built on Ilha do Mel was intended to not only protect the island and nearby Paranaguá port, but the entire nation.

By the mid-sixteenth century, sugarcane had overtaken brazilwood to become the country's major export. To cope with increasing demand and the need for more labor on the sugar plantations, slaves purchased in West Africa became Brazil's biggest import. When sugarcane production declined, the discovery of gold led to a rush in the 1690s that brought thousands of Portuguese immigrants, and conflicts between newcomers and old settlers.

Other European powers tried to colonize parts of Brazil during the sixteenth and seventeenth centuries, which the Portuguese fought against: the French in Rio and in the state of Maranhão, and the Dutch in Bahia and Pernambuco. Portuguese expeditions, known as *bandeiras,* pushed the colony's original frontiers outward. To ensure order, the

Portuguese colonial administration held two objectives. First, control and eradicate all slave rebellion and resistance. Second, repress all moves on behalf of slaves and indigenous people towards autonomy and independence.

Napoleon's invasion of Portugal at the turn of the eighteenth century thrust the Portuguese monarchy into peril. King João IV and his entire court relocated from Lisbon to Rio de Janeiro, then a provincial backwater located along a strip of the Atlantic coastline. When the first Europeans had entered these waters on 1 January 1502, they named them Rio de Janeiro, meaning the *January River*. Sixty years later, the city itself was founded.

From Ilha do Mel Tamara and I took a bus to Brazil's legendary capital and plunged into the heart of Rio. The outstretched arms of Christ the Redeemer, one of Rio's most iconic sights, welcomed us from atop Corcovado Mountain. Cariocas–inhabitants of Rio–pursued pleasure like no others, though sobering statistics underwrote the Dionysian revelry. In an average month in Rio, three thousand vehicles were stolen, one hundred people were murdered, and another hundred kidnapped. Many violent crimes were committed by or against poverty-stricken street children inhabiting *favela* shantytowns.

From the *rodoviário*–bus station–a half hour ride brought us to the bustling neighborhood of Catete. We were warned to choose our lodging carefully based on location, security, and the availability of a safe to store valuables. We had also been told by Lourdes not to answer our hotel room door until we had positively confirmed who was on the other side by looking through the peephole or calling the front desk. There had been several recent incidents in Rio of mass holdups of guests at hotels. In the hotel we settled on, our room had a view over the street and, comically, a round bed. As we later learned, less humorous was the raucous bar below our window. Tamara chased mosquitoes long into the night and I awoke multiple times to see her poised in various positions of attack, until she slapped my leg so hard I yelped. By this time, the all-night bar below the window was rocking, and sleep impossible.

Soon after first light, and with our valuables locked in the hotel safe, we walked along Rua Buenos Aires, past elegant, colorful buildings fronted with wrought iron balconies, to Campo de Santana Park where feral cats lay under vine-covered banyan trees. Peacocks, ducks, and swans swam in the ponds, and hairless rodents called agouti roamed the paths. Shops selling Carnival rhythm-maker instruments, jewelry, and wine lined the old street of Rua da Carioca. A stunning coffee and pastry shop provided us with an unexpected taste of turn-of-the-century Vienna. Satiated, we hailed a bus to Copacabana. In low season, the famous Copacabana dental floss bikinis were not abundant, but coconut vendors and muscled volleyball players still dotted the wide crescent of powder-white sand.

Later that afternoon, the air became thick and heavy; the leaves of the *Licania* tree outside the hotel rustled and the sky threatened rain. At the hotel bar, over Antarctica beers, we were busted for playing cards. The same thing had happened to us in Curitiba when a bar owner had told us that the police would shut him down if he were caught letting us play.

"It's so strange," I commented to Tamara. "You can legally drink in the street, and legally pay for sex, but forget about playing rummy in public."

Tamara had been dreaming about chocolate cake for the last few days, and I had dreamt that a sumptuous buffet was served on our Rio-bound bus. So many days on the road without any comfort food manifested in odd cravings and appetites. We found a *churrascaria* restaurant with an endless buffet and *rodizio*-style service, meaning that for a fixed price roaming waiters brought cuts of filet mignon, sirloin, roast beef, and lamb on skewers which they sliced onto our plates. We felt like royalty, and the lavish spread made me think of the Portuguese King João IV.

"When the threat of Napoleon invading Portugal faded," I explained over dinner, "the Portuguese aristocracy demanded that the king return. It was improper, after all, for the ruler of so ancient and esteemed a monarchy to reside in a colony! But

João IV liked Brazil so much that rather than return he elevated the colony to the status of a kingdom and established a multi-continental transatlantic state."

The aristocracy kept pestering the king, however, so in 1821 when João IV could hold out no longer he left his son, Dom Pedro I, behind as regent, who declared Brazil's autonomy the following year.

Unlike many Spanish territories which had revolutions and split into smaller regions upon independence, Brazil remained a single intact sovereignty. But as with the Spanish colonies, a war of independence erupted in Brazil. When the last soldiers finally surrendered in 1825, Portugal officially recognized Brazil as an independent nation. Worn by the years of turmoil and dissension, Dom Pedro I returned to Portugal and abdicated the Brazilian throne in favor of his five-year-old son and heir, Dom Pedro II.

The new emperor couldn't exercise his constitutional powers until he was eighteen. So, in lieu of a strong figurehead, a series of rebellions—coupled with social tensions typical of such a vast, slaveholding nation—caused political and social upheaval that were not overcome until years later, with Dom Pedro II's premature coronation. Nevertheless, during his fifty-eight-year reign, Brazil won three international wars and, more importantly, at last abandoned the Atlantic slave trade.

28

INTO THE AMAZON

Political and social unrest in Brazil continued well into the twentieth century. As the military plotted a coup d'état against the president, João Goulart, American President Lyndon Johnson told his aides, "I think we ought to take every step that we can, be prepared to do everything that we need to do [to support the overthrow of Goulart's government]." Following the successful coup in 1964, the new regime ramped up its suppression of the press and guerilla groups by including opponents, artists, and journalists in the clandestine campaign of political repression and terror known as Operation Condor.

At the age of eighteen, Rio-born Carlos Lamarca graduated from a military academy near the bottom of his class. In spite of this unimpressive start to his military career, Lamarca supported the coup that overthrew Goulart and, when he was eventually promoted to the rank of captain, his future with the new military regime was secured.

Or so it seemed. Lamarca deserted from the army, stole a truck filled with armaments, established a guerilla camp in the south of the state of São Paulo, and became the only man in

Brazil's republican history to be labeled a traitor. MR8, a Marxist-Leninist urban guerilla group, assigned Lamarca to the state of Bahia to expand the rebellion beyond the cities and ignite a revolution in the countryside–the same countryside Tamara and I passed through after leaving the banana palms and vine-covered rainforest hillsides north of Rio.

The landscape turned more arid as we made our way through Bahia. Crude red and white shacks clustered along the hillsides. No matter how basic, each had a round dusty satellite dish bolted to its roof. Trash littered the roadsides. The villages we passed through held a restless air. Poverty-stricken and remote, the northeast of Brazil seemed a perfect base for MR8 to foment rebellion against the regime during the early 1970s. We reached São Salvador da Bahia de Todos os Santos, Bahia's capital, in the late afternoon. The colonial capital of Brazil until it was succeeded by Rio, Salvador is among the oldest cities in the Americas.

As twilight fell, a soft glow blanketed the city. Down the Rua Miser Vordia and Praça da Sé, past decaying churches and empty, time-warped buildings, soulful denizens filled the streets. A drunk bummed a cigarette, then coaxed a few strains of Mozart and Bach from his wooden flute. Some Afro-Brazilians sold necklaces, others begged for coins. A couple of policemen frisked us on the edge of the Pelourinho, Salvador's historic core. Armed officers guarded every corner.

An air of desperation permeated the Pelô, as locals called this district. Named for the downtown whipping post–*pelourinho* means *pillory* in Portuguese–Pelô was the site of the first slave market on the continent. For centuries indigenous people and imported African slaves were punished, disciplined, and sold here by Portuguese colonists. Sugar plantation slave laborers, and the customs they brought from their homelands, contributed greatly to the city's rich cultural history. Vibrant music, dance, and culinary traditions–such as *moqueca*, a Bahian regional dish of saltwater fish, coconut milk, palm oil, and peppers cooked in a covered clay pot–were still very much alive, as we discovered firsthand.

It was here in Salvador that Carlos Marighella, the writer and guerilla fighter, was born to an Italian immigrant father and an Afro-Brazilian mother, the descendant of Sudanese slaves. At the age of twenty-three Marighella left his studies to join the Brazilian Communist Party. Unlike Lamarca, who showed no signs of youthful rebellion, Marighella was first arrested when he wrote a poem criticizing a Bahian administrator. After a second arrest and accompanying torture, he went underground. He was arrested again following the 1964 coup; in 1966 he wrote *The Brazilian Crisis,* which promoted armed struggle against the dictatorship, and in 1969, he published the *Minimanual of the Urban Guerilla,* which contained advice on how to overthrow an authoritarian regime through revolution.

His works inspired countless revolutionary groups and movements from the Irish Republican Army, to the Greek N17, and Basque ETA separatists. In coordination with MR8, in 1969 he helped kidnap a United States ambassador. Two months later, following a series of robberies and kidnappings, police ambushed and shot Marighella. Two years later Carlos Lamarca was killed by the army while resisting arrest. Following the elimination of these two key leaders, the regime fully unleashed Operation Condor.

From Bahia, a twenty-hour bus ride north brought Tamara and I to Teresina, the capital of Piauí state. The heat hit us like a hammer and no one that we spoke to knew any Spanish. Despite Venezuela's unstable security situation, we both looked forward to getting there for no other reason than my ability to communicate with locals again. Teresina's information office had long ago gone defunct. A hotel across the road drew our attention, but we could not find a single eatery.

"Não," said a man downtown selling oranges and shaking his head from side to side. "Sem restaurantes." *No restaurants.* We settled on a snack food dinner.

In the morning, a bus carried us across searing Africa-like landscapes with spare, simple red tile roof villages set amongst rolling scrubland. Children bicycled past mounds of trash littering the roadsides. Vultures soared overhead on hot, lazy thermals. Dark clouds began to gather in the late afternoon, and a noisy rain spattered the windows. Shirtless men sat in doorways and naked brown boys swam in tepid water holes as the ochre dust turned to mud.

At São Luís, capital of Maranhão state, staff at the *rodoviária's* information desk had no information about accommodations or places to eat and seemed puzzled that we were asking for any. We eventually stumbled upon a little hotel on a quiet cobblestoned side street and took a simple third-floor room that overlooked the Río Anil and the red-roofed dwellings of the São Francisco neighborhood on the other side of the river. Breezes from the Atlantic blowing through our wide wooden doors caressed the wood-plank floors and whitewashed walls. Rubble littered the ancient alleyways and deserted, decaying streets. Not a single shop or store was open. Many buildings and businesses seemed to have been closed for a long time.

"Are you sure there isn't a volcano around here somewhere?" Tamara asked, only half-jokingly.

Many of the edifices crumbling into disrepair did have laundry hanging from open windows, and *azulejo*–tile–facades of some neo-European buildings along the dilapidated waterfront seemed partially restored, so there were signs of life. Still, when I asked the hotel clerk when restaurants would open, his reply was simple: "They won't." Tamara and I walked across the bridge to São Francisco hoping to try our luck there. More black clouds gathered and soon a barrage of rain filled the streets. We found nothing open in that neighborhood either.

In the morning, I took a long circuitous walk through the deserted historic core and returned to the hotel to meet Tamara. At the lobby, checking in, stood Gustav. I had not seen him since leaving Calama, in the north of Chile. We arranged to meet him at dusk for beers at a waterfront hole in the wall. He had taken a different cross-continental route than us, but coincidentally arrived in São Luís at the same time. He told us that he had been mugged at Copacabana in Rio.

"Two guys tripped me on the beach, and when I fell to the ground they tore my pocket open and grabbed my cash. It was over in seconds."

"That's so scary," said Tamara. "We've been lucky, so far."

"What brings you to São Luís?" I asked.

"History, mostly," replied Gustav. "Did you know this is the only Brazilian capital founded by France, and one of only three located on an island? The French built a fort here, which the Portuguese soon captured. A quarter of a century later the Dutch–who, like the French, disagreed with the Pope's decree dividing the Americas between Spain and Portugal–invaded, but left almost no evidence of their occupation."

"It seems like this place was once pretty wealthy?" Tamara said.

"It was," nodded Gustav. "French and Dutch colonists never made it into the interior, but the Portuguese grew sugar cane, cacao, tobacco."

When the American Civil War interrupted cotton production in the United States, Brazilians filled the void by exporting cotton to Great Britain via the port at São Luís. The city grew rich. Weekly news from France kept citizens updated on world affairs. The first Italian opera in Brazil was built here and successful businessmen and shipping merchants sent their children to study in Europe. But, as demand for agricultural products declined, the city fell into decay. Over much of the past century, the buildings around us had slowly crumbled into dust.

After sharing some more travel yarns, we agreed to meet again in Belém, several hours to the northwest. As promised, a few days later, we spotted Gustav walking in the street below our Belém hotel room balcony. We met up with him and wandered together to check out the food stalls. Morning heat prickled our skin like a scratchy woolen blanket. Tree-filled squares, churches, public gardens, and historic blue-tiled buildings filled Belém's colonial quarter.

"This town was founded by the Portuguese after the French were driven out of São Luís," Gustav said as we walked. The sugar trade underwrote Belém's economy until the end of the seventeenth century. Afterward, cattle ranching replaced sugar. Rice, cotton, and coffee followed. Prosperity rose and fell with each new export. Belém suffered as farms started relocating to the southern savannah, but a rubber boom put this Amazon river port back on the map. Today aluminum, iron ore, Brazil nuts, pineapples, cassava, jute, black pepper, and other goods still pass through Belém's harbor.

At the food stalls, locals were drinking sixty-cent beers and dancing to music that poured from oversized speakers. The crowd cheered and clapped as two young women danced a samba. The Amazon River flowed past, just a few feet away. Located near the Atlantic Ocean, Belém is the gateway to the Amazon. This nearly four thousand-mile river and its many tributaries carry twenty percent of the world's fresh water, and discharge more water into the ocean than the next seven largest rivers combined. Belém is separated from the larger part of the Amazon delta by Ilha de Marajó, or Marajo Island. Massive clouds piled high over the river and thunder boomed overhead as we searched the waterfront for the boat that was scheduled to take us on an Amazon sunset cruise.

"Don't worry," said one crewman as we leapt aboard. "This is normal."

The storm marched downriver with us, churning frothy waters in its wake. But as evening fell the deluge dissipated, the clouds took on bright white then orange hues, and a three-quarter full moon rose over the Amazon.

We still needed to decide how to negotiate Brazil's interior. No buses went farther than Belém, and no roads connected Belém with Manaus, the primary city at the heart of the Amazon. We had gotten a sampling of life on the river during our sunset cruise splurge, but the basic boats traveling between Belém and Manaus had few, if any, facilities. Tamara was willing, but not keen, to travel ten days upriver aboard a filthy riverboat with no bathroom. I began to waver as well when

Gustav told us about a Brazilian woman he had met who had a bad experience on one of these boats.

"After two days of waiting, no fresh water had been brought aboard, the toilets did not work, and her boat had still not left," said Gustav.

One morning, near the waterfront market where vendors sold fish of all shapes, sizes, and colors, a Dane told us his story.

"I waited four days in Manaus on a boat that broke down twice and never left port," he said. "I finally gave up and caught a flight to Belém."

Tamara glanced at me. I knew what she was thinking. Since there were no actual roads to travel on, I decided that flying would not violate the overland integrity of our journey.

"Okay," I relented, as we walked together along the docks. "I'll find us a flight to Manaus."

"Yay!" she exclaimed happily.

Manaus nestled near the confluence of the Negro and Solimões rivers. Founded by the Portuguese in 1669 as a fortress, the bastion of rock and clay functioned for the next century as protection from the Dutch who at that time were headquartered in present-day Suriname. In 1832 the fort's status was elevated to that of town with the name Manaus, meaning "mother of the gods" in tribute to the indigenous Manaós nation. The settlement received city status in 1848 with the name Cidade do Barra do Río Negro, Portuguese for "The City on the Margins of the Black River." Eight years later the name reverted to Manaus.

While Belém benefited from the Amazon's nineteenth-century rubber boom, the epicenter of trade was Manaus, which, for a time, ranked among the gaudiest spectacles on Earth. Rubber barons seeking to out-compete each other devised ever more extraneous displays of wealth. A grand opera house with domes, gilded balconies, and European marble, glass, and crystal was erected at a cost of ten million dollars. The death of half the members of one visiting troupe from yellow fever accentuated the irony of the city's ostentatiousness. When rubber tree seeds were smuggled out of the Amazon, Brazil lost its monopoly and Manaus fell into poverty. The boom had brought electricity to the inner Amazon ahead of most European cities. But, after the bust, and with generators too expensive to run, the city at night sat as dark as the Río Negro.

A delay with our flight meant we would arrive in Manaus, nicknamed "filet mignon" for the condition of some of its murder victims, well after midnight. Soon after takeoff, the vast rainforests of Amazonas state passed beneath us in a carpet of green. We had traversed so many perilous cities by now that we were almost nonchalant about our impending late-night arrival. Sipping a bottle of complementary cabernet during the flight likely helped soothe our concerns. The fact was that we had come so far I almost believed we might actually survive South America fully intact.

"Cheers," I said, "to a remarkable trip."

"Cheers," smiled Tamara. "But let's not count our chickens before they're hatched. We're not out of this yet."

29

COMING INTO CARACAS

After surviving Manaus, we left the city on a northbound bus that drove onto a series of wooden ferries, one after the other, in order to cross the rivers flowing down from the Guiana Highlands. Pools of water on the roadside reflected a brilliant shade of orange. Palm savannahs stretched to the edge of the highlands. That day we would reach Venezuela, the last country on our itinerary.

"Five years ago," said a young man on the bus whose parents worked with indigenous villagers in the region, "the journey from Manaus to Boa Vista took three days. The mud stood knee-deep. Buses pulled each other through the muck."

Road conditions had improved somewhat since then, and soon after Boa Vista, we left Brazil behind. The sun burned hot in Santa Elena de Uairen, on the Venezuelan side of the border and we stood north of the equator for the first time since Panama. We passed pristine rivers and waterfalls, lush gorges and valleys, and the impenetrable jungle of La Gran Sabana. Palm groves carpeting rolling savannahs led to mountain-covered horizons. Grand cumulus clouds piled high into a cobalt blue sky and tabletop tepuis rose abruptly from the jungle. From the local Pemon language meaning "house of the gods," tepuis such as Neblina, Autana, and Auyantepui–the latter the source of Angel Falls, the world's highest waterfall–stood as testament to the sandstone plateau that once stretched from the Amazon to the Orinoco River. As the land eroded around the tabletop mesas, flora and fauna unique to each tepui evolved in isolation. The cooler, wetter upper plateaus were cut off from the warmer tropical forests at their bases by imposing rock walls, making the tops ecological islands.

Until recently, no public transport existed anywhere in this area, though travelers could sometimes catch sporadic rides on a jeep or truck. When the fuel station ran dry in Santa Elena, as it often did, petrol was sold from barrels. All motorists were forbidden to travel without twenty spare liters.

At a remote outpost a contingent of soldiers and locals rushed onto our bus, but without enough seats, most stood. We continued on, through a pristine landscape, before stopping in the midday heat at a military checkpoint where guards in camouflage searched all the passengers' bags. We skirted past Venezuela's roadless eastern border, beyond which the unbroken jungle stretched to Georgetown, the capital of the country of Guayana. To our west, rainforest sheltered the borderlands between Brazil and Venezuela.

"Somewhere over there," said Tamara, pointing westward, "is where anthropologist Napoleon Chagnon lived while researching his controversial work *Yanomamö: The Fierce People*. Chagnon challenged Rousseau's romantic notion that in a state of nature humans are altruistic and peaceful."

"I remember learning about the Yanomamö in my high school sociology class," I said. "But I forget the details."

"Chagnon presented the unknown tribe to the world as a violent culture in which males derived status and obtained women by killing rivals. He reported that a fourth of adult Yanomamö men were murdered by other men from the tribe and that the tribal region was almost constantly at war. But his claims were fiercely challenged by his peers."

"What do you think?" I asked.

"It doesn't really surprise me," Tamara said. "Why should an ancient tribe be any different from the Spanish and Portuguese conquistadors who came after them? Human nature seems capable of, well, nearly anything."

Massive thunderclouds let loose as we talked. Raindrops splattered the windows of the bus, and dribbled through in places that were held together by tape. After ten hours of open countryside we passed the town of Upata, then San Felix. Long after the golden cumulus clouds towering above the horizon had faded into darkness, we reached Ciudad Bolivar on the edge of the Orinoco River.

Christopher Columbus sailed near the Orinoco in 1498 during his third voyage to the Americas. Amazed by the volume of freshwater deflecting his course, he thought he had reached Heaven on Earth. The following year, an expedition led by Alonso de Ojeda visited nearby Lake Maracaibo. Stilt houses in the area reminded de Ojeda's Italian navigator Amerigo Vespucci of Venice, so he named the area *Veneziola*–"little Venice"–from which derived the name Venezuela. In an alternative story of the origin of the country's name, a member of de Ojeda's crew stated in his work *Summa de Geografía* that the expedition encountered an indigenous tribe calling itself Veneciuela. An undisputed fact is that the Americas were named for de Ojeda's navigator, Amerigo Vespucci.

By the time we arrived, most restaurants and hotels in Ciudad Bolivar were shuttered for the night. When we eventually found a hotel, a cranky, tentative oldster opened the door. We waited on a balcony with a pair of Brits who were drinking bottled Brahma beers and watching local television announcements by Venezuelan President Hugo Chávez, followed by the opening ceremony of the Sydney Olympics.

The old man led us to a concrete-walled room, which had a bed with broken springs, and doorless, blocked toilet; the plumbing problem meant we couldn't shower until the next day. Our door had no number, handle, or lock, and a languorous fan feebly shifted stale air around the room.

Instead we sat on the balcony and drank Polar beers until the old man glanced at his watch too many times. We took the hint and headed inside.

Clouds mushroomed into an early morning sky above the Orinoco, which flowed swift and silent to the waiting Atlantic. We watched the passing watercraft that were transporting tonka beans, animal skins, gold, diamonds, and chicle and balata gum. Down to our last twenty Venezuelan bolívars, we were desperate to change money. Of three central banks, two were closed and one had a long line snaking away from its entrance. We then learned that the only place to change money was a *casa de cambio* at a hotel near the airport. On the local bus, rather than shout or pull a cord to be let off, we clapped twice as the locals did. The sign at the *casa de cambio* kiosk was lit, but there was no one present.

"She will be back," said a desk clerk.

A German woman passing by told us that the cashier had been there earlier, but declared she was out of money, so that was it for the day. The German, too, was out of cash.

"I have been in Venezuela six weeks," she said. "I've had enough of this place. I tried to change my plane ticket, but no one answers the phone," she shrugged. "So I can go nowhere."

We started to walk away, but the desk clerk insisted the cashier would be back. A local woman wandered in. She needed American dollars for her father, who had to fly to the States.

"Would you like to exchange?" she asked. "We can go to my car where my husband is waiting, or we can do it here."

The woman, Bibi, pulled from her bag a suspiciously handy calculator and a thick wad of bolívars. Her story held no water, but she gave us a phenomenal black market rate and enough bolívars for us to survive the weekend.

We returned to our dump of a room. The toilet still didn't flush. It was so hot that we took cold showers every few hours and let the lethargic fan dry the water from our skin, but after a few minutes away from the fan, sweat again poured from our brows.

The next day we hopped onboard another bus, heading for Cumaná, and trundled through flat green countryside beneath a sky decorated with puffy clouds. No air moved through the dilapidated bus so our clothes became sopped in sweat. After a quick stop in Puerto La Cruz we continued over jungled headlands and past islands that dotted the clear blue waters of the Caribbean Sea. Venezuelan weekenders thronged sandy beaches beneath swaying palms. At Cumaná, on the very northern edge of South America, a *carrito*–or Venezuelan version of a trolley–carried us through quiet, empty streets to the colonial downtown.

As many as a million Carib, Auaké, Caquetio, Mariche, and Timoto-cuicas indigenous peoples lived in present-day Venezuela when the Spaniards established Cumaná, the first permanent settlement in South America, in 1522. Legendary indigenous leaders such as Guaicaipuro and Tamanaco fought the earliest incursions, but were no match for the Spanish. Later, colonists pushed farther inland along the Orinoco. The Yu'kuana people later revived resistance in 1775, to no avail.

Following independence from Spain in 1811, Venezuela experienced decades of political turmoil and dictatorial rule, which culminated in a civil war in the 1860s that killed hundreds of thousands–in a country with less than a million citizens. During the First World War, the discovery of crude oil deposits in Lake Maracaibo forever altered Venezuela's future. The oil boom was on. Enticed by the prospect of untold wealth, a series of dictatorships ruled well into the twentieth century.

Unrest plagued the nation through the 1960s, which led to a series of military uprisings and the suppression of basic freedoms. The worldwide oil crisis of the 1970s triggered an explosion in Venezuela's national revenue, along with a glut of debt. The collapse of oil prices in the 1980s again reversed the nation's fortunes. The value of the bolívar plummeted, which reduced living standards and ensured that corruption, poverty, and crime were rife. Two years before our arrival, military leader Hugo Chávez gained the presidency.

Despite Chávez's ambitious socialist agenda, the country remained mired in an economic quagmire, and everywhere we traveled we could see that Venezuelans struggled. Inflation had skyrocketed. More than half the population lived well below the poverty line. Venezuelans were, in effect, poorer than they had been two decades ago. The frustration evident on so many faces suggested to us that watching wealth vanish was harder than never having known affluence at all.

Again low on local currency, but with all banks in Cumaná closed, we waited outside one with a band of locals. We asked if there was a line. No, they said. When the guards unlocked the doors, the same locals pushed their way inside ahead of us and shoved us aside. No one would let us into the queue and the guards yelled at us for trying to break the ragged line.

We gave up and walked aimlessly along trash-filled streets lining garbage-covered riverbanks, before eventually finding a tour agency. The woman inside claimed that a *casa de cambio* lay seven blocks down. Half-full microbuses didn't stop or acknowledge us, so we found the place on our own. I emerged with half a millions bolívars stuffed into my pockets, enough cash to make it to Caracas.

A battered bus filled with sweaty bodies pulled to the curb. One of the seats in front was missing entirely. Another leaned back nearly to the floor. A man told us to put our rucksacks in the hold, but we refused—the hold's door didn't even latch, and kept flapping open as the bus barreled off with us aboard and our gear in our laps. On the edge of town the motor cut out. The driver removed his shirt and lay under the bus on a couple strips of cardboard. He banged at the undercarriage as two others stared into the engine. After a while one gave the thumbs up, and we all got back on board.

Coming into the town of Barcelona the driver had to negotiate gnarled, clogged streets. Dilapidated buildings were filled with trash and rubble cluttered the roadways. Beyond Barcelona we bounced sickeningly from side to side as the driver passed trucks on blind curves. During our one break at a roadside shack we bought unshelled peanuts to hold us over.

As day turned to night we crept into the outskirts of Caracas, then one of the most dangerous cities in the world. Pickpockets were common around the crowded railway and bus stations, such as Capitolio. Destitute neighborhoods on the outlying hills, known as *barrios*, were off-limits. Most criminals carried guns or knives, and readily used them. In addition to armed robberies and attacks, fights often broke out among *caraqueños*–Caracas locals. The city had the second highest large-city homicide rate in the world, so arriving at night and walking the narrow streets after dark was not only ill-advised but potentially suicidal.

I intended for us to sleep in the first hotel we found, but our driver swerved into a terminal on the eastern side of the city with no accommodation anywhere nearby. I gleaned from a group of chattering locals that a microbus might take us closer to where we wanted to be. We flagged one down and puttered along until the driver pulled to the curb and pointed to a metro station. He said the stop we wanted was Capitolío, but having been warned against going there, we instead found a cluster of hotels in the Grand Sabana district. The first two hotels crawled with roaches. One *cucaracha* actually chased Tamara out the door. The third hotel seemed roach-free and even had air conditioning, to Tamara's delight.

In the morning we tried to make our escape from the city. We learned that we might be able to buy bus tickets for the town of Mérida by going to the central bus station located in the La Hoyada neighborhood. By day La Hoyada was disconcerting; wandering the grimy streets past crumbling buildings at night was out of the question. Rain began to fall as the thunder and black clouds building all morning had threatened. While we sheltered from the deluge, we watched a man snatch the purse of a woman standing nearby. Pedestrians grabbed him before he could escape, and a melee erupted. They punched, kicked, and beat him until he lay unconscious on the concrete. A passerby fanned the purse snatcher's swollen face as the rain drummed onto his sprawled, inert body.

We scurried onto a microbus. Brown muddy water overwhelmed the sewers and gutters. The bus plowed through streets flooded to the curbs. When someone yelled at us we hopped off. Where the public station was, if one existed, we had no idea. We stumbled instead upon a private bus terminal and bought two bus tickets to Mérida. We waited out the rain before we left beneath a red overpass, where vendors sold sneakers and watches. Taunting men whistled and made crude gestures at Tamara, until a flurry of shouting and a crowd of people running towards us distracted the catcallers. Another purse snatcher darted past, followed by a gang of *caraqueños* in hot pursuit.

30

EXODUS

Before leaving Caracas, I had purchased two Miami-bound plane tickets from a downtown sales agent for a flight departing one week out. With time to spare, we decided to explore the northwestern portion of the country. We had, in essence, come full circle. We had touched all four edges of the South American continent—from the Pacific shores of Peru in the west, to the Strait of Magellan at the southern tip of the Southern Cone, to Brazil's eastern Atlantic coast, and now on to Coro on the northernmost brow of Venezuela.

On the way to Coro we stopped in Mérida, where thick mist covered lush mountainsides that rose just beyond our hotel window. We took the Mérida Cable Car, highest and longest *teleférico* in the world, to the peak of cloud-shrouded Pico Espejo fifteen thousand feet above. Yelling locals, howling dogs, and soldiers chanting to the rhythm of a calisthenics regime made for a restless night. In the early hours, the deafening din created by morning rain falling onto our corrugated tin roof stifled the street noise, and we slept at last within our swath of mosquito mesh.

For lunch, we chose a nearby third floor restaurant with a menu of the day that served a scary cannibal stew of bones, fat, and skin. The next course was little better, with ragged chunks of carnage accompanied by macaroni, yucca, and plantain. For dessert we visited an ice cream parlor with a Guinness World Record for most ice cream flavors–over eight hundred. We sampled a range of unusual delights, from trout, steak and cheese to sardine, and brandy. For good measure, the man added samples of whiskey and black bean.

A recurring theme throughout Venezuela was that restaurants, cafés, and bars consistently overcharged. In Caracas they charged for *refrescos*–beverages–that we never ordered. In Mérida, a place around the corner charged triple for beers. At lunch one day, a family sitting nearby watched with quiet eyes when our astronomical bill was presented. I argued, but lost. As a peace offering, staff that evening brought a complementary plate of soggy fries and watery cheese.

Another certainty was the ubiquitous cockroach. In Curaná I killed a dozen *cucarachas* in the time it took for Tamara to have a shower. Their babies scurried in the sink. Medium-sized teenagers clung to the walls. Three-inchers lurked in the bath. At a beer place in Mérida, five-inch-long monster cockroaches clung to the trunk of a sapling behind Tamara. They were some of the largest we had seen. Yet Tamara barely noticed. She only shrugged when I mentioned them.

"Guess I'm used to them," she said.

Just before we reached Coro, the second-oldest city in Venezuela, our bus stopped at a military checkpoint. We blearily pulled our rucksacks from beneath the bus and Tamara slung hers at the armed soldiers as though tossing an overstuffed pillow. The soldiers rooted around and then waved us on. When the zipper on Tamara's bag jammed, she forced it shut, flung the bag in the hold as the driver revved his engine, fell–unfazed–into her seat, and within moments was asleep.

The hotels in Coro were much the same as elsewhere in the country. We couldn't find our first choice, and our second no longer existed–only an empty shell of concrete and rubble remained. Farther on, we found one with scummy windows, holes in the walls, and a toilet choked with excrement. Next was a pair of love hotels with stark, filthy rooms. An uninterested man picking his nose outside one of them responded to our questions with gruff grunts. He made more by the hour than night and had no need for us.

We stood on a street corner, sweating in the sun, unsure where to turn. Tamara queried two nearby policemen wearing khaki shirts and blue pants. We followed them down an unmarked side street. From there, a long-haired Frenchman led us through a palm, fig, and banana tree-lined courtyard to a quaint room with wood beams, bedside lamp, and hand-stenciled decorations on the walls. We were saved.

For dinner, Tamara and I ordered fried white snapper. All of it, including the head, tail, and fins, arrived. Tamara never flinched. As we readied to leave the restaurant I noticed her bottle of hand sanitizer—she had nearly left it behind. I realized that she hadn't even touched it before we ate. It seemed as though the concerns that had haunted her for much of our trip had simply dissolved away.

The days were breezeless and uncomfortably hot—over ninety degrees Fahrenheit in the shade and nearly one hundred ten in full sun. In the room, the fan just pushed the hot air around in a suffocating swirl. The heat became too much even for the cockroaches but, in their place, hundreds of ants crawled across the floor, and into our rucksacks and clothing. We tried to shake them out. When they naively bit Tamara on her feet and hands they created a deadly new enemy. We ventured to some sand dunes on the north side of town, but couldn't linger long. The sun we could tolerate, but a gang of knife-wielding boys had recently tied up and robbed three Frenchmen there, so we were advised not to dally.

With the weekend approaching and not enough bolívars to buy tickets to our next destination, Maracay, we again needed to change money. The ATM at the lone bank was out of order, the lines extending from the bank entrance were long and unmoving, and we knew that the tellers likely would not exchange foreign currency anyway. After a lunch of cheese *arepa*–fried maize mixed with salt and water–we headed to the airport to try our luck there. A man pointed towards the *casa de cambio*. The sign was lit and doors unlocked but the curt woman sitting inside refused us.

"Estamos cerrados. Indefinidamente," she said. *We are closed. Indefinitely.*

We returned to the man who had pointed out the *cambio*. He whistled, and a guard approached. They conferred. The guard looked left, right, and behind him, and then motioned us to follow him. He led to a doorway and pointed towards three men sitting beneath a tree next to a battered Ford LTD taxi.

"Allí," the guard pointed. *There.* Then he disappeared.

I traded one hundred fifty dollars and promptly bought two bus tickets to Maracay. Five hours later, in Maracay, a sudden downpour flooded the streets. Waves splashed by passing buses onto the sidewalks swirled over our feet as we stumbled beneath our loads. Eyes bored into us at every turn. A man reeking of alcohol feigned a handshake and grabbed my hand. I backed away but he clenched more tightly and pulled me close.

"Dólares," he barked gruffly. "¡Quiero dólares!" *I want dollars!*

I dodged this ruffian, but later, when I attempted to place a phone call, a limping, scab-faced youth accosted me for money again. In the bathroom of a restaurant, an ape of a man stared at me with his nub in his hands. At a beer joint, a drunken, overeager middle-aged man joined us. He bought us a round, and we bought him a beer. After a while his slurring grew worse and the conversation circular and redundant.

We escaped Maracay aboard a school bus that ran us and a load of youngsters into the mountains of Henri Pittier National Park. With every song that blared over the speakers, the schoolchildren sang and danced in their seats. In the park we walked a trail to a near-deserted building where two khaki-uniformed park rangers stood by a dusty desk. One held a blue-bodied butterfly in his hand. I asked the other to draw us a map of the park.

We wandered an overgrown, empty trail into pristine rainforest far lusher and more dense than Alto Madidi of Bolivia. Massive trees covered in bromeliads and lichens reached into the sky. In the distance, large red-bodied monkeys, sounding ferocious, called to each other. A red-tailed squirrel dashed across a tree trunk. On the path, brown-shelled snails clung to each other. Two yellow-bellied birds flit silently among the branches. Orange and crimson flowers brightened the understory, as did the sun for brief moments. This was the rainforest we had come to see, but only found in our final days.

"This jungle," mused Tamara, "is a good reminder that often the vision of a place we hold in our minds is only a fragment of that place."

We pushed on. Our Choroní-bound bus ascended lush, mountainous slopes past an untouched, unbroken carpet of fern, bamboo, and banana. A rowdy child climbed over the seats, took Tamara's cookies and cried incessantly before eventually collapsing into sleep. From the jungled pass we descended to the coast and into Choroní's narrow streets lined with picturesque pastel-painted homes with blue, yellow, and orange window frames. Venezuelans milling about in bathing suits drank Polar beers and played music as the surf crashed onto a sandy, coconut palm-shaded beach. We met two young Austrian men who shared some hair-raising travel yarns.

"One night a man offered to help us cross the border from Colombia into Venezuela," one of them said as we drank beers in their room. "He said he had a proposition, and later stopped by our hotel, where he asked us to run cocaine across the border. We agreed to meet him at eleven the next morning. But by seven, long before he arrived, we had left for the border. We were ready to be out of there!"

"We met one couple that flew into Caracas," related the other Austrian, "caught a taxi, and then was forced by the driver to go from ATM to ATM until all their money was gone. We heard about another woman who was kidnapped and tied up in a room. Every day men took money from her account until it was all gone."

Following our departure from Venezuela, the country's plight only worsened. Some socialist policies enacted by Hugo Chávez had positive impacts, but others such as price controls backfired. His goal of making basic goods more affordable for the poor by capping the price of flour, cooking oil, and toiletries spurred many businesses to stop production altogether because they no longer made a profit, which then led to chronic shortages.

Chávez was succeeded after his death in 2013 by his right-hand man, Nicolás Maduro. Under Maduro, Venezuela's economy completely collapsed. Shortages of basic supplies, food, and medicines became even more widespread. Blackouts were frequent. In parts of the oil-rich country, fuel incongruously became scarce and drivers queued for days at petrol stations. Yet Maduro was re-elected to a second six-year term, in part because many candidates had been barred from running while others were jailed or fled the country for fear of being imprisoned. One of Venezuela's main economic problems under Maduro was hyperinflation. The price of a cup of coffee in Caracas increased by nearly ten thousand percent in the span of a year. A monthly wage could barely buy a bag of rice. Some enterprising Venezuelans sold worthless hyper-inflated bolívars as souvenirs. Others created ingenious bags, wallets, and bracelets out of the worthless bills.

Many people simply left. By early 2020, five million Venezuelans had fled their country. A five-year-long exodus meant Venezuelans were one of the single largest population groups in the world to be displaced from their homeland. The majority of those leaving crossed into neighboring Colombia, from where some moved on to Ecuador, Peru, or Chile. The Venezuelan *caminantes*, walkers or wayfarers, who trekked across the Andes were no doubt overcome with fear, grief, nostalgia, resignation, and uncertainty. Some joined friends or family member who had already migrated. But many were adrift, walking for hundreds of miles until reaching a place where they might find a job and begin sending money back to relatives left behind in Venezuela.

I could not imagine how it would feel to leave my family, country, and life under such difficult circumstances. The Venezuelans we encountered were a struggling, unhappy, and often grumpy lot. Safety, stability, and security might all be illusions but, while they endure, I realize they must not be taken for granted. In one fell swoop, everything can change. There are no guarantees in this life. Economies crash. Wealth disappears. Those born into prosperous nations or conditions have no assurances that their fortunate circumstances will endure. That lesson was indelibly reinforced time after time as we made our way across Venezuela.

31

THE LYNCHPIN

The time came for Tamara and I to join the exodus. Our last day in South America was not filled with sadness, so much as a desire that nothing at the last minute foul our plans. Taking off from Caracas, we banked and soared over the cobalt-blue waters of the Caribbean. Six months ago the nations of Latin America had been a mystery to me. Now they seemed like old friends—with one notable exception. It had been four decades since Cuba's revolution shook the United States. In that time, and for much longer after we had finished our journey, Americans could not freely visit the island nation. Restrictions loosened under the Obama administration, but tightened again in the Trump era.

"What is it about Cuba," I wondered aloud to Tamara as our jet passed over the country, "that is of such paramount concern to the States?"

Cuba's modern history began with Columbus' first voyage. After setting foot on one of the islands of the Bahamas on 12 October 1492, he next landed on an island that he thought was China but was in fact the present-day country of Cuba.

Believing he had touched Asia, Columbus had no idea that a massive landmass, unexplored by Europeans, lay just a few leagues away. The first Spanish settlement on Cuba was founded in 1511. Others such as the future capital of San Cristobal de la Habana soon followed. The native Taíno people, known to Spaniards as the Arawak, fell under the oppressive *encomienda* slave labor system. Within another twenty years, most had succumbed to smallpox and measles.

Three centuries later, while the rest of Spain's Latin American empire revolted, Cuba remained loyal. Uprisings and rebellions intent on achieving independence from Spain prompted a Spanish campaign of suppression in the late 1800s. The military governor herded the rural population into *reconcentrados*, described as fortified towns but often considered the prototype for twentieth-century concentration camps. A quarter of a million people died from starvation and disease.

In 1898, the United States dispatched the battleship *Maine* to protect American corporate interests, which owned forty percent of the sugar production, including seven of the ten largest estates, along with ninety percent of the telephone and electricity utilities, the oil refineries, most of the mining industry, and some of the banks. Soon after arrival in Havana harbor, the battleship exploded suddenly and sank quickly. Though the cause was unknown, popular opinion concluded the Spanish were to blame, and demanded action. Spain and the United States declared war on each other, and after Spain's subsequent defeat in the Spanish-American War, the United States retained the right to intervene in Cuban affairs.

Strikes, student protests, and army revolts led to the rise of Fulgencio Batista. After his successful coup in 1952, a young activist lawyer named Fidel Castro sought to overthrow him, initially via legal petition and then by armed revolution. Argentine revolutionary Che Guevara joined the movement, and for three years Che and Castro waged a guerilla war. When their forces entered Havana in 1959, Batista fled into exile.

Castro's legalization of the Communist Party irked the United States. After Castro signed an agreement with the

Soviet Union, President Dwight Eisenhower approved a CIA plan to invade and overthrow the Cuban government. The CIA's failed invasion at the Bay of Pigs in 1961 during President John F. Kennedy's tenure prompted Castro to request that Soviet missiles be positioned in Cuba to thwart future United States invasions, which led to the tense Cuban Missile Crisis of 1962.

"Castro's move towards communism meant Cuba had become the only openly socialist country in Latin America," explained Tamara, "and the first to ally itself with the Soviet Union and turn its back on the United States. Castro's Cuban Revolution skewed United States foreign policy by making the prevention of another 'Cuba'–a communist ally of the Soviet Union, armed with missiles aimed at American soil–virtually the only goal of the United States. Cuba became an ideological battleground in the Cold War between the United States and Soviet Union."

The Soviet Union pumped billions of dollars into Cuba, which in turn provided aid and weapons to Maoist revolutionaries in the Americas. After the dissolution of the Soviet Union in 1991, Castro found new sources of aid and food from China and new allies in Venezuela and Bolivia.

"Given a choice between a wobbly Latin American pro-freedom democracy versus an anti-communist military regime, the United States almost always opted for the latter," explained Tamara. "This policy polarized Latin America and led to the civil wars which spread across the region in the 1960s and 1970s."

Covert regime change–the overthrow of foreign governments, the training of insurgency groups, and anti-regime CIA propaganda campaigns–became a common practice of the United States in the late-twentieth century. Sometimes direct orders came from above. At other times, non-transparent government agencies misled, or did not fully implement the decisions of, elected civilian leaders. On occasion, the United States accomplished regime change by direct military intervention.

"Cuba was the lynchpin and the reason why the United States intervened in the affairs of nearly every Latin American nation during the second half of the twentieth century," said Tamara, shaking her head. "America's fear of communism altered the fates of dozens of nations. Successive administrations acted in the name of democracy and freedom, but often at the expense of life and liberty for those actually living in the affected countries."

"It can't be easy to manage a world power," I mused. "Running any country no doubt requires sacrifices, compromises, and decisions we can't imagine. I wonder whether the effects of America's covert style were better or worse than those of the out-in-the-open dictatorships, which silenced their people and the media to achieve their ends?"

"Hard to say," replied Tamara.

I wondered: Were these tactics merely two sides of the same coin?

At sunset we descended through brilliant orange cloud over Florida's southern panhandle, which lay flat as a pancake in the Gulf of Mexico. Tidy developments clustered around square lagoons on the edge of the Everglades and wisps of cotton candy-like cloud drifted past the jet moments before we touched down in Miami.

At customs, a Haitian man beckoned Tamara aside and ordered me to sit. I had jokingly forewarned her about the possibility of body cavity searches, but did not expect customs officials to separate us. One agent grabbed our passports and, as hordes of fellow passengers streamed freely past, another hulking official grilled Tamara about our mode of travel, and how we were able to do this and pay for that. Still more officials pulled every item from Tamara's carefully packed bag while barraging her with more questions. Once they had flustered her enough, the officials brought me over and executed the same routine. Since we were merely wayward travelers, they had no choice but to eventually let us go.

Thanks to numerous kindly, albeit misinformed Cuban-Americans, at three in the morning we caught the final bus of our adventure. The thirty-hour journey carried us north, through the scarlet and golden hues of an East Coast autumn. Tamara and I had traveled overland from the northern edge of the Americas to its southern tip, excluding two roadless sections, against all odds and uncertainties. Our own fastidiousness, the kindness of strangers, and a little luck had allowed us to survive, or avoid, razor blade artists, corrupt police, terrorist organizations, despotic governments, political unrest, gun and tear gas-wielding guards, pistol-waving bandits, strikes, and protests—all functions of the American dichotomy— in addition to Arctic blizzards, breathtaking heat, unreliable transportation, shady used car salesmen, roach-infested hotels, erupting volcanoes, reckless bus drivers, the occasional earthquake, tropical diseases, torrential rains, mudslides, altitude sickness, and dicey border crossings.

I had learned that underdogs could overcome powerful oppressors, that David could overtake Goliath, that the weak could rise to the occasion and tackle any obstacle that arose before them. I had seen how both ends of the political spectrum had contributed to Latin America's violence and unrest. I had immersed myself in the places we encountered along our journey, seen the impacts of United States policies, and let the facts speak for themselves.

"Have your political views changed at all?" Tamara asked me, as the bus carried us through the Carolinas.

Before we left, I had not attached myself to any political party. I shook my head.

"I'll still support the issues and vote for the leaders that most closely align with my values and what I believe. I don't want to label myself by identifying with a particular party, nor do I want to close myself off to someone else's ideas because of the party they choose to affiliate with."

"Even after everything we've seen?" she pressed.

"Political ideologies shift," I replied. "I don't want to limit myself or vote along party lines. I want to think independently. This trip has only strengthened my feeling that our choices must depend on the situations we find ourselves in."

"I respect your open-mindedness," Tamara said, "but I know now that leftist guerrillas versus military-backed right wing dictatorship—often supported by the United States—is a story that has played out over and over again throughout Latin America, and that this tension fed much of the violence of the twentieth century. The reason guerilla groups rose up was usually because of the heavy handedness of the oppressive dictatorships they were trying to overthrow. I can't support fascism, far right ideologies, or autocracies that prioritize power over the needs of the people."

"I completely agree," I nodded. "Any extremist ideal, left or right, is bad news. Moderation is always the key in life. I'm talking more about daily interactions with rational people."

Before this trip I barely knew the difference between conservatism and liberalism in contemporary America. Now I know that, generally speaking, conservatives favor smaller government, lower taxes, and punishments that fit the crime. In their eyes, a person's life is the result of the choices that person has made, whereas liberals generally see individuals as products of society.

We don't choose our genes, our parents or teachers, the social class we were born into, or what television shows we were sat down in front of as toddlers. The world has influenced us from the start, which is why liberals often believe in spreading the wealth.

"Like the historical religions, the cores of both political philosophies make sense to me," I mused. "Something I've been thinking about lately is the idea of translating the best parts of both ends of the moderate political spectrum into living a better life. Kind of like picking the best teachings from all religions and incorporating them into my personal philosophy. For example, when good things happen to me, I'll be a liberal. Any successes in my life can't happen without the opportunities provided by the world around me. So hopefully this attitude will inspire in me humility, graciousness, appreciation, and generosity."

"So when would you be a conservative?" Tamara asked.

"When trouble inevitably rears its head, I'll be a conservative. I won't blame others. I'm fully responsible for the conditions in my life, and I can solve my problems and prevent them from happening again."

"That makes sense."

"When I see others struggling, I'll be a liberal. I'll recognize that every person's choices are a result of their socialization, and that their failings represent the failings of the society they're part of. I'll have compassion for other people's misfortunes and seek out ways to help those around me. When I see others doing well, I'll be a conservative. I'll respect hard work, good decisions, and talent. I'll honor the efforts of others, congratulate them on their successes, and feel encouraged and inspired by their achievements."

"Sounds pretty noble," remarked Tamara.

"Not noble. I just want my choices to reflect my values, not necessarily the ideologies of any particular political party."

"I can get behind that," she agreed.

32

FULL CIRCLE

As we continued into Virginia, I reflected further on what we had seen on our journey. Though I could appreciate both sides of the political spectrum, I realized what I could not support.

"One thing I've learned is that the primary obstacle to eradicating poverty and inequality in much of Latin America is an -ism I cannot support, and that is authoritarianism," I said to Tamara. "What I cannot stand behind are narcissistic, corrupt, racist, hateful, or self-serving autocrats."

The history of the Americas primarily centers on the struggle to gain freedom from the political, economic, and spiritual shackles that too often bind humanity. These battles were fought by those who wanted new liberties versus those who had privileges to defend. United States politicians have often stepped in to support dictators who enabled their own agendas, and in the course of supporting such authoritarian regimes, went against their own country's ideals of freedom and democracy. This was my strongest complaint with the role the United States has played in Latin America. The issue, from my perspective, was a failure of leadership at the highest levels.

"What is it in men that fosters such an insatiable lust for power?" pondered Tamara. "Is it their strength...or a fundamental weakness and inability to experience life lovingly?"

"I'm not certain," I replied. "As importantly, what is it that has compelled millions to surrender their freedoms to such men, to autocratic leaders and authoritarians?"

Democratic societies require negotiation and concession. Setbacks are inevitable, and victories always partial. In a democracy, leaders must have patience. They must be able to compromise. They must abide by the legislative and judicial checks and balances put into place for a reason. And they must be able to lose.

Authoritarian leaders refuse to acknowledge the parameters of constitutional rule. Media criticism, legislative oversight, and adverse judicial rulings leave them feeling besieged. These leaders find the mechanics of democratic politics unbearably frustrating. Totalitarianism is an extreme form of this type of government. Both types discourage individual freedom of thought and action. Totalitarianism does this by exerting total control over its citizenry through absolute, oppressive, one-party rule, in which the army and police operate outside the constraints of law in a purposefully unpredictable manner.

Authoritarianism is less extreme, in that some social and economic institutions remain outside government control. Such governments lack the power to control every aspect of society, but given the chance, leaders will take it. Authoritarianism is easier to implement, more common, and harder to prevent. Both are likely to be led by a tyrant, dictator, or despot.

Authoritarianism is most apparent on the left-right political spectrum as fascism, a form of radical right-wing ultra-nationalism characterized by dictatorial power, forced suppression of opponents, and opposition to liberalism. The first fascist movements emerged in Italy during the First World War, and then spread across Europe and South America. When Benito Mussolini was hanged in Milan in April 1945, and Adolf Hitler committed suicide in his bunker beneath Berlin two days later, it appeared fascism had died with them.

Seventy-five years later, the prospect of fascism was not only alive, but appeared to be thriving. Far right governing parties around the world—many of them United States allies such as Brazil and Hungary—had grabbed power. And autocracy abounded. In 2018, China's leader Xi Jinping persuaded the party-controlled National People's Congress to lift the constitutional limit on his time in power. In the same year Vladimir Putin, an acknowledged political assassin, was re-elected to yet another term in Russia. Bashar al-Assad retained his grip over much of Syria. Around the Mediterranean, hope for democracy was quashed by leaders such as Egyptian President Abdel Fattah al-Sisi, who routinely jailed reporters and political opponents.

In order to obtain and retain power, autocrats often use actual or fabricated national emergencies to overturn democracy. Security crises build public support around a common cause, because citizens are more likely to tolerate or even support authoritarian power grabs when they fear for their safety. Such crises often are used to silence opposition, since criticism can be seen as unpatriotic. Crises also loosen normal constitutional constraints because legislators and judges tend to defer to the executive leader's decisions at such times. Alberto Fujimori of Peru used a Maoist insurgency and economic crisis to justify the dissolution of Peru's constitution and Congress. President Getúlio Vargas of Brazil used the "discovery" of a communist plot—later revealed to be fake—to dissolve the constitution and establish a dictatorship, rather than leave office the next year as term limits required.

In Latin America in the twenty-first century, authoritarian rulers had become less common but their legacies remained. Chile, Peru, Mexico, El Salvador, Guatemala, Nicaragua, and Brazil all transitioned to democracy without punishing former authoritarian elites for their past misdeeds or even excluding them from positions of power. As such, over time, authoritarian influence led to broad unrest.

The United States veered sharply towards authoritarianism during the era of Trump, who revealed his autocratic instincts soon after assuming the presidency. His administration became synonymous with deception and lies. He lacked the patience or negotiating skills needed to deal with divided government; he would not compromise, and threatened to not leave office even if he was not re-elected. True to form, Trump refused to concede defeat after losing the presidential election in 2020, and afterward tried to overturn the election result and democracy itself through frivolous lawsuits and intimidation.

Even that bastion of democracy, the United States Constitution, cannot prevent a slide towards autocracy. As long as one major political party and a solid majority of the population support an authoritarian shift, it is virtually unstoppable. The Founding Fathers knew that without a virtuous citizenry, the Constitution was just a piece of paper. Benjamin Franklin believed that the American experiment in self-government, "can only end in despotism, as other forms have done before it, when the people become so corrupted as to need despotic government, being incapable of any other."

"At its best, America is a place where people from a multitude of backgrounds work together to protect the rights and enrich the lives of all," I said to Tamara soon after we crossed the Maryland state line. "I think that's the model many people around the world want to see."

After our journey across Latin America, a shift in United States international policy seemed to occur. Covert CIA missions gave way, more or less, to a more overt form of control. America seemed to be flipping to the other side of the coin.

"You asked why people willingly surrender their freedoms to authoritarian rule," Tamara reflected. "I think it's because they're afraid. This is how autocrats gain power: by stoking our innate fears. Most people are not as independent, rational, or objective as they might believe. Propaganda, intimidation, suppression of free thought, fear…these are how governments control populations."

I agreed with her. Religious institutions, corporations, and governments often rob people of their freedoms because humanity, by and large, worships power, money, and the nation-state. Religion has faded a bit since the Middle Ages, but still shapes most humans' beliefs. Identifying with corporate brands and falling prey to marketing influences how people spend their cash. And patriotism, to paraphrase Erich Fromm, is a form of incest. He wrote that, just as love for one individual which excludes the love for others is not love, love for one's country which is not part of one's love for humanity is not in fact love, but idolatrous worship.

"These institutions can't be avoided, though," Tamara said. "They are the infrastructure of society."

"That's true. But we can always be mindful that their ulterior motives are often to control our behavior and suppress our freedoms. If, when we are fearful, we turn towards authority figures for guidance rather than make our own decisions, we must beware of autocrats who try to divide us. If we allow our fears to guide our decisions, then we run the risk of falling prey to their manipulation."

"Abuse of power comes as no surprise," Tamara said dryly.

"If we do give up our freedom in the name of security and begin the slide towards authoritarianism," I added, "there are questions we must ask. What damage will be done? What freedoms will be lost? What liberties will be eroded? Can those freedoms and liberties be regained? Was the tradeoff worth it?"

"I think leaders in any era could take a lesson from the ancient Taoist philosophers," Tamara opined. "Lao Tzu wrote that the best leaders are not noticed. The next best are honored and praised. The next, people fear and the next, people hate. When the best leader's work is done, the people say, 'we did it ourselves'."

"Well said," I smiled. I later read about a prince, known as the sage of Huainan, who lived in China two thousand years ago. He often invited Taoist thinkers to speak about virtue and enlightened leadership, and later compiled these teachings into a text called the *Huainanzi*. The key to good government lies in the quality of leadership, says the *Huainanzi*. If the leader is not virtuous, the rest of the government will be an unwieldy bureaucracy. A leader acts by not forcing, leads by not bragging, and commands respect by not threatening. The highest act of a leader is to leave with no trace when his or her work is done.

This means being courageous and leading authentically, in alignment with our true self. Living and leading in accordance with our highest values. Not being ego-driven. And influencing in a way that makes a difference, enriches the lives of others, and creates value by virtue of relationships. Effective leadership is not about unilateral control and giving orders, but the art of inspiring and revealing the best talents and abilities in others. As Lao Tzu writes, when the job is done, followers will believe the accomplishments are their own. That, to me, is effective leadership.

"I used to believe every person must be a pebble in an avalanche of change," said Tamara. "I see now that not everyone needs to change the world. At the very least, be a decent person. Treat others authentically, justly, and humanely. That in itself would change the world."

After we returned to Maryland, we settled back into the rhythms of home life. Over the coming weeks, I moved into the top floor of a late nineteenth-century brick and mortar on West Main. Tamara rented the lower portion of a historic home in the outlying countryside. The city house and the country home, we called them. She did not get a monkey, as she had always wanted, but a few months later did buy a gorgeous smoky grey Himalayan kitten that she named Inca.

After Mexico, Tamara hadn't fallen sick again, but after returning home she caught pneumonia. Despite the dangers along our journey, we were never robbed. But one night at work, someone filched the stash of cash in her purse. The lesson was that misfortune can happen anywhere, at home or abroad.

As winter descended we contemplated what lay ahead for us as a couple. One night in Ecuador we had been lying in our bed watching a series of B-grade movies featuring lonely insecure people desperate for love. Tamara had lamented that she didn't want to start a new relationship.

"In the beginning it's all a game," she had said, "all acting. You hide the bad traits and highlight the good ones. You don't really know a person until a year or two into it. It's a deception, really, a lie that leads to lust and maybe love."

She was right that it took time to get to know someone. As we had learned, traveling with another person was one of the best ways to do that. Our journey had taught us each a few things, perhaps too much. In the spring Tamara and Inca stayed in Maryland. I flew to the land of midnight sun and moved into a one-room cabin in the spruce forest atop Karma Ridge. I had come full circle.

The summer passed quickly, as it always did in the Alaskan interior, but this time I did not leave when the season ended. I decided to stay for the winter. One chill, moonless night, I stepped outside the door of my cabin to look for the Northern Lights. The sound of wolves howling nearby sent shivers up my spine. The air was still and clear, and I knew they were near. I did not fear wolves, despite their portrayal in fairy tales and cinema. For me, their howls evoked the very essence of the wildness that I originally came to Alaska to find. I had traveled across the Americas and found a kind of freedom, but I realized my utopia was right here, where nature ruled, where humanity's influence was insignificant, and I could be whomever I wished. I had found my inspiration.

I was reminded of my drive to the Arctic Ocean five years earlier. As we had started back from Prudhoe Bay, a rainbow arced overhead and half a dozen snowy owls flew past. These had seemed to me like good omens. Then, a huge white wolf had appeared. He had stopped, watched us, moved off, stopped again, and then slowly continued on, before disappearing over a shallow rise. As I watched him disappear, I knew I did not want to be a lone wolf. That was the moment I decided to bring Tamara on my overland journey across the Americas to the southern tip of Argentina, and back again.

Life does not always go as planned. Tamara joined me on my journey as I hoped she would, but did not come back with me, full circle, to Alaska. I was a lone wolf after all. Yet she had come most of the way, and though we decided not to stay together as a couple, we remained the best of friends. Our bond only strengthened over the years; traveling together across the Americas had cemented a lifelong friendship between us. Sometimes, I realized, that is the best gift we can ask for.

SOURCES

Abrahamian, Atossa Araxia. *The Real Wall Isn't at the Border.* New York Times. 27 January 2019.

Albertus, Michael, and Deming, Mark. *Pinochet Still Looms Large in Chilean Politics.* Foreign Policy. 5 November 2019.

Baker-Hernández, Paul. *Eleven Killed in Massacre in Siuna.* Nicaragua News Service: A Service of the Nicaragua Network. Vol. 8, No. 21. 15-21 May 2000.

Barone, Michael. *How JFK's Assassination Changed Politics.* Washington Examiner. 4 November 2013: 16.

Barraclough, Geoffrey, ed. *Atlas of World History.* Ann Arbor, Michigan: Harper Collins. 1999.

Betts, Richard K. *Conflict After the Cold War: Arguments on Causes of War and Peace.* Fifth Edition. New York: Routledge. 2017.

Blair, Laurence. *A Leftist Loss in Uruguay Wasn't Exactly a Conservative Triumph.* World Politics Review. 3 December 2019.

Blair, Laurence. *Bolivia Crisis: How Did We Get Here and What Happens Next?* The Guardian. 15 November 2019.

Burkholder, Mark A. and Lyman L. Johnson. *Colonial Latin America.* Oxford: Oxford University Press. 2010.

Cáceres, Marco. *Is Socialism the Answer for Honduras?* Honduras Weekly. 24 May 2013.

Chambers, Bala. *Bolivia: A Complex Picture of a Political Crisis.* TRT World. 28 November 2019.

Costa, William. *Past Weighs Heavy as Paraguay Struggles with Ghosts of Dictatorship.* The Guardian. 10 December 2019.

Cristaldo, Mariel. *Paraguay's President's Popularity Plummets Amid Brazil-linked Political Crisis.* Reuters. 14 August 2019.

Faiola, Anthony. *Volcanic Troubles Shaking Ecuador.* Washington Post Foreign Service. 22 April 2000: A10.

Fromm, Erich. *Escape From Freedom.* New York, New York: Holt Paperbacks. 1969.

Garmany, Jeff, and Pereira, Anthony. *A Year After Jair Bolsonaro's Election, Why He's Not Solely to Blame for Brazil's Toxic Politics.* The Conversation. 28 October 2019.

Gresh, Alain. *The Dream of a Better World is Back.* Le Monde Diplomatique. 8 May 2009.

Hammer, Joshua. *Amazon Warriors.* Smithsonian. March 2013: 45.

Held, Jacob M., ed. *Dr. Seuss and Philosophy.* Plymouth, United Kingdom: Rowman & Littlefield Publishers, Inc. 2011.

Kornbluh, Peter, ed. *Brazil Marks 40th Anniversary of Military Coup.* George Washington University National Security Archive. Retrieved 20 August 2007.

LaFeber, Walter. *Inevitable Revolutions: The United States in Central America.* New York: W.W. Norton and Company. 1993.

Lanier, Alfredo S. *Ecuador Pins Hopes On Dollar As Cure For Ailing Economy.* Chicago Tribune. 16 September 2000.

Lewis, Martin W., and Karen E. Wigen. *The Myth of Continents: A Critique of Metageography.* Berkeley: University of California Press. 1997.

Lewis-Kraus, Gideon. *Game of Bones.* The New York Times Magazine. 20 January 2019: 44.

Miles, Elizabeth, and Gramer, Robbie. *Why Chileans Are Still Protesting Despite Reform Promises.* Foreign Policy. 23 October 2019.

Misculin, Nicolás, and Jourdan, Adam. *Argentina's Peronists Sweep Back Into Power as Macri Ousted.* Reuters. 28 October 2019.

Petropoulos, Aggelos, and Engel, Richard. *A Panama Tower Carries Trump's Name and Ties to Organized Crime.* NBC News. 17 November 2017.

Rohter, Larry. *Ecuador Junta Exits: Vice President in Power.* New York Times News Service. 23 January 2000.

Rubin, Jeffrey, W. *From Che to Marcos.* Dissent. Summer 2002.

Schemo, Diana Jean. *In Paraguay Border Town, Almost Anything Goes.* The New York Times. 15 March 1998.

Taladrid, Stephanie. *Argentina Considers a Return to Peronism.* The New York Times. 28 August 2019.

Unattributed. *Ecuador's Quickie Coup.* Chicago Tribune. 25 January 2000.

Wiarda, Howard J., and Harvey F. Kline, eds. *Latin American Politics and Development.* Boulder, Colorado: Westview Press. 2007.

ABOUT THE AUTHOR

The Americas Overland

Toby D. Smith, a financial consultant and writer, holds a Bachelor of Science degree in Zoology, and an MBA, both from the University of Maryland. During an eighteen-year Alaska-based career, he led multiple non-profit organizations focused on wilderness preservation, education, and advocacy. He has driven through fifty U.S. states, traveled across five continents, and visited over seventy countries. *The Americas Overland* is his second book, and begins where the adventures in his first book, *Across Eurasia*, end.

Made in the USA
Middletown, DE
02 August 2021